THE CRITICS SAY...

THE CRITICS SAY...

*57 Theater Reviewers
in New York and Beyond
Discuss Their Craft
and Its Future*

MATT WINDMAN

Foreword by ROBERT SIMONSON

McFarland & Company, Inc., Publishers
Jefferson, North Carolina

LIBRARY OF CONGRESS CATALOGUING-IN-PUBLICATION DATA

Names: Windman, Matt interviewer.
Title: The critics say : 57 theater reviewers in New York and beyond discuss their craft and its future / Matt Windman ; foreword by Robert Simonson.
Description: Jefferson, North Carolina : McFarland & Company, Inc., Publishers, 2016. | Includes index.
Identifiers: LCCN 2016011461 | ISBN 9780786496709 (softcover : acid free paper) ∞
Subjects: LCSH: Dramatic criticism—United States—History—20th century. | Dramatic criticism—United States—History—21st century. | Theater critics—United States—Interviews.
Classification: LCC PN1707 .C85 2016 | DDC 792.01/5—dc23
LC record available at https://lccn.loc.gov/2016011461

BRITISH LIBRARY CATALOGUING DATA ARE AVAILABLE

ISBN (print) 978-0-7864-9670-9
ISBN (ebook) 978-1-4766-2469-3

© 2016 Matt Windman. All rights reserved

No part of this book may be reproduced or transmitted in any form or by any means, electronic or mechanical, including photocopying or recording, or by any information storage and retrieval system, without permission in writing from the publisher.

Cover image © 2106 iStock

Printed in the United States of America

*McFarland & Company, Inc., Publishers
Box 611, Jefferson, North Carolina 28640
www.mcfarlandpub.com*

Acknowledgments

First and foremost, I would like to thank each critic who spoke with me for this book and Robert Simonson (who was the editor of *Playbill.com* when I was a college intern there) for writing the foreword. I would also like to thank my wife Heather (who was usually sitting a few feet away from me on our couch, watching television, while I worked on this book), my parents Joseph and Robin Windman (had they not paid for me to go to theater camp as a teenager, my life would have been very different), the editors of *amNewYork* (including Scott Rosenberg and Pete Catapano), the friends I turned to for feedback (particularly David Meyers), and the recent college graduates who helped me to transcribe the interview transcripts (including Lindsey Sullivan, Alice Wertheimer, Nathan Popejoy, Margarita Nehme, Chris Olszewski, Anna Borgida, and Jennifer Sandler).

Table of Contents

Acknowledgments	v
Foreword by Robert Simonson	1
Preface	3
Meet the Theater Critics	7
1. Why We Exist	13
2. How I Became a Theater Critic	30
3. Education and Personality	48
4. The Theater Community	70
5. Ethics	82
6. The Writing Process	94
7. Readers	125
8. Evaluation	135
9. Crisis	162
10. Economics	180
11. Online	193
12. *Spider-Man*	205
13. Regrets and Advice	213
Epilogue	223
Index	225

Foreword
by Robert Simonson

This book has arrived at exactly the right time. The relevance of drama critics has been a common topic of discussion in the theater over the past decade, as newspapers and magazines have either replaced staff reviewers with green, low-paid stringers or eliminated critics positions altogether. Twenty-five years from now, or even 10, it's doubtful that Matt Windman could have compiled this survey, as there would be few practitioners left to interview, and even fewer readers to care what they had to say.

What is the purpose of theater critics? Why do we have them? What is their job? What role do they play in the greater theater community? Are they even part of that community or not? These are questions I found ample occasion to wrestle with from the 1980s to the early 2000s, when I plied the age-old (but by then already-dying) trade at various publications in the Midwest and New York. And these are the questions that Matt Windman puts to his subjects—basically, every significant drama critic in New York, and some from beyond the tri-state area.

The answers are fascinating. Every response shows these writers and reporters—who work at daily newspapers, weekly magazines, and websites with ever-rolling deadlines—to be everything one would hope a critic might be: intelligent, thoughtful, funny, and well-spoken, with a deep knowledge and interest in their profession and the art they cover. Some of them, believe it or not, even come off as damn likeable. This is encouraging to someone like me, who still believes drama critics serve a necessary purpose. And I have no doubt it will be surprising to others who like to dismiss critics *en masse* as untalented hacks.

Matt Windman has done a skillful job of arranging the transcripts from the interviews. The book is not divided by critic, with one long Q&A following another—which would have been deathly dull. Rather, the text is sectioned off by topic, with each critic's response to a specific question (i.e. What constitutes unethical behavior for a theater critic? Do you feel guilt at writing very negative reviews?) grouped together. This allows him to juxtapose widely divergent takes on important critical matters, often to wonderfully comic effect. Thus, Peter Filichia's assertion that he functions as an "audience matchmaker" is follow by John Simon's biting comment, "Being a consumer guide is the most pathetic and inadequate way of looking at drama criticism."

Moreover, it aptly illustrates just how complex the critic's task can be, since so many smart people obviously think about it so differently. I was not interviewed by Matt Windman; I gave up my seat on the aisle years ago. But my long years in that chair gave me more than enough time to come up with my own answers to the queries he poses. And, perhaps not surprisingly, my view of critics is rather charitable. To my mind, they are easily the most selfless members of the theater world. For, as much as actors, directors, playwrights, and producers love the stage as a whole, they must ever advocate a very narrow, very particular artistic viewpoint, one that matches with their specific skill set and services the furthering of their career. They are survivalists by necessity. Critics, by comparison, love the whole of the theater. They're open to the charms of the drama, the comedy, and the musical; the lush, traditional revival and the mold-breaking experimental piece; the megamusical and the chamber drama; the ham actor and the minimalist performer; solo art and sprawling epic; Broadway and Brooklyn Academy of Music. The only ax they grind is in the pursuit of quality, as they perceive it.

And they love the theater more than the artists they review. An audacious claim, I know. But they must. If not, why would they put themselves through night after night in darkened rooms, surrounded by people with scant respect for what they do? Unlike artists, they stand nothing to gain. Free theater tickets and a byline aren't much in the final accounting of things. Critics will never get rich. They will never be famous. They will never be truly powerful. And they certainly won't become beloved. They're lucky if they're even liked. They do nothing less than sacrifice their lives at the altar of the theater.

As for that most common and simple-minded of all questions put forth by theater artists, "Why have theater critics at all?" to me, the answer has always been clear. Do you consider what you do, your art, to be worthy of thoughtful response, of analysis? Well, so do drama critics. And that's why they exist.

From the late 1980s to the early 2000s, Robert Simonson was a theater critic for Time Out New York, *the* Village Voice *and* TheaterWeek, *and otherwise wrote about the stage for the* New York Times, American Theatre, Variety, *and many other publications. He has published four books on the theater. He has since become one of the nation's leading cocktail and spirits journalists. His standard joke is that a career in writing about theater drove him to a career of writing about drink.*

Preface

During the summer of 2008, I came up with the idea of putting together a book composed of interviews with theater critics. At that point, I had already worked as the theater critic of the free daily newspaper *amNewYork* for a few years—even as I was simultaneously a full-time student in college and then law school. I started to work at *amNewYork* in 2004 as a college intern and, through a combination of endless pitching and nagging and lucky breaks, graduated to becoming its regular theater critic.

I was anxious to speak to other critics in order to learn more about the craft. I interviewed about 20 critics and asked them how they became critics, how they went about their jobs, and about their thoughts on the theater, including how they evaluate the work of playwrights, directors, actors, and designers when attending plays and musicals for review.

I thought that no similar book had ever been attempted before. But after some searching around, I did find a similar collection of interviews completed more than two decades ago: *Who Calls the Shots on the New York Stages?*, written by Kalina Stefanova-Peteva and published in 1993. Although quite interesting, these pre-Internet era interviews reflect an extremely different professional landscape than the one we see today. There is also *Under the Cooper Beech: Conversations with American Theater Critics*, written by Jeffrey Eric Jenkins and published in 2004, which focuses primarily on the formation of the American Theatre Critics Association.

After the summer of 2008, I abruptly stopped working on the book. I was about to start my final year of law school, and I was facing the storm and stress of studying for the New York State Bar Exam and graduating without a job at the height of a recession. I also didn't have a publisher for the book—nor did I even have anyone to help me transcribe the interviews I had conducted so far.

By the winter of 2014, I was still writing theater reviews as a freelance journalist every week for *amNewYork* while simultaneously working by day as an attorney (which remains my primary means of financial support). The interviews I conducted with theater critics back in 2008 were sitting on a digital recorder in my sock drawer. I often thought of restarting work on the book, but how could I manage that? Between being a lawyer and a theater critic, I was working day and night. I had also just gotten married. But I wanted the book to be seen—now more than ever—considering the extent to which theater criticism has changed in recent years. But to do so, I needed to discard the old interviews and start all over again. Too much had changed since 2008.

Now, it wouldn't be enough to just ask critics about how they landed their jobs and what they believe are the ingredients of a great play or musical. Since 2008, prominent critics such as David Rooney, Howard Shapiro, Peter Filichia, Jeremy Gerard, and Michael Sommers have lost their jobs in layoffs or forced retirements. Having a theater critic (or at least a full-time or a paid one) is now seen as a luxury rather than a necessity by many, if not most, publications. At the same time, the number of people writing about shows on Internet message boards, blogs, and social media sites has exploded, raising questions of whether it's still necessary for a publication to employ its own critic, whether message board users are legitimate critics, and whether anything could be done to make professional theater criticism more valued by both readers and employers.

I got back in touch with virtually every critic I spoke with in 2008. I also spoke with other New York critics and prominent regional critics like Peter Marks of Washington, D.C., Robert Hurwitt of San Francisco, Christine Dolen of Miami, and Chris Jones of Chicago. For a touch of Canada, I called up Richard Ouzounian, whom I was familiar with based on my annual trips to the Stratford Festival in Ontario.

I also interviewed Michael Riedel of the *New York Post*. Although he is technically a theater gossip columnist rather than a critic, he has no qualms about sharing his own appreciation—or lack thereof—for the latest shows in his weekly columns. (As I write this introduction, Riedel is skeptically questioning all of the rave reviews for the hit hip-hop musical *Hamilton* and the perception that it is a "game-changer.") I even interviewed Perez Hilton, who originally trained to be an actor and has posted theater reviews on his popular gossip blog alongside the latest on the Kardashians.

In all, I conducted over 50 interviews, each of which lasted anywhere from a half hour to two hours. They were done in person or by phone, plus one or two by email correspondence. I transcribed the interviews myself, along with some invaluable help from friends and various college students with an interest in theater and/or journalism.

Rather than present each interview separately, I wanted to organize the book by topic, with each chapter containing responses from the various critics to the same questions. That way, readers could easily compare and contrast the conflicting positions taken by the critics on each issue. While one critic sees himself as a member of the theater community, another sees herself first and foremost as a journalist. One sees himself as a reviewer, another sees herself as a critic, and a third person thinks there's no difference whatsoever between the two terms.

Whether you agree with the opinions expressed by critics such as John Simon or Ben Brantley, these are people who love the theater and who understand it just as well as—and maybe even better, or at least differently than—many actors, producers, directors, playwrights, designers, producers, press agents, and other prominent industry professionals. Although a critic may get press tickets to high-profile shows, he or she also has to endure plenty that are far less interesting or artistically successful, and the critic is expected to write about all of them. It's part of the job. And many—if not most—theater critics working today are not getting paid for their writing. They're doing it because they love the theater.

Even to this day, the theater critic maintains a unique, seemingly glamorous position—delivering a verdict-like final judgment on the work of trained, perhaps even famous actors, writers, and directors. Who are these people? Where do they get the right to say whether David Mamet's new drama is a dud or whether a Hollywood star doesn't have the chops to handle a Shakespeare comedy? I've got to imagine that anyone who's ever been stung by a bad review would be interested in learning more about these people and where they're coming from.

If the profession (is it even still considered a profession at this point, as opposed to a lucky gig for a select few?) continues to die out, if opportunities to be a professional critic continue to fall by the wayside, I believe that the theater will be very different—and most likely, not for the better. Without the support of critics, it's hard to imagine *Hamilton, Fun Home, Spring Awakening, Doubt,* and so many other well-reviewed Off-Broadway shows transferring to the Great White Way and enjoying mainstream success. The loss of critics could change which shows get to Broadway and, once there, which ones are able to enjoy healthy runs.

Then again, maybe theater criticism doesn't need to be a professional gig anymore. After all, countless people on Internet message boards are more than willing to take the time to share their thoughts about new shows without any sort of financial compensation. Some of them write just as well as, if not better than, the so-called professional critics. But who are those people on the Internet message boards, who go by usernames rather than their real names? Can they be trusted? Do they work for the producer of the show they're writing about—or perhaps a rival producer?

I think it's best to imagine this book as the transcript from a massive symposium on theater criticism in which I act the moderator. In order to focus squarely on the critics I interviewed, I have refrained as much as possible from adding my own responses to the questions being posed. I hope that the book is coherent and readable from start to finish. However, feel free to skip around between chapters or to look for the responses from the critics you like the most.

Writing any book on this subject leads to the issue of how to spell it: "theater" or "theatre"? I flipped a coin and decided to go with "theater," except when referring to any specific publications, venues, or companies that use the other spelling.

Thank you for picking up this book and taking the time to think about theater criticism—its past, present, and future. I do not claim to be an expert—only someone who has written theater reviews and who cares about theater criticism. If you have any feedback, feel free to email me at mattwindman@gmail.com.

Meet the Theater Critics

These identifications are current as of March 2016. Considering how unpredictable the publishing industry has become, at least some of them may have become outdated by the time this book is released.

Hilton Als is the chief theater critic of the *New Yorker*. He was previously a staff writer at the *Village Voice* and editor-at-large at *Vibe*. He is the author of *The Women, Justin Bond/Jackie Curtis*, and *White Girls*. He has taught at the Yale School of Drama, Wesleyan University, Wellesley College, and Smith College. He received the 2002–03 George Jean Nathan Award for Dramatic Criticism.

Don Aucoin is the chief theater critic of the *Boston Globe*, where he was previously a political reporter and television critic. He is a co-author of *Last Lion: The Fall and Rise of Ted Kennedy*. He teaches writing at Boston College.

Dan Bacalzo was the managing director of *TheaterMania.com*. He is now an assistant professor of theater at Florida Gulf Coast University. He has written for academic publications including *TDR* and *Theatre Journal*. He is a playwright, performer, and dramaturg.

Ben Brantley is the chief theater critic of the *New York Times*. He has written for *Women's Wear Daily, Elle, Vanity Fair*, and the *New Yorker*. He is the author of *The New York Times Book of Broadway: On the Aisle for the Unforgettable Plays of the Last Century* and *Broadway Musicals: From the Pages of The New York Times*. He received the 1996–97 George Jean Nathan Award for Dramatic Criticism.

Scott Brown was the theater critic for *New York* magazine from 2010 to 2013. He received the 2012–13 George Jean Nathan Award for Dramatic Criticism. He has written for *Entertainment Weekly, Wired, GQ*, and *Time*. He is also the co-author/composer of *Gutenberg! The Musical!* He is currently a writer for the television drama *Manhattan*.

David Cote is the theater editor and chief theater critic of *Time Out New York* and a contributing theater critic on NY1. He has written for the

Guardian, the *New York Times*, and *Opera News*. He is also a playwright and opera librettist.

Gordon Cox is the theater editor and reporter of *Variety*. He previously wrote for *Newsday*.

Michael Dale is the news and features editor of *BroadwayWorld.com*. He has been reviewing for the website since 2002. Before then, he spent 20-odd years singing, dancing, and acting in summer stock and dinner theaters.

Christine Dolen was the theater critic of the *Miami Herald* for 36 years. She was formerly a critic and editor with the *Detroit Free Press*.

Joe Dziemianowicz is the theater critic and reporter of the *New York Daily News*.

Robert Faires is the arts editor of the *Austin Chronicle*. He is also an actor, director, and playwright.

Robert Feldberg is the theater critic and reporter of the *Bergen County Record* in New Jersey.

Adam Feldman is a theater and cabaret critic for *Time Out New York*. He has served as president of the New York Drama Critics' Circle since 2005.

Peter Filichia is the New Jersey theater critic emeritus for the *Star-Ledger*. He currently writes online columns for Music Theatre International, MasterWorks Broadway, and Kritzerland. His books include *The Biggest Hit and the Biggest Flop of the Season*, *Broadway MVPs of the Past 50 Seasons*, *Strippers, Showgirls and Sharks*, and *The Great Parade*. He is chairman of the Theatre World Awards.

David Finkle writes about theater for the *Clyde Fitch Report* and *Huffington Post*. He was the chief drama critic for *TheaterMania.com* for 12 years. He has written about theater for scores of publications including the *Village Voice* and the *New York Times*.

Elysa Gardner is an entertainment critic and reporter at *USA Today*, where she writes about theater and pop music. She has also written for *Entertainment Weekly*, the *New Yorker*, the *Los Angeles Times*, and *Rolling Stone*.

Thom Geier was a senior editor and theater critic at *Entertainment Weekly*. He is now the deputy managing editor at *TheWrap.com* and a writer for *CultureSauce.net*.

Jeremy Gerard is the executive editor and theater critic of *Deadline.com*. He has written for *Bloomberg News*, the *New York Times*, and *Variety*. He is the author of *Wynn Place Show*.

Jesse Green is the theater critic of *New York* magazine. He has also written for the *New York Times*. He is the author of *O Beautiful* and *The Velveteen Father: An Unexpected Journey to Parenthood*.

Eric Grode was the theater critic of the *New York Sun*. He has written for the *New York Times*, *Broadway.com*, the *Village Voice*, and *New York* magazine. He is the author of *Hair: The Story of a Show That Defined a Generation*.

He teaches at Syracuse University as part of the Goldring Arts Journalism Program.

Perez Hilton is the entertainment blogger behind *PerezHilton.com*.

Robert Hurwitt is the theater critic of the *San Francisco Chronicle*. He previously wrote for the *San Francisco Examiner*. He received the 1994-95 George Jean Nathan Award for Dramatic Criticism.

Charles Isherwood is a theater critic at the *New York Times*. He has written for *Variety*, the *Times of London*, *The Advocate*, and *Backstage West*. He received the 2005-06 George Jean Nathan Award for Dramatic Criticism.

Leonard Jacobs was the national theater editor and a critic at *Backstage* and a theater critic for *New York Press*. He founded the *Clyde Fitch Report*, a website on arts and politics, and authored *Historic Photos of Broadway: New York Theater, 1850-1970*. He is currently the Director of Cultural Institutions at the New York City Department of Cultural Affairs.

Chris Jones is the chief theater critic of the *Chicago Tribune*. He previously covered Broadway and the road for *Variety*. A former academic and associate dean, he is also the director of the National Critics Institute at the Eugene O'Neill Theater Center.

John Lahr has been a contributor to the *New Yorker* since 1992. He was the magazine's senior drama critic for 21 years. He has twice won the George Jean Nathan Award for Dramatic Criticism. His books include *Notes On a Cowardly Lion: The Biography of Bert Lahr*, *Tennessee Williams: Mad Pilgrimage of the Flesh*, and *Prick Up Your Ears: The Biography of Joe Orton*. He has edited the diaries of Joe Orton and Kenneth Tynan. He is the first critic ever to win a Tony Award for co-authoring *Elaine Stritch at Liberty*.

Brian Lipton was the editor-in-chief of *TheaterMania.com*. He currently writes for *IN New York*, *Cititour.com*, and *Theater Pizzazz*.

Peter Marks is the chief theater critic of the *Washington Post*. He was previously a theater critic for the *New York Times*.

Matthew Murray is the chief New York theater critic of *TalkinBroadway.com*. He has also served as an editor for *TheaterMania.com* and *Stage Directions* magazine and contributed to *Backstage*.

Michael Musto writes the column "Musto! The Musical!" for *Out* magazine and pieces for the "Style" section of the *New York Times*. He wrote the entertainment column "La Dolce Musto" for the *Village Voice*. He is the author of *La Dolce Musto: Writings by the World's Most Outrageous Columnist* and *Fork on the Left, Knife in the Back*.

Jesse Oxfeld was the theater critic of the *New York Observer*. He has also been an editor of *Tablet* magazine and *New York* magazine.

Richard Ouzounian was the theater critic of the *Toronto Star*. He has also worked as a director, lyricist, and playwright.

Michael Portantiere has been a theater journalist and editor for more than 35 years. He is a panelist for the weekly Broadway Radio podcasts on *BroadwayStars.com*. He is also a theatrical photographer.

Andy Propst is the founder of *AmericanTheaterWeb.com*. He has written for *TheaterMania.com*, the *Village Voice*, and *Backstage*. He is the author of *You Fascinate Me So: The Life and Times of Cy Coleman*.

Ronni Reich was an arts reporter and critic for the *Star-Ledger*. She has also written for the *Washington Post* and *Backstage*.

Michael Riedel is the theater columnist of the *New York Post*. He is also the co-host of *Theater Talk* on PBS. He is the author of *Razzle Dazzle: The Battle for Broadway*.

Frank Rizzo is the theater critic and arts reporter of the *Hartford Courant*. He also writes for *Variety*, *American Theatre* magazine, and the *New York Times*.

David Rooney is a film and theater critic for the *Hollywood Reporter*. He was previously the chief theater critic and theater editor of *Variety*.

Frank Scheck is a theater critic for the *New York Post* and the *Hollywood Reporter*. He has also written for the *Christian Science Monitor*, the *New York Daily News*, and *Time Out New York*.

Michael Schulman has contributed to the *New Yorker* since 2006 and covers theater in its "Goings On About Town" and "Talk of the Town" sections.

Howard Shapiro was the theater critic of the *Philadelphia Inquirer*. He currently writes about theater for *NewsWorks* and reviews Broadway on the radio for the Classical Network. He teaches arts criticism at Temple University.

Helen Shaw is a contributing theater critic for *Time Out New York*. She also works as a dramaturg and teaches drama at New York University.

David Sheward was the executive editor of *Backstage*. He currently writes reviews for *ArtsinNY.com* and *TheaterLife.com*. He is the author of *Rage and Glory: The Volatile Life and Career of George C. Scott*.

John Simon was the theater critic of *New York* magazine from 1968 to 2005 and of *Bloomberg News* from 2005 to 2010. He is currently the theater critic of the *Westchester Guardian* and *Yonkers Tribune*. He received the 1969–70 George Jean Nathan Award for Dramatic Criticism.

Alexis Soloski is a theater critic and reporter for the *New York Times*. She also writes for the *Guardian* and the *New Yorker* and is the former chief theater critic of the *Village Voice*. She holds a doctorate in theater from Columbia University.

Michael Sommers is a former president of the New York Drama Critics' Circle and was chief critic for the *Star-Ledger* and the Newhouse Newspapers. He is currently a freelance regional critic for the "Metropolitan" section of the *New York Times* and covers New York theater for *NewJersey Newsroom.com*.

Meet the Theater Critics

Marilyn Stasio is a theater critic for *Variety*. She is the author of *Showtune*, a biography co-written with songwriter Jerry Herman. She is also the "crime columnist" of the *New York Times Book Review*.

Zachary Stewart is the chief critic and features reporter of *TheaterMania.com*. He has also worked as a playwright and director.

Steven Suskin is a theater critic for the *Huffington Post*. He has also written for *Variety* and *Playbill*. He is the author of 14 books including *Show Tunes*, *Second Act Trouble*, *The Sound of Broadway Music*, and *The Book of Mormon: The Testament of a Broadway Musical*. He has worked as a theatrical manager and producer.

Terry Teachout is the drama critic of the *Wall Street Journal* and the critic-at-large of *Commentary*. He is the author of biographies of Duke Ellington, Louis Armstrong, and George Balanchine. He is also a playwright and opera librettist. He won a 2014 Bradley Prize.

Roma Torre is a theater critic and news anchor at NY1 News.

Elisabeth Vincentelli is the chief drama critic of the *New York Post*. She was formerly the arts and entertainment editor of *Time Out New York*. She is originally from France.

Rob Weinert-Kendt is the editor-in-chief of *American Theatre* magazine. He has also written for the *Los Angeles Times* and the *New York Times*.

Matt Windman is the theater critic of *amNewYork*. He is also an attorney.

Linda Winer is the chief theater critic of *Newsday*. She has also written for the *Chicago Tribune*, the *New York Daily News*, and *USA Today*.

Jason Zinoman writes about theater and comedy for the *New York Times*. He is the author of *Shock Value: How a Few Eccentric Outsiders Gave Us Nightmares, Conquered Hollywood, and Invented Modern Horror* and *Searching for Dave Chappelle*.

Richard Zoglin is the theater critic of *Time* magazine. He is the author of *Hope: Entertainer of the Century* and *Comedy at the Edge: How Stand-Up in the 1970s Changed America*.

1

Why We Exist

MATT WINDMAN: *Why do we have theater critics in the first place?*

Michael Sommers: Theater criticism goes far back, even in informal ways—like the English court wits that sat around and made cutting remarks during performances in the 17th century. I'm sure there was a lot of grumbling on the amphitheater steps at Epidaurus.

Helen Shaw: Theater criticism is about the human response to write about theater. Many of us take other jobs so we can do it. We are not doing this to be wealthy, to be known, to be liked, or anything like that. It's just a primal response.

Zachary Stewart: Theater critics lead the conversation after the curtain has fallen. They sift through the junk (so that people with limited time and money don't have to) and connect important work to the larger cultural conversation.

Chris Jones: People sometimes say to me "critics are dead" or "we don't need critics," or variations of that. But consider the *American Idol* phenomenon and all its spinoffs. *American Idol*, at its core, is a group of critics. There's still a broadly accepted sense that this is a good thing and a healthy thing—even if people don't find a particular review or a particular critic to be all that good or healthy.

Michael Riedel: There's no real reason for theater critics. It's not a job that's essential to the wellbeing of mankind. It's just that during the late 19th to early 20th century, when Broadway was coming along and becoming a big part of the entertainment business, newspapers decided they wanted to cover the shows that people were going to see.

Jesse Green: Magazine and newspaper editors got it into their heads that people are interested in reading reviews—though perhaps less so now than previously. It's part of a package of cultural information that appeals to an audience that advertisers want to target. I don't think there's a lot to say about theater criticism as an art form. It can be done well, and it can be done poorly. But fundamentally, it's a business, just like any other. Even Shaw did it for the money.

Peter Marks: Traditionally, theater criticism was a service for the readers, to let them know which shows to see. It then grew beyond being just a consumer guide. As the theater became more diverse and complex, as the stories and the forms became more varied, there was more reason for someone to have a conversation with the audience about what was going on in the art form.

Frank Rizzo: I used to review rock concerts, which would come into town and leave the next day. And I would think, Why are we covering this? After all, the show's gone. But people want to know what it was like to be there—to be part of that experience. Theater has a lot more to offer than concerts. Shows have longer runs, so people can read a review and become inspired to go to the theater. But even if they don't go, they can still feel like they're part of a cultural community. I read reviews from all over the country. I'm not going to see those shows, but I can feel what it was like to be in that audience.

Jeremy Gerard: Critics offer a skeleton key into thinking about a subject. They help us to see things with open eyes, open hearts, and open minds. Good critics are not people I agree with all the time. Often, they're people I disagree with, but whose intellect I respect, and who help me see things in a show that I hadn't thought about before.

Elizabeth Vincentelli: From a pragmatic point of view, there are a lot of shows out there and tickets are not cheap. People's time and money are at a premium, so you want to direct them towards the shows that are worth their attention. A big Broadway show is not necessarily worth their attention. They may be better off with a small, experimental thing that tries to do something and succeeds in its own universe.

David Cote: Criticism and reviews provide a direct response to works of art. There's nothing worse than putting art out there, putting your soul out there, into a void. Even if you can afford the most expensive marketing and advertising, it's still a void. We also serve the function of telling people what we think of certain works and shaping the discourse around them. If critics went away, it would be a horrible blow to art.

Michael Dale: Theater critics provide an informed opinion. While it's true that that any opinion can be a valid one, a theater critic working in New York will review well over 100 productions a year. They don't just see what they want to see. They commit themselves to seeing every major production and a wide variety of other productions, so their reviews come with a thorough knowledge of what is happening and developing in the theater.

Howard Shapiro: Critics provide more than just comments from friends. While everyone can have ideas about a show, usually they don't. Usually they just say, "I liked it" or "I didn't like it." That's not being a critic.

Chris Jones: There is a need within the artistic enterprise for somebody to deliver some kind of verdict. In the theater, you start with an idea. Maybe you have a workshop or a tryout and then a full production. At that point, someone has to say, "This is good" or "This is not good," or maybe even, "This is great." That person can't have a stake in the production. It has to be somebody who is unbiased but has the context to be able to judge that production and relate it to other work.

Ben Brantley: In the best of all possible worlds—one where people went to the theater without reading reviews—theater critics would be there to continue the conversation, start an argument, give a nod of affirmation, or whatever. I like to read other kinds of criticism after I've seen a movie or read a book. I think there are people like me who enjoy reading criticism—even of things that they won't see—if the critic can recreate the experience in writing. Ideally, that is what criticism should do. Sometimes you can kind of get off on someone else's enthusiasm.

Peter Filichia: Not everyone agrees with me, but I say we're here to let people know what they'd enjoy. I want to be an audience matchmaker. Most of my reviews are positive because I specifically slant them to the people who will enjoy a certain show. I see no reason why critics should only give their own opinions. They're writing for an audience. It's about the reader. It's not about me. I don't care if I have a good time or not. I am there to determine who would like the show.

John Simon: Being a consumer guide is the most pathetic and inadequate way of looking at drama criticism. Unfortunately, that is the way many publications—perhaps even most—look at it. That is the last thing that matters. What matters is trying to understand what the work is and what it isn't and to reveal that to your own satisfaction—assuming that you apply high standards to your own work, which you should if you're a critic.

Linda Winer: For me, the consumer guide function has always been the least interesting part of the job. I don't want to devote my life to telling people whether or not to spend $50 or $100 or even $500 on something. I think we have theater critics to continue the conversation. Everybody walks out of the theater talking about plays, and we are part of that conversation. I think a good critic is someone with an interesting mind. It isn't the yes or the no that matters—it's the *why*. Everything we do is about trying to explain the *why*. That is harder and harder to do with reduced space. But for me, that's the goal.

Roma Torre: I go back and forth about this. Sometimes it's consumer-oriented, in that you're steering people to see or not see something based on its quality and its cost, but I think the main function of a theater critic is to assess the intrinsic merit of a piece of theater. There are many aspects to that, and a lot of intangibles as to what make for good theater. But if we do our jobs correctly, we can help maintain a sense of quality control within the art form.

Steven Suskin: How do prospective ticket buyers decide what to see? If you're in a town with only two theaters operating at any given moment, you can find out easily enough what's playing. But in New York, there's so much out there. It's easy to say, "I want to see *The Book of Mormon*. That's supposed to be really good." But there are a lot of Off Broadway shows, and even Off Off Broadway shows, that are worthwhile. I don't think there is any way that theatergoers will find out about them unless they read something urging them to go, and that's what theater critics do. I don't think our job is to tell people whether it's good or bad. Our job is to give the readers enough information so that they can say, "Oh, I'm interested in this."

Michael Schulman: If it's done well, criticism is certainly more than providing a kind of consumer report. Critics are people with an analytical ability who deconstruct the experience of seeing theater. Criticism deepens the art and deepens the experience for all audience members. And since theater evolves and is ephemeral, we need theater critics to document and analyze what's happening with the theater as an art form: how it changes, how it grows, where it missteps, and where it finds insight into the human condition.

Leonard Jacobs: More than evaluating or passing judgment, the main function of theater criticism is to teach—whether that's teaching the public, the industry, or other critics.

Andy Propst: In the ideal world, a critic is someone who is at one corner of a triangle. From that corner, there are the two lines that go out. On one line, there's the critic speaking to the potential audience member about why he or she should go to a show, and hopefully telling the audience member a little bit more than he or she would have known about the piece, its style, and all that. The other line goes out to the artist, and the critic is saying to the artist, "This is what I saw. This is what I liked and why. This is what I didn't like and why. This is how I think you achieved your goals." Then a line forms between the audience and the artist because of those two dialogues that have happened.

The classic example I use is Richard Christiansen of the *Chicago Tribune*. At the beginning of the Chicago Theater Movement, Christiansen went to some tiny theater and saw a play by a writer no one had ever heard of. A few days later, he wrote that he'd seen this play, that he didn't think it was a terribly good play, but that audiences should see it because this playwright needed support and would be someone someday. That playwright was David Mamet. That kind of support of an artist at an early juncture is incredibly important.

Robert Faires: I like to refer to a celestial metaphor, where the artistic experience is the sun and the audience is the Earth. Sometimes the audience isn't facing the sun directly. It's turned around, and maybe it's not receiving the light. A theater critic can be the moon, reflecting that experience onto the dark side of the Earth, and giving the audience a sense of what that light was like coming from the artists. I feel like I am at my most valuable when I'm providing that function—when I can reflect as powerfully as possible my experience at the theater and what I think it meant.

Rob Weinert-Kendt: We all have a critical impulse: we see a show and then we want to talk about it. We want to supplement the experience of seeing theater by arguing about it and reading about it, and we turn that over to people we think are really interesting, authoritative, or funny. I'm not saying that we need theater critics to tell us what to go see. I really believe that theater criticism is only going to survive if it's seen as part of the theater experience, and not just as something you read before you go to a show. In my idealized world, people would be seeing a lot of shows, and criticism would be in the mix of that. It would be the icing on the cake, something to help people think about what they already saw.

Theater also needs to be recorded. It's the same with dance. It needs reporters. It needs someone to say, "This is what happened. This is what we saw." I can't go back and look at old plays. I can look at old films, but I can't see the original production of *Oklahoma!* It's lost to history. All we have is the review, and that's an awesome responsibility.

Jason Zinoman: I see theater criticism as a branch of reporting. Going to see a production is like going to see a presidential debate. If some new, really interesting actress has a great role, that's important to mention. If the play contains an idea that's in the zeitgeist, you want to talk about that. It's also an act of translation. It makes connections and puts the show in a context that makes it more meaningful than whether it's just good or bad. It could be a historical context, a political context, the context of the playwright's work, or the director's work.

Linda Winer: I love reading critics. I love newspapers. I still get four newspapers delivered to my door. I love picking up the paper and reading what my colleagues said about something, and how often it sounds as if all of us have been to totally different events. The lesson there is not that critics are stupid, but that human beings are complicated, and the arts are complicated.

MATT WINDMAN: *Who is your favorite theater critic of the past or present?*

Terry Teachout: The critics who have meant the most to me wrote in other fields: Fairfield Porter and Clement Greenberg in the visual arts, Arlene Croce and Edwin Denby in dance, Edmund Wilson in literature, and Virgil Thomson in music.

Ben Brantley: The critics I've been most influenced by are probably film critics—certainly Pauline Kael and James Agee.

Adam Feldman: I love reading Pauline Kael on movies. Her passion for the art form is exciting, even when—or especially when—I disagree with her.

Michael Sommers: I certainly enjoy reading criticism, all the way to James Gibbons Huneker, the great progenitor of the American theater critics. He was a music and theater critic for various publications in New York at the turn of the last century. He had an urbane, modern style. I also admire the *New Yorker* style that Robert Benchley had in the 1930s and the amiable persona that he put out.

Aside from Brooks Atkinson and George Jean Nathan, if you look at many of the New York critics, their careers didn't last more than 10 or 20 years. They went off and wrote about something else, or they died. I guess there's some burnout, too. I've been very fortunate to have been able to do this for so long—and I still love it. You should give it up once you don't love it anymore. John Simon's going to go out of the theater feet first. I think that's how all drama critics want to go. When drama critics retire, they usually die. Look at what happened to poor Jacques le Sourd. Howard Kissel didn't last that long after he stopped writing. We have to go forward like sharks or else we die.

Alexis Soloski: The golden age critics of the 1920s are my heroes: Robert Benchley, Alexander Woollcott, George Jean Nathan, and Dorothy Parker. They have a sense of play and delight that's informed by a pretty staggering intelligence.

Elisabeth Vincentelli: I just bought a collection of Mary McCarthy's theater reviews. I wouldn't say she's my favorite, but her reviews are wonderful. It's like opening a packet of bonbons.

John Lahr: Mary McCarthy is hilarious. She's always wrong, but she's quite stimulating, and she can make an absolutely great argument.

Ben Brantley: I was recently reading Mary McCarthy's theater criticism. She's interesting in the sense of someone whose judgment doesn't reflect what would be considered good by posterity. She dismissed pretty much everyone, including Arthur Miller and Tennessee Williams, but she's great fun to read because of the intellectual energy that she brings.

Steven Suskin: George Jean Nathan, who worked from 1910 into the 1950s, was good at citing past shows to help put things in perspective.

Linda Winer: Claudia Cassidy was the music, theater, and dance critic of the *Chicago Tribune* for maybe 25 years. She was famous and infamous and extremely tough. She was the closest thing I had to a mentor. By the time I got to the *Tribune*, she was semi-retired. But of all the people who could have patronized me, she always said, "Just call me Claudia." She would go to a theater, dance, or music event, go back to the paper, pound out a review on her manual typewriter, and then go out dancing with her husband. She had long red hair that, as the mythology goes, Brenda Starr was modeled after.

Tennessee Williams said that he owed his career to her because they opened *The Glass Menagerie* in Chicago, and he was an unknown. Claudia Cassidy went to see it and loved it. She reviewed it and reviewed it and reviewed it until the New York producers had to go and see it. Her name is now connected to Tennessee Williams forever.

Chris Jones: For me, it would be Claudia Cassidy, who had my job, and in whose footsteps I am proud to follow in. She was an incredible critic, but she is not as well-known in New York as she should be because she wrote in Chicago. If people do know her, they know her as "Acidy Cassidy," as a hatchet woman known for trashing second-rate touring shows and irritating New York producers—which is certainly true. Nobody could write a more vicious pan than her. But when she loved something, she could write about it with astonishing passion and eloquence.

She understood Tennessee Williams better than anybody. I think it's fair to say that without her, Williams would not have become the writer he became. Williams was writing ahead of his time. If you look at the recent Broadway revival of *The Glass Menagerie*, what you're seeing is people finally understanding his brilliance. The play was too soon for a lot of people, but Claudia caught it in the moment.

David Cote: Kenneth Tynan is the top. His writing is concise, witty, and explosive. He didn't hide his political convictions or his passion. Besides Tynan: William Hazlitt for perspective, Stanley Kauffmann for intellectual rigor, Walter Kerr for bedside manner, Robert Brustein for balls, and George Jean Nathan for arrogant bitchery. There aren't many living theater critics that I admire.

Richard Ouzounian: I love Kenneth Tynan, but I don't think he can be your model if you write in North America. You can love his style and prose, but he did say that the job of the theater critic is "to make way for the good by demolishing the bad." I don't know if it's quite that draconian anymore. I may be an incredibly negative critic when I hate a show, but I am also the most incredibly positive critic when I love a show. You have to be able to give as well as take away. You have to bring people into the theater as well as keep them out.

Jeremy Gerard: In terms of knowledge and insight, I would say Walter Kerr in his prime—which was not his time at the *New York Times*, but before that at the *Herald Tribune*.

Roma Torre: I loved Walter Kerr. He was so measured. His criticism was never personal or snarky. He understood the nature, structure, and general elements that made for quality theater. His criticism was always constructive. There was a time when producers would look to certain critics to fix their shows. There aren't too many critics who could serve in that function anymore—partly because of the current nature of criticism today. The emphasis on glibness, the reduced space, and economic pressures prevent us from being able to present the kind of consistently thoughtful, studied assessment that embodied Kerr's writing.

Steven Suskin: The best theater criticism creates an impression of what you're seeing in words. Walter Kerr could describe an actor in two or three sentences and make you feel like you were experiencing the performance.

Linda Winer: The person I read for wonderment—on how theater can be made alive through words that bounce off the page—is Walter Kerr. The *New York Times* used to have a daily theater critic and a Sunday theater critic. When I was in Chicago, I would wait for the Sunday *Times* to come out to read Walter Kerr. He was on the third page of the "Arts and Leisure" section above the fold. He would write essays about what he saw the week before, and he could contradict the daily critic. It was good to have two voices since the *Times* has so much power. Kerr had a rich, individual way of describing an event. He could zero in on the way a particular actor did a particular thing, and from there, open it up until you got a picture of the entire play. I thought it was magic. I miss having someone in that slot. But most of all, I miss Walter Kerr.

Richard Ouzounian: I used to worship Walter Kerr as a kid. He was the great combination of the smart and populous, which is what I strive to be. Walter Kerr was the guy who said *Gypsy* was "the best damn musical I've seen in years." On the other hand, he was a professor at Catholic University. He could write smart, but he could also write zippy. I also learned a couple of tropes from him. He used to begin with a telling scene or an image from a show. He also loved to wind up a review by making it very clear what he had said. There was never any doubt about what Walter Kerr said in a review.

John Lahr: When I was young, the book I thought was the bee's knees was *Seasons of Discontent* by Robert Brustein. I used to write out sentences from it just to feel the rhythm. Brustein's style was a bit florid and dense when he wrote for the *New Republic*, but at least he was in the ballpark of wanting a discussion.

Helen Shaw: I think of Robert Brustein as the ideal critic. One of the reasons I went to the A.R.T./MXAT Institute for Advanced Theater Training was to be there before he left. Being taught by him, and looking at the naughtiness and the liveliness of his mind, was certainly my biggest influence.

John Simon: I like Robert Brustein quite a bit, but we have significant differences. He claims that I don't understand American humor.

Rob Weinert-Kendt: My favorite critic of theater of the past is Eric Bentley. He's still alive. I think he's 98 years old now. His books about theater are must-reads. Even though they're dense, they're really well-considered and substantive. He's very hard on a lot of the great playwrights of the 20th century (his stuff about Eugene O'Neill is unforgiving), but they're really valuable. He writes about big, important subjects that take in so much of the world.

Andy Propst: I've always responded to Frank Rich. I will actually pull out *Hot Seat*, the collection of his *New York Times* reviews, and read it just for fun.

Matthew Murray: Frank Rich fused the fan's adoration with an unswerving critical eye in a way almost no one else has.

Charles Isherwood: Frank Rich brought me to the paper. I go back to his reviews all the time. He's an amazingly exciting theater writer.

Helen Shaw: Scott Brown writes this kind of baroque, Joycean prose that is a gorgeous keyhole to go down.

Matthew Murray: My favorite of the current crop is probably Jesse Green of *New York* magazine. Just like his predecessor, Scott Brown, he turns out intense, intricate, and insightful analyses of new shows that don't seem to be matched anywhere else.

Jesse Oxfeld: I do enjoy Jesse Green's criticism in *New York* magazine. He's so deeply enmeshed in the theater world of New York, and he has such an understanding of its history and people. He really brings a lot of insight that goes beyond, "This was a nice performance" or "The set was pretty but the lighting was ugly."

Frank Scheck: John Simon has always been a favorite of mine. He can be way over-the-top and vindictive and nasty, but he's so entertaining and brilliant. He's so much fun to read that I can't resist it.

Michael Sommers: It still gives me a little thrill to see John Simon stomp into a theater.

Michael Riedel: I've always thought that John Simon, in his heyday, was the best. His brutal putdowns of shows were always fun.

Jesse Green: I grew up reading John Simon in *New York* magazine. That's part of the reason I took the job. I was horrified by the hatefulness of his reviews, but he was a stylish and obviously intelligent writer.

Matthew Murray: John Simon was erudite and willing to say anything and everything he wanted about anyone. He got a not-entirely-undeserved rap for being hard on people. I'm not sure there's ever been anyone with a more scalpel-edged view of theater and method of reportage than he.

Terry Teachout: I've known John Simon since I came to New York, and I truly admire him. He's the senior critic in town. I don't always agree with him—in fact, I frequently don't agree with him—but he knows more than I'll ever know. And if you don't respect that kind of knowledge, you need to be taught a lesson in why you should.

Elisabeth Vincentelli: I'm ambivalent about John Simon. He's such a great stylist and writer, but his meanness is just too much. It was delicious to read, but sometimes it got in the way of his critical acumen, and that kind of spoiled the pleasure of reading him. I didn't feel like there was any generosity behind it. He often wrote about very real issues that nobody else would touch—the stuff that's very tricky to deal with—but he wrote about it with such a lack of empathy.

Robert Faires: Benedict Nightingale influenced me very early on. There was a period when he left England and spent a year writing in New York. Out of that, he produced a book called *Fifth Row Center*, about not being in his home country and trying to understand theater from a different perspective. It really struck a personal chord with me. I had a sense of both the work he had seen and of his personal journey through that work. I can't say I've stayed on top of his work throughout the years, but I do find myself going back to that book periodically, reading passages from it, and finding it very inspiring.

MATT WINDMAN: *Is there any kind of difference between the titles of theater critic and theater reviewer?*

Jeremy Gerard: It's just semantic bullshit.

Zachary Stewart: While the former title suggests an effort to critique a work within the context of theatrical tradition and the latter suggests something closer to a consumer report, it actually really depends on the branding of the publication (with critic connoting something more highbrow).

John Simon: This is something I've always been fairly fastidious about. Reviewers—either because it's their kind of mentality, or because it's the kind of job they have, and it's what is expected of them—manage to like a whole lot of pretty cheesy, wretched things. It may be purely to stay at their jobs. The *Daily News*, or perhaps even the *Times*, couldn't stand to give as many bad reviews for so many things that a true critic would have to give.

Elizabeth Vincentelli: Some people say the reviewer is more of a consumer guide. They see the reviewer as having a lesser status than the critic, who's highbrow. I think that's very self-serving—as is so much in theater. It's bullshit.

David Cote: A review gives a quick impression of what the show is. It is written under greater time constraints, and probably with less intellectual energy expended and less context. The critic writes longer, and isn't concerned with spoiling elements of the plot. There's more space in criticism, but that doesn't necessarily make it more valuable or insightful than a review. I write reviews, but there's criticism embedded in the review.

Michael Dale: I think we mostly use the term critic because it's short and sweet, but reviewer is probably more accurate. Critic implies that the writer is offering a complete analysis of every aspect of the production. But given the limitations of time and space, that's impossible to do on a regular basis. Reviewer implies that you're simply giving an overview of what you saw.

Steve Suskin: A theater critic isn't so much concerned about the plot as a show's value and what it's like. Walter Kerr was a critic. John Chapman and Burns Mantle of the *Daily News* were reporters. They were giving reports to their readers. They weren't giving keen, analytical viewpoints. The question being asked was, "Should you see it or not?" The theater reviewer is really a theater reporter. A reporter covers the show and tells you what it's about and who's in it.

Don Aucoin: I respond directly to the work in front of me and spread the word to my readers as quickly as possible. Whether that makes me a reviewer or a critic is not important to me.

Helen Shaw: A reviewer writes about something that is still open and includes a directive of "go" or "don't go" to the show. Criticism is what happens as soon as the show has become history. If you find yourself writing about a production that you saw last year, which no one will ever have a chance to see again, that's *de facto* criticism. I am a reviewer who wants to be a critic. I hope my writing will be useful after the show has closed, but I also want to issue an invitation to people to come and be changed by whatever the show is.

Howard Shapiro: Some people say that you can't write a piece of criticism with only 500 words, but I don't really see any difference. I don't see a difference in the old term drama critic either. We all do the same thing.

Jesse Oxfeld: What I did for the *Observer* was really being a reviewer, not a critic. Criticism is not service journalism. Criticism is engaging with the art form and having a conversation with the artist. Reviewing is saying, "This was nicely done, and it's worth your money." There was a period of time when I would call myself the *New York Observer*'s theater reviewer instead of its theater critic, but the distinction was just too tiresome to make.

Andy Propst: It comes down to how you view your own work. On my best days, I approach criticism. On the worst, I'm a reviewer.

Ben Brantley: The terms are used pretty much interchangeably. My title is chief theater critic. I think criticism is not consumer reports. It should give a little more. It should let the reader figure out for himself or herself how they would respond were they in the critic's shoes, even if they don't necessarily agree with the critic.

Chris Jones: I consider myself a critic. It's true that I write for a daily newspaper, so maybe my criticism is not as considered, and it does not have the hindsight of history. It's immediate, but I don't think that makes it any less valuable.

Peter Filichia: The critic tells the show's creators where they've gone wrong. The reviewer tells people whether a show is worth their time and money. For newspapers, I'm a reviewer. In my books, I'm a critic. A lot of pros in the business tell me that they enjoy reading what I write because I try to find solutions for problems in a show. It's not enough for a critic to say that something stinks.

Roma Torre: A reviewer is somebody who just says whether a show is good or bad without going into any real depth. A critic is somebody who analyzes the show in a methodical fashion. I hate to admit it, but I am more of a reviewer—only by virtue of the time and space limitations that have been imposed upon me. It's thoroughly disconcerting to me because I have so much more I want to say about each work I see. On the other hand, it has forced me to be far more economical in my writing. I have very little room to wax poetic on anything. It's a constant frustration, but it's the nature of the beast.

Adam Feldman: The critic may have his or her own set of standards stemming from a particular approach. That can often be seen in academic work, where people delve into a particular work of art or a set of works within a specific intellectual context. They often have more space in which to do it, and it can be more analytical and have less to do with a recommendation or non-recommendation. For those of us who write reviews fairly quickly, it's a balancing act to describe what the show is and let audience members find the right shows for themselves while also making critical judgments about the quality of shows.

Scott Brown: That's a pretty artificial distinction. What's important is that you're saying something that's relevant and interesting, and that you're fully engaged with the material. I don't want to be preachy and say, "Theater reviewers just check the boxes of what the show did or didn't do and have snarky comments, while theater critics spin glorious curlicues of wisdom into the air." It varies show to show, too. I've turned in things that were just reviews and other things that might be classified as criticism.

Jesse Green: I prefer to be called a critic. That said, I don't think criticism (as I would define the term) really exists anymore. I may be disrespecting the great work of many people, but if criticism does still exist, it's not popular. I'm sure there are academic journals where you can find drama criticism, but the only thing I would like reading less than a manual on how to work a toaster oven would be academic dramatic criticism. The days when dramatic criticism stood as a popular conversation, when it was part of what a writer delivered to interested readers, are long gone. Even in monthly magazines, it's extremely rare to get any kind of writing that looks at the larger picture of the theater.

John Lahr: I do think there's a difference between a reviewer and a critic, and I've gotten flak from some quarters about this. In our culture, a reviewer is really there for a marketing function: to give a thumbs-up or a thumbs-down. They're not having a discussion so much as treating the show as a news story. They're writing for the readership. Criticism has an entirely different function. A critic treats the theater as a metaphor to be interpreted. A critic puts the play into a larger context. Historically, there's been very little criticism in America. There have been a few places you can point to, like the *New Republic*, or the *Nation* when Harold Clurman was writing for it.

I wrote a polemic recently for the *Nieman Reports* where I talked about the difference between critics and "crickets." A lot of today's newspaper reviewers are just bluffing. They don't know what they're talking about in any deep sense. They tote a similar line. They talk about Pinter pauses or Tennessee Williams being all about sex. They codify all the major styles in a way that makes them uninteresting to the audience. There's no space for discussion. As a result, the narrative of the theater gets impoverished.

Michael Schulman: The *New Yorker* certainly aspires to criticism rather than reviewing. Hilton Als's and John Lahr's essays go beyond whether a play is good or Tony-worthy or whether people should buy tickets. The term reviewing implies that it's a consumer service. I think that's what the *New York Times* does. The *Times* reviews shows, but on a very high level. Criticism stems from a kind of intellectual discourse about any number of things. If you read some *New Yorker* reviews, they don't necessarily tell you whether to go out and buy tickets. They tell you something about the larger questions of the arts.

John Lahr has described his job as being like a shrink. He sits back and listens to the play, as if it were a patient. And when there's something wrong with it, he diagnoses it. It goes a lot deeper than a checklist of looking at the set, the lighting, and the lead performance. Michael Feingold sort of steps back and looks at something in a much larger historical context. I think of it as looking at a painting from various distances. There's a normal distance where you go up to a painting, look at it, take it in, and decide if you like it or not after five seconds. Michael Feingold is looking at paintings from different angles, looking at something from across the room and seeing how it reflects all the other paintings. John Lahr is looking at something very up close and observing the texture of the craft.

Michael Sommers: I'm a reviewer, not a critic. When you get 500 to 750 words to write about a show, and sometimes as little as 250 words, that's being a reviewer. You're basically telling people what the show is and giving them some flavor of it. A critic is someone who looks at the show in a more leisurely fashion. The critic brings more outside elements into the review. As a reviewer, I've got no room to talk about how the show relates to other circumstances. I don't know how many real critics there are anymore. A great critic was Eric Bentley, even though I disagree with most of the things he wrote. That was criticism. There isn't much of that anymore. Who's got the time to read it?

David Finkle: I think of myself as a reviewer. When you call yourself a critic, you're asking to be taken very seriously. I like the idea of not necessarily seeing yourself as important.

MATT WINDMAN: How does being a theater critic compare to being a different kind of arts critic?

Elysa Gardner: It's all different media with different elements. But at the end of the day, it's about the visceral impressions that the art makes on you—whatever art that is.

Michael Sommers: With any kind of criticism, what you're trying to do is put a work in some sort of context and give people an understanding of what it is.

Jesse Green: Theater is not a vibrant economy anymore. Film is extremely vibrant, and TV is even more vibrant than film. I get a breakdown every day of the hits on the *Vulture* website, which is *New York* magazine's cultural web presence, and it's organized by cultural category: film, music, TV, theater, books, and art. Without giving away any trade secrets, I can tell you that TV is almost always at the top and theater is almost always near the bottom, unless James Franco was involved in whatever I reviewed the previous night. Perhaps it's a reflection on my writing, but I don't think so. It's just the way it is.

Charles Isherwood: Because film is such a ubiquitous part of our culture, film critics don't have as much direct influence. People go to the movies no matter what the critics say. Sometimes you get the feeling that film critics are talking to themselves or to each other. That's less the case with theater critics. As much as we like to complain that people don't go to the good shows, people really do look to critics when they're going to spend $100 or more to go to the theater. They're not going to slavishly follow any one person's opinion, but you can feel like you're having some sort of impact.

Zachary Stewart: Compared to a mass media critic, theater critics write for a much more boutique audience who can afford to go to the theater and have a desire to do so. This can be quite liberating when it comes to writing with specificity for a targeted audience.

Michael Schulman: As far as the financial prospects of a movie are concerned, film criticism is negligible. Theater exists in this small community where a *Times* review can make or break you. That puts a lot on the shoulders of one person or two people.

Don Aucoin: When I wrote about TV shows, I could safely assume that thousands of my readers were going to see the show in question, or that they at least had the ability to see it by clicking a remote control. With theater, you're speaking to a much smaller, but often more committed audience.

Frank Scheck: The experience of watching film is different than watching theater, and the art form is different, but the process of writing about them is the same.

Robert Feldberg: Theater is different than movies. Every Friday, another romantic comedy opens. They're written according to formula. They're not even meant to be reviewed. They're all variations of the same thing. When I was reviewing movies, only one out of 10 movies was really engaging. Movies are aimed at a certain audience for one weekend, like teenage boys or couples or whatever. Theater is much more individualistic. And in the majority of cases, the playwright is trying to create something artistic. Every show you see is likely to be different from other shows, so the writer deserves your patience and attention.

Joe Dziemianowicz: Stage productions are fleeting. The review is often the only record of the production, its cast, its direction, its look, its interpretation, its vision. Sure, some productions are filmed, and there are books and photographs, but reviews are an essential part of the theater history of any given season.

Michael Riedel: If you review a movie, everyone else is going to see the same movie that you saw. But if you review *Angels in America* on Tuesday night, the performance on Wednesday night is not going to be the same. You're describing a live event that's going to be seen only once. You're capturing a passing moment. In some ways, your job is to capture it as a reporter.

Andy Propst: You walk into a theater and sit there for two and a half hours. That's a whole lot of sensory overload to bring in, distill, and then pump out into words. With a CD, you can savor it once, twice, maybe even three times. A lot of film critics now have the ability to screen a film from home, so they have the same option.

Scott Brown: Nothing compares to the intensity and immediacy of theater. Nothing compares to the incredible social stress of being trapped in a room with people who are performing for you. It's different than sitting back in a chair in a screening room, watching something at home, or slapping on a pair of headphones. It's different to go to a specific location where you're locked into gladiatorial combat with each other in a weird sort of way. Actors talk about press nights that way. I don't think there's anything that compares to that. It's really thrilling, and it can be very graphic. Theater criticism is more of a contact sport. It's always going to be taken more to heart by the people who are involved with it.

Chris Jones: There's something about staring in person at an artist that creates a more intense relationship than being in a screening room and watching people in a movie.

Robert Feldberg: Theater criticism is local. If you review a movie, it's opening all over the country. If you review a play, it's only of immediate interest to New Yorkers, other people living in the metropolitan area, or tourists who happen to be in New York. Someone might want to see it months later when they visit New York, but it's happening locally.

Ben Brantley: Because theater, either rightly or wrongly, is perceived as an art form in jeopardy, a certain amount of cheerleading is required. We also have to work a little harder at getting people to pay attention or be interested. You probably have to be a little clearer, a little less self-referential, than you might be in other disciplines. If you read art forums, they're very academic and hermetically-sealed.

Richard Zoglin: I really have to really justify why a show deserves space in *Time* magazine. I'm writing about something that most of my readers can't see right away because they don't live in New York. I can't do a piece just because there's a show opening this week.

Linda Winer: Classical music critics don't get to write about new work very often. On the other hand, the work they get to write about has stood the test of time. They spend more time bathing in real art—in masterpieces. What I've always loved about theater criticism is how often we get to bump up against new work. Of course, we're currently getting more and more revivals. My husband has said that my job as turned into "comparing this Willy Loman to that Willy Loman."

Frank Scheck: Music is more subjective because there are musicians you like and ones that you don't like. If you don't like the music, you're not going to like the concert, so you have to step back and just evaluate the music on its own terms, and whether or not it's working for the people who appreciate that type of music. If I'm reviewing *American Idol* in concert or the Jonas Brothers, I'm not the target audience. You have the same scenario in the theater, too. There are some shows that are not geared to your sensibilities, so you have to evaluate them on their own terms. For example, is it working for the teenage girls?

John Simon: The good thing about music criticism is that you really have to know a lot about music. Anyone can write drama criticism. Indeed, it often happens that way, where someone who's been writing obituaries for years suddenly gets the drama critic job. It's absurd, but there you have it. But with music criticism, you have to put in someone who, however peculiar or questionable his opinions may be, has a solid knowledge of music, and that requires discipline and learning and some kind of mental level that not every Tom, Dick, or Harry has.

Terry Teachout: In the case of music or art, the difference lies in the words. Ned Rorem has a neat line on this: "Critics of words use words. Critics of music use words." If I'm writing about a symphony, I have to find a way to translate the event into words, but without using the kind of technical language that I might use if I were writing for musicians. There is no paraphrasable content in a symphony or a plotless ballet. But a play is about something, and it is written in words, and it usually has some kind of intellectual content. That makes writing about theater easier than writing about abstract music or a painting. There are more ways to go at it. You have more hooks to hang your hat on. But because I've written about art forms where verbal content is nonexistent or less important, it's loosened up the way I perceive what happens up in a play. It causes me to be more aware of certain kinds of nonverbal aspects of a theatrical production that other critics might not notice.

Helen Shaw: I have written about dance, and trying to explain just a movement through language is so bloody difficult. With theater, you can always hang your hat on the interplay between text and image. It's a dialogic art. It invites us to write about it. It wants us to have a dialogue with it. You've been sitting in a room for two hours with these combating voices, and then you get to add your voice to the fray.

Linda Winer: In terms of difficulty, writing about dance is somewhere in between writing about theater and writing about music. With dance, you're writing about something abstract, but you have arms and legs to talk about, and you've got so many pictures that you can create in your writing. Creating pictures about what the violin may have been meaning is meaningless with music.

Eric Grode: I once got a job offer to be a theater, dance, art, and classical music reporter and critic. I would be grotesquely underqualified for that job. In fact, I don't know if anyone exists who can handle all those different things.

2

How I Became a Theater Critic

Matt Windman: How did you become a theater critic?

Peter Filichia: One day in college, I was walking up a flight of stairs, and this guy I knew from high school saw me and said, "Hey, I've just been made editor of the school paper. I remember from high school how much you love theater. Why don't you write reviews for us?" I had never thought about it. I didn't know yet about press tickets. The first show I reviewed was the Broadway production of *Hair*. I paid with my own money to see it: $7.50 for a third row orchestra seat at a Sunday matinee.

Then I got a freelance job working for a new publication called *Boston After Dark*, which was essentially the *Village Voice* of Boston. I was 23 years old, and like today, they wanted people with a youthful slant. Because they were just starting out, paying the writers was a struggle. And when I went to get paid, they'd always say, "We can't pay you this week." I gave an ultimatum and threatened to quit if they didn't pay me. And when they didn't pay me, I quit. Next to my marriage, it was the biggest mistake of my life. It took a while before I realized that I wouldn't get free tickets anymore. And more importantly, my name wouldn't be in front of the public. I vowed that if I ever got the chance to do this again, I would not blow it over money.

Seventeen long years pass. It's now 1987. I'm walking down the street, and on the newsstand I see *TheaterWeek*, volume one, number one. I immediately bought it and thought, They must be looking for writers. I went over to my girlfriend's house and said, "I'm going to call them tomorrow, and I'm going to write for them." She said, "You're crazy. They're not going to pay you any decent money. Why don't you call up the *New York Times*? They'll definitely give you a freelance assignment." I said, "Yes, but only every now and then. What I want is a regular gig."

I went to see the editor-in-chief of *TheaterWeek*. He said, "You don't want to write for us because we don't pay enough." I said, "The money isn't important. I just want to get my name out there." I truly believe that if you do what you love, eventually, the money will come. Of course, the free tickets were nice, too. I got an assignment, and then I kept getting them. The people who succeeded the original editor-in-chief kept me on, one of whom was Michael Riedel. It was Michael who asked me if I wanted to write a column, and I kept doing a column until the paper went out of business in 1996.

In 1993, the position of New Jersey theater critic opened up at the *Star-Ledger*. Michael Sommers, who had been the New Jersey theater critic, was being promoted to the New York spot. When I went in for the interview to be the New Jersey critic, they said, "The reason we want you is because you are positive. We want the arts to grow in New Jersey. We don't want a mean critic. We want somebody who is really interested in seeing theater flourish in this state."

Richard Ouzounian: I was born and raised in New York. I'm 64 years old, so I was a kid during the days when there were still seven daily papers in New York. My dad, who ran a bar, would bring home the four morning papers when he came in every night. We also got the three afternoon papers. Somewhere along the way, I started reading theater reviews in the papers, and I realized that someone got paid to see plays.

I wrote reviews in high school and college. At the time, there was a very reputable television critic, Leonard Harris, who taught a course in arts criticism at Fordham University, where I went to college, and I took it. I realized that no one was going to hire a 20-year-old theater critic, so I became a theater practitioner. For roughly the next 20-odd years, I worked as a director-writer-actor across Canada. I was very lucky. I got a lot of jobs as an artistic director when I was very young, and I wound up running five major theaters.

By the time I was 40 years old, I had two kids and had discovered that my younger son was developmentally challenged, so I thought I should get a permanent job. I didn't immediately go over to the dark side, but I started doing work in TV and radio. I did a weekly radio show that was broadcast across Canada where I would play musical theater songs, set them in context, and talk about them. It's what inspired Bob Martin to create the character of Man in Chair in the musical *The Drowsy Chaperone*. Then I got a weekly theater critic slot in Toronto on CBC, our equivalent to NPR, and it became very popular and powerful. I realized that when Garth Drabinsky opened his first production of *Joseph and the Amazing Technicolor Dreamcoat* with Donny Osmond. The major daily newspapers in Toronto all hated it, but I liked it. And the next week, a full-page ad appeared with my quote across the top. I thought, This is pretty good: a brand-new career in my forties.

In 2000, as I turned 50, the theater critic of the *Toronto Star*, the country's largest paper, walked in one day and said, "I'm tired of this. I want out." It was the same day that my department at TVOntario, my major employer, got slashed, and I was without a job. The arts editor of the *Toronto Star* called me up and said, "I listen to you on the radio. Have you ever thought of doing it in the newspaper?" And I said, "That was actually my childhood dream." So at the age of 50, I became a daily newspaper critic.

John Simon: If you like to write (which I obviously do), and if you like theater (which I obviously do), and if you put those two things together, they spell theater critic. I was taken to the theater when I was a very small boy, and I fell in love with it. At any rate, I fell in fondness for it. So given my critical nature and my wanting to be closer to the theater, this is what came out of it.

The first publication I wrote for—if you can call it that—was a little pamphlet called *Audience*, which a young graduate student at Harvard started. It was a nice little giveaway. The first major publication I worked for was the *Hudson Review*. Robert Brustein, who was moving from the *Hudson Review* to the *New Republic*, recommended me. There are other things I did which I can barely recall. After all, I'm now 90 years old, and my memory isn't what it used to be.

Clay Felker, who was the editor at *New York* magazine, noticed something I had written for the *Herald Tribune*. It was a humorous piece about a supposed writing school sponsored by *Reader's Digest*. So when the *Tribune* died and Clay Felker went on to become the editor-in-chief at *New York* magazine, he took me on because Harold Clurman, who had been the drama critic, was not, in his opinion, a very interesting writer (which I concurred with). It worked out well. It worked out for 36 and two-thirds years.

John Lahr: I don't think anyone grows up thinking, I want to be a theater critic—or at least they didn't when I began doing this, which was around 1965. It wasn't taught at university. You couldn't take a course in it. You can now take a course in drama criticism, which is ironic since there's hardly any work anymore.

I had just come back from Oxford and was writing a biography of my father. At the time, I happened to have something I wanted to say about *Marat/Sade*, which I had just seen in England. I wrote an essay about it and sent it to *Manhattan East*, a local giveaway paper. It had a circulation of 50,000 because they gave it out in the lobbies of Park Avenue apartments. The editor then asked if I'd be interested in being the theater critic. I'd get free tickets and $10 for each review. Since I had no money, I thought that was great. I didn't know anything about drama criticism, but I had spent two years writing critical essays with Christopher Ricks, one of the great English literary critics.

From the outset, I wanted to do something different with my drama criticism. My idea was to invite the artists into the article and let them speak. I really wanted to create a sense of the life of the theater. Within about a year,

2. How I Became a Theater Critic 33

I was hearing from people who I never thought I'd get a response from, like Harold Pinter and Jules Feiffer, and I realized that this was something I could do. I progressed to writing for an underground paper called the *New York Free Press*. When Grove Press bought it, they agreed to pay me the astronomical fee of $250 apiece. Grove then made me its theater editor, which meant I could get plays published. By 1971, I was also the lead critic for the *Village Voice* and the literary manager of Lincoln Center Repertory Theatre, which meant that I could put on a play, review a play, and publish a play.

When the book about my father came out, it was reviewed on the front page of the *Times*. Then I left town. I had to get vaccinated from ambition or else I'd explode. I lived in England for seven years and worked on what became *Prick Up Your Ears*, my book about the playwright Joe Orton. That led to writing for a wonderful magazine called *New Society*, which all the major English critics worked for.

I was tapped for the *New Yorker* job in 1992. I told Tina Brown, the editor at the time, that I wanted to write a new kind of drama criticism—more of a discursive encounter that both described the play and informed the reader about theater culture. I also wanted to keep theater professionals in the discussion. I wanted to change how theater was reported, and Tina agreed with that. She was bored by conventional theater criticism.

For instance, when I went out to cover *Angels in America* at the Mark Taper Forum, I talked to Tony Kushner before the show and went backstage afterwards and described what was going on. I quoted a gorgeous letter that Tony had written to the cast. Anyone who wants to know what it was like to be in that theater at that great moment in our theater history will find it in my review. I was discussing the play, making connections to society, and getting all these voices into the piece.

Linda Winer: Everybody comes in through a different backdoor. I was a classical music major, with no thought about what I was going to do with it. I read about a two-year program that the Rockefeller Foundation had set up for the training of classical music critics. The first year, we were out in California, around the University of Southern California and the *Los Angeles Times*. We spent the whole year writing practice reviews. Critics from all over the country and England came and spent time with us. Virgil Thomson spent a week with us. They would tear at our stuff and help us understand what went into a review. The great thing about it was that there was no party line. The more people we talked to, the more we realized that everyone went about it in a different way, and that we were going to have to find our own way. But at least we learned what the basic standards were.

During the second year of the program, I was an apprentice at the *Chicago Tribune*. I grew up in Chicago. After the apprenticeship year, they kept me on as an assistant music critic. Then I got more and more interested in dance. It was right around the time of the so-called "Dance Boom," so the *Tribune* sent me to a program for the training of dance critics at Connecticut College. Martha Graham would sit there with her turban in the cafeteria. Again, we wrote reviews, and all these different critics would come in and tear our reviews apart.

At the time, the theater critic at the *Tribune* was an old pro named William Leonard, who reviewed touring companies and dinner theaters. That's pretty much all there was in Chicago at the time. But what we now know as the Chicago Theater Movement then began. There were all these people who lived in my neighborhood and were putting on plays in little storefronts. We were all the same age and seemed to have the same interests. The *Tribune* wasn't covering them, so I said, "I'll do it." I had taken a lot of theater courses in college, but I was not a trained theater professional. The first play I reviewed was *The Duck Variations*, David Mamet's first play in Chicago. I started at the *Tribune* in 1969, and I left in 1980. During my last seven years there, I was the chief theater and dance critic.

I really wanted to move to New York. The repetition in Chicago was getting to me. I couldn't review *Warp!*, this sci-fi storefront extravaganza, one more time. The *Daily News* was starting a separate afternoon edition of the paper. They were trying to reach the readers who read the *Times* on their way to work. They hired about 300 really good people, and they brought me to New York. I was called a cultural affairs specialist, which was a kind of critic-at-large. The afternoon edition only lasted about 10 months, but fortunately, the *Daily News* kept me on as the dance critic at the regular part of the paper.

Then I got a call from some people I had never heard of. They took me out to lunch at the Oyster Bar, and they said, "We're starting a national newspaper. Would you like to join us?" And I thought, This is only going to last six months, but at least it'll be something else. And that was *USA Today*. I offered to be the theater, dance, and music critic of the country. I was there for five years. At the beginning, it was really fun because they didn't have the form set in stone yet. There was more of an opportunity to have an individual voice. By the time I left, it was this big, established national newspaper.

Meanwhile, editors from *Newsday* called and said, "We're going to start a New York edition of the paper." They hired about 400 people. It was going to be an upscale New York edition called *New York Newsday*, completely separate from the Long Island edition. Allan Wallach was already the theater critic, but they asked if there was something else I wanted to do there. I said, "I would like to write a twice weekly column about the politics of the arts." They said, "Great, come over," and that's how I joined. I had all this writer energy that had been building up because *USA Today* was not a writers' newspaper. *Newsday* had these wonderful editors, and they let us write the hell out of everything.

2. How I Became a Theater Critic 35

New York Newsday lasted seven or eight years. They killed it, but not because it deserved to die. It was actually starting to pay for itself. But the *Los Angeles Times*, which owned us, got a new head of the board who wanted to show that he could save a lot of money quickly, so he folded *New York Newsday*. It was the last real chance of having a daily newspaper in New York that could compete with the *Times*. Eventually, I became the theater critic of the Long Island edition of *Newsday*.

Michael Riedel: It was really just a fluke. I had no ambition to be a journalist or to do anything in the theater. I went to college at Columbia, planned on going to law school, and was hanging out with a bunch of people who were involved in the theater, including a guy who became the editor of *TheaterWeek* magazine, who asked if I wanted to become the managing editor. I thought I would do it just for the summer, but it turned out to be a career.

I was at *TheaterWeek* for three years. Then I got friendly with a lot of gossip columnists, like George Rush and a woman named Charlotte Hays, because I had pretty good theater stories that I would give to them. Then Hays got a column at the *Daily News*. I figured she would need an assistant or leg man, so I applied for the job and got it. She was a bit of a disaster and got fired, but they kept me on. I worked for George Rush for a few months, and then they made me a feature writer. Then they gave me a regular weekly theater column. A year later, the *New York Post* lured me away and gave me a twice-a-week column, and I've been there ever since.

Ben Brantley: It was a long, circuitous route. It was the job I always wanted. It combined the two passions in my life: theater and writing. Journalism is a trade in my family that goes back a few generations. First, I was an intern at the *Village Voice*. After college, I worked for *Women's Wear Daily* and *W* as a reporter, editor, and fashion critic, first in New York and later in Paris. It was the best graduate school I could have gone to. Then I was a writer for *Vanity Fair* and then the *New Yorker*. I also wrote movie reviews for *Elle*. My first editor at *Elle* was Alex Witchel, who at that point was dating Frank Rich, whom she subsequently married. The *Times* had been looking for a second-string theater critic for a long time. I met Frank through Alex, and we bonded over our love of theater. He called me at one point and said, "You know, we're looking for someone. Would you mind if I threw your name into the hat?" I had to do some audition pieces, but it happened very quickly.

Charles Isherwood: I didn't aim to be a theater critic. It really wasn't a lifelong dream. I didn't study criticism or journalism. But in a way, it's something that drew on all of the various interests I'd been cultivating for years. I grew up in Northern California in the suburbs. I didn't go to the theater very often, but I think my critical instincts were there from a very early age. I was a huge movie fan as a kid. I was completely obsessed with Pauline Kael. I wrote movie reviews just for fun. After college, I graduated and moved to

Los Angeles, thinking I was going to either work in the movie industry or in magazines, and I ended up getting a job at a magazine.

I started going to the theater a lot when I was in Los Angeles. It was the late 1980s, when movies had started getting really bad. When the magazine I worked for folded, I ended up at *Variety* as an editor. At the same time, a friend of mine became the editor of *Backstage West*, and I volunteered to write reviews for five dollars each. A couple of years into that, *Variety* was very unhappy with its L.A. theater critic, so I went to the editors and said, "I've been doing these reviews. Why don't you let me do it?" And that's how it started.

Terry Teachout: I come from a small town in Southeast Missouri. When I was in junior high school, I saw a couple of college productions and became fascinated. I did theater in high school and college. I played the Noël Coward character in *The Man Who Came to Dinner*. I was the Artful Dodger in *Oliver!*, and my voice changed midway through the run. I was the fiddler in *Fiddler on the Roof*, and I fell off the roof on the last night as the curtain came down. (I held the violin over my head, and nothing got broken.)

I've been writing for publications since I was in high school. I was the *Kansas City Star*'s jazz critic and second-string classical critic while I was still an undergrad. I was also a working musician. Although I decided to concentrate on being a writer, I've always thought of myself as a musician first because that's what my training is in.

I remained interested in theater. I wrote about it quite a bit when I had a *Washington Post* column about the arts in New York. I wasn't new to it by any means when Paul Gigot of the *Wall Street Journal* asked me to lunch to discuss the paper's arts coverage. A half hour into the lunch, he said, "We'd like to start a drama column. Would you like to write it?" I was completely blindsided. I said, "Let's try it as an experiment." We started running columns every other week, and it very quickly became weekly. It then became a permanent arrangement, and I've been doing it ever since.

Alexis Soloski: A lot of us, at some point, were actors, directors, or playwrights. As an undergrad at Yale, I trained as an actor, while also studying the history of ideas. My major in college was the humanities—basically Western thought—and there were some nice crossovers, like the aesthetic theories of Lessing, who was a dramaturg in Hamburg. I was also dragooned into reviewing plays for the school paper, including undergraduate work, plays by Yale School of Drama students, and productions at Yale Repertory Theatre and the Long Wharf Theatre.

When I was a senior, one of my professors, Marc Robinson, who used to write for the *Village Voice*, came to me and said, "The *Voice* needs a theater intern." I said, "I'm a work-study kid. They don't pay their interns, and I can't afford to take the train back and forth to New York twice a week." When I went home, I remembered how I used to run to the library to get the copy of the *Village Voice* every Wednesday. It was very much my resource. It had a focus on experimental and avant-garde art and theater, which was what I was interested in. I called Professor Robinson's office voicemail at two in the morning and said, "Of course, I'll do it." I signed up for some science experiment that tested my startle reflex and made enough money to start taking the train back and forth. After a couple of weeks, the editor at the *Voice* started assigning me very short pieces. Once I graduated, I started copyediting, and eventually, I became a writer there.

Chris Jones: I started out as an academic. I got a PhD in theater 35 years ago. I taught classes, directed, and lived the life of a college professor. But when I was still very young and in graduate school, I started covering out-of-town shows for *Variety*. I became fascinated by the whole nature of touring theater. To this day, I have a real interest in and affection for the idea of taking your show out on the road, even though that business has become a pale shadow of its former self.

About 12 years ago, Richard Christiansen, my predecessor at the *Chicago Tribune*, retired. The job became open, and I thought, This is an amazing theater city, and there are very few of these jobs. So I quit everything else. I gave up tenure and the academic life and became a journalist. And here I survive, despite all the frustrations of the profession.

David Rooney: I fell into journalism almost accidentally. I studied film and had a lifetime interest in theater. During my high school years in Australia, I got involved with theater companies. I flirted with the idea of becoming an actor, but I made bad choices with my audition pieces for the National Institute of Dramatic Art. Everybody said, "Don't do Tennessee Williams," and I did Tom in *The Glass Menagerie*. Everybody said, "For your Shakespeare piece, don't do Romeo," which is exactly what I did. It wasn't to be, and now I'm relieved that it didn't happen. It's too much of a struggle.

When I first left Australia, I traveled around the United States for a year. I spent six months in New York and discovered the city's wonderful theater landscape. Then I moved to Europe and spent 20 years there. I had friends working in theater, so I saw pretty much everything in the West End and beyond. I came to New York once a year during those two decades and caught as much as I could.

After I moved to Italy in 1990, I started working for *Variety* as a freelancer. I took over as the Rome bureau chief in 1993. I had little journalistic experience prior to that. I had written a handful of book reviews for *Time Out* while I was in London and some pieces for an Australian independent film publication. I started covering European and North American film festivals. After 14 years there, I was looking to leave Italy, and Peter Bart, the editor-in-chief at *Variety* at the time, offered me a transfer to New York as a film reporter and reviewer. A year later, Charles Isherwood left *Variety* to go to the *New York Times*. Peter knew I had a passionate interest in theater and liked my reviewing style, so I became the chief theater critic and theater editor.

David Cote: I was an actor doing experimental plays at venues such as La MaMa, P.S. 122, and the Ontological-Hysteric Theater at St. Mark's Church. While I was doing that, I became angry about the lack of media coverage of Off Off Broadway, so I co-founded a self-produced pre-blog called *OFF*. That was in 1996. It was basically manifests and reviews, photocopied and stapled and left for free at downtown theaters. In 2000, a position opened up at *Time Out New York* for a theater writer. Jason Zinoman knew me from Off Off Broadway, and that's how he contacted me. I had never written a formal theater review before. I learned the journalism ropes at *Time Out*.

David Sheward: I wanted to be an actor, so I got a job at *Backstage*, thinking that I could find out about audition notices. I started doing reviews there, and then I became an editor, and that gradually became the focus on my attention. I was at *Backstage* for over 20 years.

Michael Dale: I became a critic totally by accident. About three months after starting a blog about attending theater, I got an email from the editor-in-chief of a brand new web site, *BroadwayWorld.com*. He offered me the chance to write about pretty much whatever I wanted. I started writing humorous essays, but then we started getting invited to review Off Off Broadway plays. I had never thought much about reviewing, but I started taking assignments. Eventually, the website was accepted by the Broadway League's press list, and I was named chief critic.

Zachary Stewart: I really did just fall into it. When I began working as the listings editor at *TheaterMania.com* in 2008 I would request to review shows I was interested in but weren't being covered by any of the regular reviewers (stuff like haunted houses, novelty gay musicals, and Off Off Off Broadway). By 2012, I started reviewing four or five shows a month. And in 2013, I became the chief critic at *TheaterMania*.

I had previously directed several shows in the city, and I never really had any intention of becoming a critic, but I've discovered that I like being a part of the conversation without having to make the personal sacrifices (lots of travel, income uncertainty, etc.) that it takes to be a working director in America. So this career path was really a happy accident.

Don Aucoin: It's been a long and winding road. Towards the beginning of my career, I worked for a newspaper in Meriden, Connecticut called the *Record-Journal* as a news reporter. But as is the case with many small newspapers, they let me do other things so long as I didn't ask for extra money, and I was interested in reviewing plays. Meriden is about 20 miles north of New Haven and 20 miles south of Hartford. I began reviewing productions at Yale Repertory Theatre, Long Wharf Theatre, and Hartford Stage.

2. How I Became a Theater Critic 39

In the mid–1980s, I began freelancing for the *Boston Globe*, which is where I really wanted to work. I had grown up in the Boston area. I was even a newspaper delivery boy for the *Globe*. I did an interview with August Wilson when *Ma Rainey's Black Bottom* premiered at Yale Repertory. I think it was the first piece about August Wilson published in the *Globe*. In 1986, I joined the *Globe* as a copy editor on the night news desk. After a year or so, I began writing theater reviews for the *Globe* on my nights off. Kevin Kelly was still the drama critic back then. But if there was a smaller production or something that he couldn't get to, I would review it.

When I left the copy desk and became a reporter, I didn't write any theater reviews for two decades. I worked as a general assignment news reporter, a reporter in the City Hall and State House bureaus, a TV critic and reporter, and a feature writer. Fast-forward to 2009. Louise Kennedy, the theater critic at the time, was on maternity leave, and the features editor (who heard that I had written theater reviews once upon a time) asked me to fill in. About eight months after Louise came back, she decided to leave the paper, and they asked if I wanted the job.

Elisabeth Vincentelli: I was the arts editor at *Time Out New York*. The job of theater critic opened up at the *New York Post* after Clive Barnes died. A former colleague of mine, who had gone on to be the features editor at the *Post*, called and asked if I was interested. They wanted to mix things up and take someone from outside the pool of usual suspects with a different background. They wanted someone who could take a show that, on the surface, didn't look accessible and make it feel exciting to a lay reader. They wanted someone who could go to everything, from the big Broadway musicals to the super-experimental European stuff, and make it all interesting and fun to read about.

Frank Rizzo: I went to the University of Arizona, where I majored in journalism and minored in theater. I didn't intend to go to graduate school right away, but I couldn't get a job in journalism at the time. When I finished grad school, I got a job at a small newspaper in Massachusetts as a general writer. That gave me the best training in the world. It was outside of Boston, so I could give myself assignments in Boston all the time. I covered the world premieres of *Pacific Overtures*, *A Little Night Music*, Angela Lansbury in *Gypsy*, and all those other great shows that were coming into Boston in the 1970s. I would also cover the fire department, the police department, school board meetings, and everything else.

I cobbled together a pretty good portfolio and got a job at the *Journal-Courier*, which was the morning paper at the time in New Haven. I was a general arts writer, covering everything from disco and rock concerts to theater. I was there during the last years of Robert Brustein at Yale Repertory Theatre. I just missed Meryl Streep's time there. Then I got hired by the *Hartford*

Courant—not as a theater critic, but as an arts journalist. By the 1990s, I was pretty much the theater writer. And starting in the late 1990s, I was reviewing more and more.

Frank Scheck: I think people end up becoming critics in the same way: they love going to the theater, the movies, or whatever. In my case, it was both movies and theater. I've always been an addict. I started writing early on for my high school newspaper. Then I went to Columbia University and wrote for the *Columbia Daily Spectator*, and it proceeded from there. It was a way to spend every day going to the movies and the theater, make a living at it, and not have to do anything else. Nothing else ever really interested me.

Like everybody else, I went through the process of starting at smaller places and moving on up by getting breaks. After I graduated college, my first job was for an independent theater magazine called *STAGES*, which was run by a doctor in New Jersey who decided to become a magazine publisher. I started out as a reviewer, then I became the editor, and I ultimately wound up co-publishing it with him for several years until economic realities finally took hold. While that was going on, I did freelance writing for a variety of publications. I got my first real break when I became the theater critic for the *Christian Science Monitor*. A couple of years later, I wound up also writing for the *Hollywood Reporter* as a film critic. Eventually, I segued over to theater and music as well, which led to a gig at the *New York Post*.

Helen Shaw: I have an MFA in drama from the A.R.T. Institute at Harvard, which leaves you qualified for literary positions and dramaturgical work, and I was doing that kind of stuff in New York. A friend of mine from undergrad, Jeremy McCarter, was the theater critic at the then-existing *New York Sun*. During the Fringe Festival, they got pretty desperate. He was trying to cover as much of it as possible, but it was too much for one man, so he was reaching out to everyone he knew who stayed with the theater and was possibly interested in criticism. I wrote a couple of Fringe reviews for the *Sun* and then became the second-string critic under Jeremy. I was very happy there. It was a very conservative paper, but it had some of the best arts coverage in the city. They were interested in weird, experimental work, which is my focus. I then went on to freelance at *Time Out*. Unfortunately, the *Sun* shut down, but I've been with *Time Out* ever since.

Howard Shapiro: I had been at the *Philadelphia Inquirer* in many positions before I became its theater critic. In the 1990s, I was the arts editor. Then I became the travel editor. At some point, both of the paper's full-time theater critics took buyouts, so the arts editor asked me to do some theater reviewing. It never occurred to me to be a theater critic. My first review was in April 2002. When I sat down to write it, I realized how little I knew about being a critic, even after having been an arts editor, but I liked it. I did one or two pieces a month, which very rapidly turned into at least two pieces a week. And at some point thereafter, I become a full-time theater critic.

Jesse Oxfeld: I grew up as a stereotypical Jewish kid from the New York suburbs. I'd always been a theater fan and a theatergoer. By the time I ended up at *New York* magazine, I had already written for several different outlets while continuing to go to the theater. When I left *New York* magazine, a friend of mine became the editor of the *New York Observer*. At the time, they were remaking the paper in response to imperatives coming primarily from its owner, Jared Kushner, and the realities of the newspaper business. John Heilpern, who was their theater critic, only wrote infrequently.

This was soon after the *New York Sun* closed, and there was a theory at the time that advertisers were looking for a smart publication that was less expensive than the *New York Times*. There was this idea that theaters, museums, and cultural things like that wanted to reach an affluent, educated New York audience, so the *Observer* was looking to beef up its cultural pages and have regular theater criticism in order to sell theater advertising. It didn't matter if the reviews were good or bad. They just needed someone who could do it and would be reasonably cheap. So my friend called me up and asked if I'd be interested. My first reaction was to say, "I can't be a theater critic. I don't know how to do that." And he said, "You're being ridiculous. You're a smart guy. You're a good writer." And then I thought, Why should I say no to this? Maybe I'd be good at it.

Michael Musto: I went to Columbia College and majored in English because there was no undergraduate journalism major. I knew I wanted to pursue writing of some kind, particularly cultural writing. I would hang out at the office of the *Columbia Daily Spectator* every day, just hoping somebody would throw me an assignment, and it wasn't happening. Then I met a woman named Jami Bernard, who years later became the film critic for the *Daily News*. She asked me to write for the *Barnard Bulletin*. Barnard is Columbia's sister school. I started writing theater reviews for the *Barnard Bulletin*, be it reviews of campus productions or Broadway shows. Then the *Spectator* took notice, and I became its theater critic. This was back in the 1970s. I was reviewing shows like *A Chorus Line* and *Chicago*. I also did interviews with people like Chita Rivera, Kelly Bishop, and Carole Shelley.

After college, I wrote for *After Dark* and *SoHo Weekly News*, which was an alternative to the *Village Voice*. I wrote things for daily newspapers in New York—not exclusively about theater, but including theater. In 1984, I got my column at the *Village Voice*: "La Dolce Musto." I had done a few freelance pieces for the *Voice*, and then there was an opening for the column. I submitted a sample column, and they liked it. They wanted something that covered the wide range of culture in New York: theater, nightlife, fashion, and beyond. They gave me the freedom to cover any entertainment or non-entertainment topics that I was interested in. I featured theater very heavily in the column for the 29 years I was there. My current column at *Out* is called "Musto! The Musical!" That pretty much says how dedicated I am to covering theater.

Richard Zoglin: I've been writing and editing at *Time* for over 30 years. Back then, our theater critic was William A. Henry III. After he died of a heart attack, *Time* had no theater critic. I had done a few theater reviews here and there, filling in when Bill wasn't around. The job fell to me because I could do it part-time. Back when Bill was writing, *Time* covered theater pretty regularly. Later, the magazine felt less obligated to review everything, so being a theater critic wasn't a full-time job, and it was kind of perfect for me.

Rob Weinert-Kendt: As a film major in L.A, I ended up enjoying the critical studies classes more than the production classes. I saw tons of films and learned how to write about them. I started working for a little newspaper in L.A. called *Downtown News*. At the time, L.A. was having a theater flowering. Gordon Davidson was putting on *Angels in America* and *The Kentucky Cycle*. Then I got a job as editor of *Backstage West*, which I had for about 10 years. L.A. is a spread out bunch of communities with theaters all over the place. It was a really fun and gratifying scene to cover.

I eventually left *Backstage West* and freelanced for the *Los Angeles Times*. I really wanted to be the paper's theater critic, but they wanted someone from New York. They went without a critic for four years—even though I was right there. Clearly, to continue being a theater journalist, I needed to be in New York, so I moved there in 2005. I've been freelancing and doing theater coverage ever since. I was the last critic that *Broadway.com* employed. You may know the story: *Broadway.com* is a ticket site, and the people selling tickets to the shows didn't really love having a critic standing alongside their ticket sales, which I can understand.

I'm now the editor of *American Theatre* magazine. I also write articles for the *Times* and *Time Out New York*. I write reviews regularly for *America* magazine, which is a Catholic weekly. I feel like there are a lot of folks in my sort of category, who consider themselves critics, even though they mainly write features and preview pieces. We cut our teeth writing reviews, but it's hard to find a place that wants to publish only our reviews. To make a living, we have to do a lot of features and other stuff.

Robert Faires: I stumbled into this. In the early 1980s, Austin was still very much a small town. There was an upstart free biweekly called the *Austin Chronicle*, and I happened to have a friend of a friend who was writing theater reviews for it. Periodically, we would talk about theater. At one point, he asked if I had considered doing theater reviews. At the time, I was doing community theater in the evening. I had done enough complaining about critics, so I thought, Well, the universe is telling me to either put up or shut up. So I gave it a try, and I found that I really liked it. At the time, there were a few other people who were also writing about theater at the paper. But within six months, I was the only one left. Before long, it was more of a calling in my life than anything else. After about 10 years, I was invited to be on staff as an arts editor, but theater has always been where my heart is. It's still what I cover most regularly.

Roma Torre: Both of my parents were involved with the theater in New York. My dad was a producer, and my mom was a columnist and a critic. For a long time, I thought I would be an actress, but that didn't work out so well. I became impatient with the whole process, but I still loved the theater. Several years out of college, I decided that I wanted to be a news reporter. My first on-air job was at News 12 Long Island. While I was there, they started a magazine called *Total TV*. Knowing of my background in theater, they asked if I could write theater and film reviews for it. One of my first reviews was of *Les Miz*.

I was at News 12 Long Island for five years, and then I got a call from NY1. It was this start-up 24-hour cable operation based in New York City. I was very happy to join it. After six months, Steve Paulus, who was the news director and a big fan of the theater, said, "I know you did theater reviews over at News 12. Would you like to continue doing that for us?" So I've been continuously reviewing theater since 1987.

Scott Brown: I've been writing criticism in one form or another since college. That led me to *Entertainment Weekly*. I was an editorial assistant, working my way up the ranks. I spent seven or eight years there and ended up writing a lot of criticism because there was bandwidth for it at the time. They had their major critics, plus a lot of other people picking up the slack. They had a stage section, which came out whenever there was a crop of new shows. There wasn't one dedicated theater critic, so I ended up doing a lot of theater reviews, filling a niche where there was one. From there, I got my foot in the door at *New York* magazine. One of my former editors had taken a job there, and they were looking for a new theater critic. Like a lot of these things, there was a great deal of luck and people you know involved.

Jesse Green: When I was at Yale in the late 1970s, I reviewed two plays for a campus publication under a pseudonym. I had some pretentious idea that Robert Brustein, who at that time ran the Yale Rep and Yale School of Drama, would get back at me if I used my real name. Between then and just recently, I haven't written any other theater reviews. I wrote a lot about theater, but always in the form of profiles, feature articles, or news stories, mostly for the *New York Times*.

After the 2008 financial crisis, the *Times* was particularly hard hit and couldn't afford to pay me what it had previously, so I started looking for other work. And lo and behold, *New York* magazine offered me a position as a feature writer, which would sometimes include features on theater, like my notorious profile of Arthur Laurents. I also wrote a lot of nontheatrical stories about sad people doing sad things. At the same time, I was getting to be known (at least by shut-ins and insomniacs) from appearing on that silly TV show *Theater Talk*. (I shouldn't say it's silly. It's actually quite good, but I feel silly on it.)

In March 2013, Scott Brown, my predecessor, decided that he wanted to take a sabbatical because his wife was about to give birth, so the magazine asked me to take over for him for three months. *New York* magazine covers every Broadway show as well as a certain algorithm of non-Broadway shows, and this was happening in March, April, and May, when the Broadway season is insane. It was sort of a trial by fire, and also a tryout because there was a possibility that Scott would eventually leave the job permanently.

Scott came back for three or four months and then decided that he wanted to give his other writing a good try, which meant giving up theater reviewing. Because he was going to work with people who were being regularly represented in the kinds of shows he had to review, it was also becoming a conflict of interest. So Scott resigned the position. He was not forced out or anything like that. I didn't poison him. Then they asked me to take over, which I did starting in October 2013.

Steven Suskin: I came about it in a roundabout way. I spent about 25 years working in the Broadway theater as a company manager, general manager, producer, actor, and stage manager. In my spare time, I wrote books about the theater. After several books, I moved into reviewing. I did a series of books called the *Broadway Yearbook*, each of which covered a full season's worth of reviews. Those books were more about analysis and after-the-fact reviewing. After that, it seemed natural to become an overnight critic. I had also been doing CD reviews for many years for *Playbill.com*. Eventually, *Variety* called, and I went to work for it.

Adam Feldman: When I was a kid, I was really interested in the history of musicals. I would go to the library and look up what people said about them when they opened. I did some theater in college, and later I was associated with a publication called the *Harvard Gay & Lesbian Review*. There were things that I wrote for it that could, in a sense, be called reviews. When I moved to New York, I had a day job. And when I was bored or had extra time, I would go online to a Usenet discussion group called *rec.arts.theatre.musicals*. There were a lot of interesting people there, including a young Jeff Marx, and we would have spirited conversations about shows we loved or didn't love. And through that, I ended up being recruited into theater criticism.

Someone from *Show Business*, a news publication which was sort of like

Backstage, contacted me and said, "Hey, we like what you've been writing online. Would you be interested in writing reviews for us?" I said, "Sure. That sounds like fun." Then I ended up meeting Paul Wontorek, the editor of *Broadway.com*, at a party. We started talking, and it came up that I was writing reviews, and he suggested I send him some. He liked them, and I started writing for *Broadway.com*. This was back in the day when *Broadway.com* had reviews; they don't anymore. (You'll see that as an emerging theme, unfortunately.) At that point, I decided to take the bull by the horns. I quit my day job and started freelancing as much as I could. In 2003, a space opened up at *Time Out*. They hired me, and I've been there ever since.

Michael Schulman: I grew up in Manhattan and always went to the theater. I acted in plays in high school, and I directed at Yale. When I graduated and moved back to New York, I had this sense that I would go to film school or pursue theater directing. Then I started looking around. And within five minutes, I thought, I have no idea how to do that professionally.

Then I got a job at the *New Yorker*. One day at the office, I went up to the woman who edited the theater listings and said, "There's this play that I think you should cover." She said, "Do you want to go out and write 100 words about it?" I did that, and then she sent me to see two other plays that same week. And it took off from there. I had a body of knowledge about theater, and they just happened to need someone at that moment to go out and see plays. Most of my criticism in the *New Yorker* is unsigned. Unlike my reporting, my theater criticism is a little more under the radar, which is kind of nice because I make fewer enemies that way.

Michael Sommers: I've been doing this for a long time. I reviewed movies for my high school paper. Then I became the theater critic for my college newspaper. I was also the football writer, which is pretty much the same sort of thing. (I always wonder how my career would have turned out if I stayed a sports writer. I'd probably be making a lot more money.) When I came to New York, I worked for Actors' Equity. I didn't like it very much. I thought there must be other ways I could wreck the American theater, so I became a drama critic (laughs).

I got a job at *Backstage* in 1981 and became an editor there. I was the first reviewer that *Backstage* ever paid. I wouldn't do it for free, so they had to pay me for my reviews in addition to my salary as an editor. I got five bucks a review. (I don't know if they ever raised those rates.) I then started reviewing as well for the *New York Native*, which is the newspaper they keep talking about in *The Normal Heart*. I started at the *Star-Ledger* in 1991. They hired me to review New Jersey theater. In 1993, William A. Raidy, the paper's New York theater critic, died, and I nabbed his old job.

Peter Marks: I acted in college. When I was coming out of college, I applied to the Neighborhood Playhouse and to a newspaper, and I got the newspaper job. In 1996, I was the theater reporter at the *New York Times*. An editor came up to me and said, "We're looking for a second-string critic. Who can you recommend?" I gave him some names, and he said, "Well, what about you?" And I said, "I'm certainly willing to try." I did a couple of practice reviews. They liked them, and voilà!

I wrote reviews for the *Times* for three and a half years. Then the *Times* thought it would be fun for a theater critic to cover the 2000 presidential election. After I did that, Bruce Weber had become the second-string theater critic, so there really wasn't a job for me anymore. Then the *Washington Post* called me in 2002 and offered me the theater critic job.

Robert Hurwitt: I wrote my first piece of criticism without actually meaning to become a critic. I was an undergraduate at NYU, where I was active in theater. Most of us in the theater community were very scornful of the reviews being printed in the campus paper, so I walked into the paper's office one day and said, "I'd like to write the next theater review," without actually having the forethought that it would be of a play that I wanted to audition for. That review is something I hold on to. It's a total embarrassment. It's full of inside-baseball jargon and is probably incomprehensible to anyone outside of the theater.

After I graduated from NYU and got a master's degree from Berkeley in English Literature, I got back into acting and worked in the San Francisco area. This was in the 1960s, when the underground newspapers were starting up, which led to the alternative press of today. A friend of mine who started one of those papers in Washington, D.C., asked if I would be his West Coast correspondent. After I started writing for him, other papers began picking up my stories. Because I knew a lot about theater, that quickly became one of my beats. I then became the theater critic of the *San Francisco Examiner*. And when the Hearst Corporation bought the *San Francisco Chronicle* in 2000, they merged the staffs, and I've been at the *Chronicle* ever since.

Matthew Murray: I studied acting and playwriting in college, and worked as an actor briefly after school until deciding that I liked eating and getting paid regularly. Not long after moving to New York for a non-theater job, I got involved with the *All That Chat* discussion board on the website *TalkinBroadway.com* and my writing attracted the attention of the people who ran the site. They had just lost their Off-Broadway reviewer and wanted someone to take over that role. They asked me, and I said yes. Within a year or so, they lost their Broadway reviewer, and so I ended up doing that, too.

Jason Zinoman: It was partly an accident, and partly something I was of born with. I grew up around the theater world. My mom founded the Studio Theatre in Washington, D.C., the year I was born, so I grew up around productions. I didn't want to act, but I did like to write, and I really wanted to be a journalist. The magazine I was really obsessed with as a teenager was

2. How I Became a Theater Critic   47

the *New Republic*. Journalism and writing about the arts seemed very exciting and high-stakes.

When I got out of school, I moved to New York. I freelanced a lot around that time. Then a deputy theater critic job opened up at *Time Out New York*. I don't know how I got the job. I was not qualified, but I knew a lot more about theater than the ordinary 24-year-old because it was all around me growing up. We sat at the dinner table talking about scenes from an August Wilson play. I worked under Sam Whitehead at *Time Out*. After he left, I took over at the age of 25. From there, I got the Friday theater column at the *New York Times*, which included news and gossip. Writing the column was tremendously valuable because I got to meet all the producers, but the position was becoming obsolete because of the Internet. Then I had nothing to do, so I did freelance theater reviewing. Three years ago, I became the *Times*' first comedy columnist.

3

Education and Personality

MATT WINDMAN: *What kind of education should a theater critic have?*

Adam Feldman: There are so many different kinds of critics, from so many different backgrounds, that I don't know if there is one set of educational prerequisites for the job.

John Simon: It's assumed that anybody can write film or drama criticism. It's based on the know-nothingism of too many editors, too many publishers, and too many publications that simply don't understand what theater is and what demands it makes on the person writing about it. I was once on an episode of *The Odd Couple* where I played a demanding theater critic. On the episode, the character of Oscar has to take over as a drama critic. Oscar is a sports writer, but his editor thinks that anybody can write drama criticism. Then there's a symposium at which he appears with some real drama critics, and he makes an ass of himself. That's what really happens.

Jeremy Gerard: I have tremendous respect for academics that have doctorates, but I don't. I wasn't interested. Plus, most academics are terrible writers.

Zachary Stewart: Theater critics should have an ever-expanding knowledge of art, culture, and current affairs, and should be able to draw upon that knowledge in reviews. That might require a high school diploma and a lot of independent study for some, a PhD for others.

Ben Brantley: I don't think going to graduate school for journalism is going to do a whole lot of good in the long run. People either can write or they can't write. Some of the smartest writers I know never got college degrees.

Rob Weinert-Kendt: There are now degrees in arts journalism. I'm sure they have value, but I don't think it's a prerequisite to being a good critic.

Eric Grode: I teach at Syracuse University as part of a one-year master's program in cultural journalism. A lot of the students there are just out of college. That generation has no compunction about voicing its opinions thanks to social media. It's a pre-professional program, and many of the skills we teach involved getting noticed and navigating the working world. I also try

3. Education and Personality   49

to instill in the students a sense of history and context, to give more depth to their opinions. We go over how important it is to back up your opinions. It's not sufficient to just say that something's great or that it sucks—the way it would be in a tweet. You need to point to concrete examples of how you came to that conclusion.

Linda Winer: I don't think you need academic training in the theater—although it certainly doesn't hurt. I also don't think you need to have worked in the theater—although that doesn't hurt either. I know brilliant critics who have not been involved in the theater, and I know brilliant critics who have been involved in the theater. Likewise, I know dull critics who have been involved in the theater, and I know dull critics who have not been involved in the theater.

Peter Marks: There is something essential about being a critic that has more to do with taste and an ability to communicate an experience in the theater. It goes beyond a knowledge base. I find that the people who are most useful to me as critics are the ones who can couch their experience in a lively, entertaining, and informed way.

Howard Shapiro: The education that a theater critic should have is the education a person gets by sitting in an audience. I'm just an audience member with a great big mouth, but I'm an experienced audience member who can write well. I think I can put my great big mouth to sensible use.

Michael Dale: Shortly after graduating college, I joined a papering organization that offered members free tickets to shows that needed to "dress the house." You just paid a very cheap service charge. There was the occasional Broadway show, but it was mostly Off Broadway and Off Off Broadway, mixed with classical concerts, dance events, opera, cabaret, jazz, performance art, or anything else that needed fannies in the seats. I would see shows three to five times a week, and made it a point to take a chance on things I knew nothing about. I was a member for about 15 years, and I think that kind of continual exposure to a variety of performing arts provided my education for being a critic.

Michael Musto: I never went to journalism school. After sitting in on some graduate journalism classes at Columbia, I realized they were all about pretend press conferences and made-up articles. At that point, I had already been freelancing for real publications outside of campus, so I was one step ahead. After graduating from Columbia, there was no reason to pursue education anymore. I wanted to immerse myself in the real world and learn by doing. If a critic's got a PhD and extraordinary intellect and 27 books under his or her belt, that's fine, but it's not necessary. There are probably some great critics in high school right now.

Alexis Soloski: You need very little education if you have the talent. I've never read Tom Stoppard's theater criticism, but I bet it was genius, and he didn't go to college. What's essential is having clear, intelligible, compelling prose. It's helpful to be able to say whether a show melds two genres, or if it's influenced by certain playwrights, but you can offer a very lively, sensitive, acute review that merely describes the work itself. I think I had the makings of a good critic when I was 19 years old, when I had read a lot less.

Helen Shaw: We are locked into a kind of closed system—this industrial-educational complex. I don't think I could point to a playwright working today who doesn't have a college degree. But for years, the best playwrights didn't have college degrees. The next theater critics might not have the education that I used to think of as being so crucial.

Robert Faires: When somebody approaches me as an editor about writing theater reviews, I prefer it when that person has been exposed to a lot of different kinds of writing and thought, and has a natural curiosity based on those things. I'd like for that person to have spent a lot of time in the theater already, seeing not just the kind of shows that he or she personally enjoys, but all kinds of shows, because that's how deep this person's love of theater runs.

Robert Hurwitt: Any theater critic who doesn't know his or her Shakespeare is that much less of a critic. Same for the Greeks. Same for Molière. As rarely as the German or Italian classics are done in the United States, you should know them. You'll want to know as much about American theater classics as you can. When you're dealing with an experimental group, you'll want to know the theory behind its practices.

Andy Propst: At any given moment in time, a theater critic needs to become an expert on the subject at hand, on whatever a play may be about. In a realm in which physics can be used as a metaphor in an award-winning drama, you had better be able to wrap your head around what that piece of physics is.

David Rooney: The key to being a readable critic is having a breadth of pop-cultural knowledge, and not being too head-in-the-sand about your specialized field. Of course, expertise in the area you're covering is essential, but the reviews I really enjoy reading are by people who are able to tie what they're reviewing into other things that are happening politically and socially—to television trends, movies, music, fashion, and all that.

Michael Riedel: They need to read a lot, and I don't mean just plays. I mean great books, great novels, great poems, great biographies, great history. I think it's a mistake for a theater critic to be totally immersed in the theater—to only listen to show tunes and read plays.

John Simon: You have to be a cultured person with many interests. You should know about the other arts because there is a relationship among the arts. If you know a lot about fiction, that could help your drama criticism. If you know a lot about music, that could help as far as musicals are concerned.

3. Education and Personality

If you know a lot of things generally, then you won't be so easily impressed by certain things that are not very good. You'll have higher expectations.

Gordon Cox: It's far more helpful to study theater than journalism. I didn't go to school for journalism. I've never even taken a journalism class, but I did study theater and writing. I use that knowledge far more than the basics of journalism, which you can pick up as you go along.

David Cote: You should have a general knowledge of theater history and practices—not just the history of the play and the musical and the development of Broadway, but of theater as an expressive form, and how it's changed over the centuries. Most critics have a general knowledge of theater and of Shakespeare. But at the same time, you need to be versatile with your viewing apparatus. You should be able to shift from one genre to another—from big, dumb Broadway musicals to the avant-garde.

Robert Feldberg: Theater is sort of an in-between. It's not high art. It's not low art. It's in the middle. So the more you know about different stuff, the better prepared you are. I don't think there's one particular kind of background, or one major in college, that will set you up better than anything else.

Terry Teachout: If you don't know about more than just theater, everything you write will be provincial. It's just going to be a fan's notes, or the reactions of a knowledgeable professional who can't connect to larger cross currents in culture.

Michael Schulman: David Denby, who's a film critic for the *New Yorker*, once said that his students often come in having a very strong sense of their critical axis (what kind of things they like and don't like), but they haven't studied language, which is the critic's medium. You have to study writing. You have to know how to use words to describe what you're seeing and what you're reacting to.

MATT WINDMAN: What kind of personality or attitude should a theater critic ideally have?

John Simon: I don't think there is a one-on-one relationship between what you are in life and what you are on the page. I wouldn't be surprised if a very mild-mannered person was a very fierce critic, or if a very violent person was a weak critic.

Steven Suskin: Whether you're quiet and calm, or enthusiastic and excited, doesn't matter. If you can write well, you can be a good critic.

John Lahr: A critic should be a feeling individual. Feeling is as important as thinking. That's where a lot of the stumbling blocks are in present criticism. I'm not sure people can parse their feelings well. Therefore, certain kinds of plays are misunderstood depending on the psychological nature of the critic. The more humanity you have, the more humanity you feel. The more limited you are psychologically, the less you can see in certain plays. It's about both intellectual and emotional sophistication.

Terry Teachout: You need to have the right attitude in order to be a good critic. There has to be a fundamental generosity and excitement. You have to want to communicate enthusiasm. You can't be there just to pick out flaws. I'm not sure you can breed that out of someone whose idea of a critic was shaped by the movie *All About Eve*.

Michael Dale: I don't think I've ever met a critic who doesn't adore going to the theater, and who doesn't take a seat sincerely prepared to possibly see the best show ever. I think that's the ideal attitude to have.

Michael Sommers: I've always been a glass-half-full sort of writer. To quote from the musical *Spamalot*, I "always look on the bright side of life." I rarely get offended. The last thing that offended me in years was *Intimacy*, that terrible Off-Broadway play at the New Group by Thomas Bradshaw. The whole thing was just so foul. Still, I did wonder how they made that ejaculation scene work. Even with the worst shows, you can always find something to be interested in.

Jeremy Gerard: I consider myself a tough critic, but not a nasty critic. I don't see shows that I don't like as crimes against art, as some other critics do. They're just shows I don't happen to like. For me, no production is a life or death issue. I think of myself as fair, and that's reflected in my ability to cover the industry in the way I do, and in continuing to write reviews that people pay fairly well for.

Zachary Stewart: A critic should be intellectually curious, constantly trying to learn more about the world beyond his limited corner.

Alexis Soloski: You need an open heart. I don't think you're doing anyone any favors if you go in without one. You need to be able to experience a show emotionally—to be disturbed by it, and confused by it, and delighted by it—and then be able to step back and evaluate that experience analytically.

Chris Jones: You have to keep an open mind. Whatever history you may have with an artist, sometimes they can surprise you. They do great work when you don't expect it. Or, they do terrible work when you expect greatness, and you have to be able to see that. You have to float above relationships and alliances, and be able to see a show for what it is on a given night. Artists change constantly. Theater changes constantly.

David Cote: You have to be wise and naïve at the same time—wise in the sense of being an educated audience member and bringing all your years of reading and viewing to the table, and naïve in the sense of never being jaded and being open to new forms and experiences. If you grow cynical and tradition-bound, your writing may not suffer (some critics have made a career out of being aesthetic dinosaurs), but your thinking will rot.

Michael Musto: Ideally, a critic should be able to separate his or her own life crises and challenges from what he or she is reviewing. When they enter the theater, they have to put everything else on the back burner. If they just came from the dentist, or if they just got jury duty, they have to objectively evaluate what they're going to see—even when shows are endlessly opening in time for Tony Awards consideration, and you're sitting through play after play. You can't let that overabundance get to you, or make you numb, or dampen your critical faculties.

Elysa Gardner: I don't believe in being snarky. Making easy jokes is something we've all done. When I'm about to write something snarky, I try to stop myself and find a better way to put it.

Howard Shapiro: You need to be open to everything. I could be a restaurant critic who hates Mexican food, but I would know when it was well-cooked and nicely presented. The same is true when covering any kind of art. Even if you don't like a general kind of theater, you should acknowledge when it's good and when it's working.

Michael Schulman: Openness is the most important part of the critic's temperament. The biggest temptation for critics is cynicism. There's a tendency for critics to get together for martinis after a show and to just start bashing the show and dragging each other's esteem for it down. But the best theater makes you vulnerable to it. If you fall in love with a play—like if you fall in love with a person—you let your guard down. There's a tendency for critics to keep their guard up and prove they didn't fall for a play. It's much harder to say that you were completely undone by a work of art.

Jeremy Gerard: It's an odd combination of knowing a great deal while not having any prejudices, and being open to new experiences while not abandoning your own history. I once had an experience with Neil Simon during a pre–Broadway tryout in Dallas. I was interviewing him, and he knew that I was not a fan of his from my earlier reviews. When the interview was over, he said, "If I knew you were the critic in Dallas, I wouldn't have let the show open here. With you, I'm batting zero, so I have to believe you've written your review before you've seen the show." And I said, "Well, I hope that whatever I write about your show, you won't think that I've written the review before I go to see it, and I assure you that I haven't written it already." As it happens, the show in Dallas was a piece of shit. It was the all-female version of *The Odd Couple*.

Robert Feldberg: Critics need to be patient and willing to go along with whatever a writer and director are doing. After the first five minutes, you may think it's going to be awful, but you need to be able to withhold judgment, sit back, and say to yourself, "I'm going to let this happen. I don't think this is going to work, but let me go with it and try to figure out what the writer intended." It may end up being terrible, but you at least need to give it a hearing.

Andy Propst: You have to be compassionate. You have to realize that, even on the worst of evenings, these are people who are doing their best. That's not to say you should be namby-pamby, but a critic needs to understand that that a company of artists—be it on Broadway or in a tiny theater in the basement on the Lower East Side—did not set out to fail.

John Simon: A critic should be very thick-skinned. As I know from experience, if you are a very tough critic, people tend to be very unkindly disposed towards you in all kinds of ways. You don't get invited to many parties. You don't get published in many places. You don't get a kind word from many people.

Chris Jones: To some degree, you have to be satisfied in heralding the work of others—which may sound strange to people who think that critics are egomaniacs. Getting really excited about someone else requires a subjugation of the self. Most people in the arts promote themselves, or their colleagues, or those for whom they work. A critic has to get excited about excellence not coming from his or herself, which is harder than it may seem. There's a certain selflessness to it. The greatest reviews are driven by the work itself, and not by your own issues. It's a delicate dance.

Michael Riedel: Critics should enjoy being a bit of a showman and attracting attention to themselves. They should have a thrill for the kill and should not be afraid to put the knife in. There's no place for someone who doesn't take strong opinions. I really don't believe in temperate criticism. I don't believe in thoughtful "on the one hand, on the other hand" writing. To really engage the reader, you have to either make a case for something or tear it apart. It's a waste of everyone's time if you just say, "It was kind of alright" or "They tried, but it didn't work very well." That's boring to read. With Frank Rich, you either lived or died. He got behind it and sold it, or he dismantled it, and that makes for lively reading.

John Simon: He should be absolutely fearless. He should not be afraid that readers will hate him, or that his editor will be uncomfortable with him. That is a very rare thing, partly because reviewers depend on their livelihood. I have great doubts about critics who start out as publicists and still have a publicist's mentality. I could name names. There is something about a critic being born rather than made. It's something in your nature, in your perspective, that makes you a critic. It's innate. It can be furthered. It can be polished. It can be developed. But the germ, the core, has to be innate.

Helen Shaw: Some of my favorite critics are the ones that get pissed off, like David Cote. When he is angry, David writes some of the best stuff you will ever read. He is so impassioned and thrilling when he is mad. On the other hand, Scott Brown is someone who is never angry, even when he is reviewing something that is absolutely appalling, and can write with crazy, intense generosity.

3. Education and Personality

Don Aucoin: The ability to be moved is important. Matthew Gilbert, the *Globe*'s TV critic, once told me, "You have to be willing to fall in love." What he meant was that if something like *The Sopranos* comes on the scene, you can't be so jaded by all the crap that came before it that you miss its greatness. You have to recognize that something pretty momentous has happened. Without being a pushover, a theater critic has to be receptive to the occasional miracles that can happen.

Howard Shapiro: You can't pull punches. This is harder for people who work in regional theater. In New York, you are unlikely to walk down the street and run into the people that you're reviewing. It's quite different in Philly. You're covering stuff from people you see on the street, so you need to have a thick-skinned temperament.

Rob Weinert-Kendt: I've known good critics of all temperaments. The thing that unifies them is courage and independence of thought—to be the kind of person who has the fortitude to go against the grain. A bit of a contrarian streak is helpful. I'm not saying you should be an asshole, but a critic should speak up for their point of view.

Matthew Murray: Critics must be able to withstand fatigue. Theater reviewing looks easy, but it's a huge time commitment, especially if you have to hold down another job to make ends meet (as I do, and as many reviewers do). In super-busy months, like November and April, it's not uncommon for shows to open on top of each other for weeks at a time. As I'm writing this, we just had something like 14 shows open in two weeks, with multiple days where two or three shows opened at once. For organizations that don't have an army of reviewers at their disposal (meaning, basically, everyone except the *Times*), in these periods, you are seeing and writing about shows during literally every free moment you have, and that can wear on you physically, emotionally, and intellectually, and can cause your personal life and non-theater relationships to suffer.

MATT WINDMAN: How important is it for a theater critic to be funny?

Michael Dale: Not at all.

Zachary Stewart: It's only important if that critic wants people to read his or her reviews.

Ben Brantley: It depends on the subject. If you're writing about a Holocaust drama, you don't want to make jokes. We're in a moment in history where you have to be pretty circumspect. Things can come back to bite you. Fortunately, that hasn't happened to me too often.

Michael Riedel: It's important for anybody, anywhere, in any profession, to be funny. Humor is necessary to relieve the general pain and misery of life. But those who try too hard to be funny are excruciating. I can't bear the *Times* columnist Gail Collins. She thinks she's so clever and witty, but she's really just smug. Paul Krugman is unintentionally funny because he's so serious and angry that you have to laugh when you read him.

Perez Hilton: I don't think it's important at all. I actually find it annoying. A critic isn't a comedian.

Steven Suskin: If you write a review in straight and dull prose, it'll be straight and dull. I realize that there's somebody reading the review. And if they're not interested, they'll just turn to the next page. I try to give them a review they'll want to read through.

Roma Torre: A lot of critics think it's good to be funny, but I don't think it's important at all. It goes with the new wave of theater criticism, which can be more about entertaining the readers than providing an intelligent assessment of the work. If I am funny, it's only because there isn't much else to say about the show. It's much easier to crack a joke at the work's expense than to critique its flaws. On the other hand, if I feel that a show's creators were way off the mark and ignoring good sense, I may consider that a license to echo their absurdity, but I'm not a comedian by any stretch of the imagination. Chances are that my attempts at being funny would backfire.

Peter Filichia: I love being funny, but I almost always do it in favor of the production. I don't like being funny in a nasty way. I am aware that people like reading nasty reviews and seeing other people fail. It's schadenfreude.

Hilton Als: When you start thinking about being funny, you're getting self-conscious, and you're not really writing.

John Simon: It helps if you can make your reviews humorous or witty, so long as it's not at the expense of truth.

Rob Weinert-Kendt: I used to say that theater criticism is part of the entertainment. It's part of the experience of the theater. You should enjoy reading it. There's some theater criticism out there that's boring as shit to read. But reaching for humor is a bad idea. If you're not naturally a wit, you shouldn't try too hard to be funny. Even some critics who are naturally funny, like Scott Brown in *New York* magazine, sometimes push too hard. You feel like you're watching a standup routine rather than reading a review. They're not taking the job seriously.

Michael Musto: Being funny is very important because people have this idea that theater is dry and boring. That's what scared me as a kid when they took us on class trips to see shows. There's a place for dry, intellectual theater critics, but there's also a place for me, who's kind of on the outskirts, looking in, and making my caustic little one-liners.

Alexis Soloski: If there is an opportunity to be funny, I can be shameless. I've written some terrible puns, and I enjoy them very much.

David Cote: It's important for a critic to have a good sense of humor because the majority of what we see is rather crappy, or just numbingly mediocre. Also, there is an assumption that the critic is a witty person, and who doesn't want to be witty? You need a certain arrogance and wit, so humor works.

Ben Brantley: Your wit should never get in the way. I've recently been reading old Dorothy Parker reviews. They're extremely funny, but they're more about showcasing her wit. I don't think there's a whole lot of transparency with her. With some critics, you feel like you're looking at the show through their words. With Dorothy Parker, all you see is her wit.

Michael Dale: No matter what the play, Dorothy Parker's reviews are all about her. I wouldn't call it responsible criticism.

Michael Schulman: Some are better at humor than others. I like to think I have a droll sense of humor. There's a kind of *New Yorker* sensibility that I've internalized. A lot of people who go into writing enjoy using their voice on the page, and humor is a part of that.

Charles Isherwood: I'm a big fan of humor in virtually all walks of life. At the same time, you don't want to be cruel and mocking. There have been times when I've been accused of stepping over the line, but I can honestly say I've never written a line with the intention of hurting anyone's feelings. It simply doesn't enter into my thinking. I get a lot of flak from people objecting to the fact that I sometimes use humor in my reviews. Artists are deluding themselves if they think a sober, boring pan is going to be more comforting than a pan that tries to entertain the reader.

Howard Shapiro: It's especially important to be funny when you're panning something. Elton John's vampire musical *Lestat* comes to mind. I had a lot of fun with that one.

Don Aucoin: Wit is a blessing in every form of writing. Even if you're writing about something tremendously bleak like *Long Day's Journey Into Night*, you can still insert some levity into the review. My reviews are the closest that most of my readers are going to get to a production, so I try to make the review not an approximation of the theater experience, but an enjoyable experience in and of itself, and wit is definitely a part of that. Of course, you don't want to take cheap shots at the good-faith efforts of people making pennies for their work.

Elysa Gardner: Critics, like playwrights, should be cautious of falling in love with their own sense of humor, and of saying things just to be cute or clever. I'm not out there doing shtick just to make a name for myself. Some movie critics do that.

Jesse Green: I am a writer, and humor is a part of the arsenal. When I'm writing reviews, I apply all of the traits I would apply to anything else I write, be it a book, a novel, a memoir, or an essay. You're instructing and entertaining the readers, just as you hope playwrights are. Even if it's very serious, I like a play that has humor in it.

John Lahr: Critics shouldn't be funny at the expense of the performers.

But if they're amusing (and very few critics are), it's a wonderful gift. I'm envious of Anthony Lane, who can be hilarious in print and still be so penetrating. Kenneth Tynan could also be hilarious and brilliant at the same time.

Peter Marks: Being entertaining is vital. No one's going to read your shit if it's just a beautifully-crafted assessment. It's also a great way to bond with a reader. When you can make them laugh, they're going to want to read more of you. But there's a difference between being funny and *trying* to be funny. Some of my *Times* reviews were uproariously nasty.

Matthew Murray: Nice? Yes. Important? No. The most important thing is to accurately express and back up your opinion, so that the reader will have the most information you can possibly give them. Humor must come afterwards. In a lot of the current reviews I read, it seems like the writers twist and turn and waste dozens (if not hundreds) of words to get to places where they can be funny, and that I have no patience for. I want to know why a show is good or bad first. And if the review does that well, then it can be as funny as the writer can make it—but not before.

MATT WINDMAN: To what extent does a critic's personal background affect his or her writing?

Michael Dale: To the same extent a playwright's personal background affects his or her writing.

John Lahr: You are what you write. You are a compendium of all your influences. Who you are as a person, your humanity, your ability to understand your life and yourself—all of that affects how you write and how you respond to a play.

Hilton Als: All writing is personal. You are giving the world an idea of your own sensibilities.

Michael Portantiere: People talk about objectivity on the part of a critic, but I don't know how realistic a goal that is.

Chris Jones: I'm a 50-year-old man, originally of British origin, who's lived in Chicago for 30 years, but I try mightily not to reflect any particular worldview. I don't think many critics will answer the question that way. They'll say, "I am who I am, and my readers know who I am," but I don't think that way. There's only one review that I write for this newspaper, and I try to make it as if I had no particular identity beyond than the search for excellence. I don't write as who I am. For me, the goal is to not be of a particular group.

I don't think it's impossible for a male critic to review a play by a woman. I don't think it's impossible for a white critic to go to an African-American theater. If you continue down that road and under that line of thinking, you end up with an absurd bifurcation of the whole reviewing process. The critic's job is to be an impartial expert on everything, and I try mightily to achieve that. Maybe it's impossible to achieve, but that's my aim.

Jesse Green: I'm in favor of gender. I'm in favor of sexuality. I'm in favor of politics. I'm in favor of critics having different varieties of all of those, and of all that informing their writing and opinions. It's healthy when there are different kinds of people seeing plays. Obviously, you can fight over it. You can say, "He's a well-known conservative, and his paper is a well-known conservative paper, and that's why he didn't like the show that I liked." That makes for good discussion, but you have to accept the fact that people don't like the same things, and that's true among the critics, too.

Richard Ouzounian: How you grew up, and the environment you grew up in, affects you very strongly. I grew up in a rough neighborhood in Queens. Then I went to an integrated university, rode the subway every day, and lived through the race riots in New York. I grew up with a much broader ethnic and social palate than a lot of my colleagues, who grew up in small towns where everything was incredibly white and proper and benign.

Robert Faires: There are parts of my background I can't escape, and there are also parts of my background that I treasure. I grew up in Texas, far from New York. That's going to have an influence on the way I perceive shows that come from New York to this part of the country, and it affects how I perceive shows that are homegrown here, too. Also, I'm a male who grew up in an era when males were running the theater and shaping what the conversation in the theater was about. That's still a part of who I am, although I feel lucky to have also experienced the tremendous expansion of the theater to cover so many more voices.

Leonard Jacobs: It's strange that the *New York Times* is comfortable having two middle-aged gay men as their top two critics. Its readership is not just middle-aged gay men. Its readership is middle-aged gay men and everybody else. A lot of people had a problem with Margo Jefferson when she was the number two theater critic at the *Times*, but at least you had another point of view with her. It was interesting to have an African-American woman step up and say whatever. There should be more female critics. There should be more critics of color. There should be younger critics and older critics.

Michael Musto: Depending on their gender and age, certain critics will get crushes on certain actors. A lot of times, the political leaning of the critic will make a difference in whether they like or loath the newest political drama. The more you acknowledge about yourself, the more open you are to review other people's work. From the beginning, I was out about myself. That kind of frees me from any hypocrisy in writing about other people.

Don Aucoin: When I see a play like David Lindsay-Abaire's *Good People*, I immediately pick up on the fact that it has characters that you don't see enough on contemporary stages: people on the economic margins. That resonates with me in a way that I think has something to do with the blue-collar jobs I had earlier in my life. I spent two years working on the General Motors assembly line, which is not the usual path for a college graduate, but it was an endlessly important experience for me, and one that still reverberates in my writing.

Frank Rizzo: I would be eager to look at reviews from other perspectives, whether based on gender, race, or geography. There's a play called *Sixteen Wounded* about a Palestinian-Israeli relationship, and I would have loved to have seen both an Israeli critic and a Palestinian critic review that show—as long as both are open, fair, and good writers.

Elisabeth Vincentelli: What we write reflects who we are, where we come from, our education, and our experiences. To me, that is reflected very obviously in how critics treat plays dealing with women-centric subject matter. I'm not saying there is some kind of systematized sexism, but it's very obvious that there's a kind of deafness to what some specific voices are saying.

Charles Isherwood: Except in extraordinary circumstances, some particular experience from your past is not going to heavily affect your response to a play. Inevitably, on a subliminal level, I'm sure it does. But if you're conscious of any potential dangers, you can guard yourself against that kind of thing. The *Times* is very vigilant about not allowing any political biases to inform your writing.

David Cote: You need to be honest in terms of your humanity. You need to be aware that certain buttons—political, ideological, and emotional—will be pushed at certain plays. You need to be aware of all possible perspectives and put your perspective on hold, if you can, or at least wrestle with your perspective. For example, if you have a reaction to a play that stems from a political view. I think some of my colleagues are conservative. I can't say I have political discussions with them, but I feel as though politics do color their reaction to certain things. If you see a play that is antiwar and you are conservative, and you think that war is not such a bad thing for big business or whatever, then I guess you might not like the play. As a liberal, I wish I saw more plays that expressed conservative views.

Michael Riedel: I hate pious liberal plays. I find them tedious and predictable. By the same token, just because a play takes a right-wing point of view doesn't mean I'm going to like it, especially if it's badly written. On the whole, since the theater tends to be a very liberal place, everybody has the same opinion, and that's not very interesting. It's refreshing to see a writer like Jonathan Reynolds, who made you think another way about abortion in his play *Girls in Trouble*. It's always about a woman's right to choose. But from his character's point of view, it was, "I'm a selfish, piggish man, and I knocked you up, and I want you to have an abortion because I don't want to have any responsibility for you or the kid."

3. Education and Personality   61

Alexis Soloski: How I respond to something is always through the filter of my knowledge and experience. I don't think it's possible to efface the personal from the work, and I don't want to. When I started working at the *Voice*, I was a 21-year-old female from Southern California, and I'm pretty sure my writing suggested that. I feel like every play this season is about real estate, and that's probably because I'm currently looking for a two-bedroom apartment. My preoccupations make their way into my writing. That doesn't meant I'll go see *Henry V* when I'm pregnant and think it's all about pregnancy, but I am often conscious of seeing works of art through my very personal lens, and sometimes I indulge in that.

David Sheward: I'm gay, but I'm not going to give every gay playwright a pass just because of that. For example, I was very disappointed with *Mothers and Sons*, Terrence McNally's recent drama about an older woman meeting the former lover of her son, who had died of AIDS years earlier. I'm also left-leaning, but I think it's important that a play isn't just a news report, and that its point of view is fully fleshed out.

Elysa Gardner: I don't have to agree with every notion that's being proposed or seems to inform a work in order to enjoy it. I've found myself attracted to things that are less than politically correct.

Helen Shaw: Watching plays as a woman, I feel like I see things that someone who isn't a woman, or who doesn't identify as a woman, wouldn't.

Jeremy Gerard: I grew up in a liberal Jewish home. I know that affects my worldview, and to pretend otherwise is silly.

Peter Filichia: At the risk of being offensive to a lot of people, I think it's very important to have a heterosexual male critic representing the public. I'm not saying that someone has to be a heterosexual in order to be a good critic. However, I do think the impression of musical theater being a gay art form has been terribly injurious. It's become something that husbands have been reluctant to go to because they don't want to be associated with the gay element. Like it or not, there are plenty of husbands who feel that way. I'm 68 years old. And when I was a kid, all through high school, nobody ever accused me of being gay because I was interested in musicals. I was thought of as being very high class because I liked this adult art form.

Adam Feldman: All of us have a certain set of opinions that reflect our personal experience. Mine are affected by the fact that I am white, Jewish, gay, and middle-class. I was born in Canada, live in New York, and went to college. All those things, and many more, will affect my experience at the theater—but that doesn't mean that my opinions are uniquely determined by a set of identity structures. If you want to be fair, you try to take the things that are only about yourself out of the evaluation. If I see an actress and I like her because she reminds me of my sister, that's meaningless to the reader. You have to understand that when you're processing it as a critic.

Dan Bacalzo: I'm a gay Filipino-American male who has a PhD in performance studies. Does my background make a difference in the way that I see and evaluate every single thing? Of course not, but it could make a difference in the way that I see and evaluate some things. I guess everyone comes from a unique perspective, and it's a matter of whether or not that perspective is worth listening to.

Linda Winer: The fact that there's only one African-American theater critic—Hilton Als at the *New Yorker*—matters. There are no Asians. There are no Hispanics. There's a greater variety of perception when you have different kinds of people looking at things.

I was so spoiled by there being other female critics in Chicago. When I joined the New York Drama Critics' Circle, it was virtually all men. If the *Post* hadn't hired Elisabeth Vincentelli, I would still be the only first-string female theater critic in New York, which is shameful. There are more women's voices now, but it's been shocking and limiting. Being the only woman on the aisle didn't make me feel special. It made me feel lonely.

We bring everything we are to the theater and to our reviews. There's no way for me to know how much of what I perceive is molded by the things that I believe and the way that I was raised. Now that we have four or five strong-voiced female critics around, we don't always agree, but we see things that men sometimes don't see. When there are plays by women in which women are just sitting around talking, my colleagues historically have written reviews saying, "This wasn't about anything," while plays where men are just sitting around and talking are always profound and hilarious.

Michael Schulman: There's been a real effort lately to produce more work by female playwrights, and I think there should be an effort to have more female theater critics. I can think of just a few, like Alexis Soloski and Elisabeth Vincentelli. I can think of one African-American theater critic: Hilton Als. We need a variety of people writing reviews so there isn't just one monolithic point of view in the critical world. If every critic is a well-off white guy, they're going to sympathize with certain kinds of things. They're going to be predisposed to like certain kinds of theater (whether consciously or not), and they'll be blind to other things. I would love to see a female successor to Ben Brantley and Charles Isherwood at some point.

A few years ago, when *Hair* was revived, Hilton Als pointed out that the black characters are not nearly as fleshed out as the white characters, and no one else pointed that out. He's the one who would notice that kind of unconscious, institutionalized racism in a musical. Of course, you can't have a widely diverse pool of theater critics if you don't have a large pool of theater critics to begin with.

Michael Sommers: One of the things that helped my career was the fact that I was fairly open about being gay. For Christ's sake, I worked for the *New*

York Native. When all those plays about homosexuality really started coming out in the 1970s and 1980s, I never had any problem writing about them.

Roma Torre: There aren't many married, straight female critics with children, so it's possible that I bring a perspective that is relatively unique when I see a show. When my kids were young, I would bring them to see children's shows and partially use them to determine if it was worth seeing or not.

Jesse Green: I'm a little unusual among my colleagues for having kids. I think that informs my reaction to many things I see, if only in an unconscious way.

Peter Marks: It's kind of embarrassing that so many critics are white guys. There should be more women. There should be more reviewers of color. There should be more Asian and Latino reviewers. There should be more young critics because different generations have different perspectives.

Robert Feldberg: You have your likes and dislikes and prejudices and influences, but a good critic will moderate all that and move to the middle. A man and a woman will have a different reaction. Depending on your sexual preference, you may have a different reaction. What you learn to do is moderate that and say, "This is something that's strongly influencing me, but I've got to step back and lessen that particular influence."

Ronni Reich: I've found myself in positions where I've criticized a female character in a new play set in the present day for seeming really antiquated, and then I won't see any criticism along those lines in the reviews written by male critics. I've seen other reviews where the critic was offended by the way that a character of color was portrayed but I didn't think of that.

Terry Teachout: H.L. Mencken said, "Criticism is prejudice made plausible." It's an exaggeration, but a very illuminating one. I write what I think. That's what they pay me to do. I try very hard to write about the show that I'm seeing, rather than the one I'm expecting to see. I know I'm doing that because I am very frequently surprised by what I see. If I was never surprised, I would know something is wrong. There are certain things that I don't like to see at the theater, like uncontrollable whimsy or propaganda. But when I say that, I'm not expressing a prejudice. I'm expressing a view of what makes art good or bad. There are things I'll never like because I don't think they're any good.

Jason Zinoman: I don't believe there's such a thing as perfect critical objectivity, but I do believe it's important to aim for it—even without ever actually achieving it. To be a critic, you have to review musicals, plays of different styles, and experimental work, and you have to give all of them a fair shake. But the eccentric, idiosyncratic background that you bring to the table is a strength. That's your critical voice. That's why people want to read you.

MATT WINDMAN: What makes you unique as a theater critic?

John Simon: I hope I'm unique. It's terrible if anybody is not unique. I'm glad that you're asking that question because I assume it means that you think that I am unique, and I very much want to be that.

Marilyn Stasio: I've never thought about it. I don't care. I just do what I do, and I pay no attention to what other people are doing.

Peter Marks: I think my value is as a communicator. I don't think my judgment is particularly stellar. I respond emotionally to a lot of things, and maybe my heart rules over my head too much, but I feel like I can communicate the experience of immersing myself in a production with a level of informed judgment.

Elisabeth Vincentelli: I'm interested in everything, and in the ways that everything connects together. My tastes in music probably also set me apart. For instance, I don't know other theater critics that are interested in metal.

Helen Shaw: The *Times*' dance critic, Claudia La Rocco, and I are both interested in interdisciplinary performance and dance-infused physical performance. There aren't a ton of mainstream critics who are interested in the really zany stuff.

Jeremy Gerard: I was an Off-Broadway baby. I grew up going to the alternative theater of the 1960s and 1970s. That's why I wrote a book about the American Place Theatre and the people I feel must not be forgotten. I have a real love for the outliers who make it possible for the theater to continue living and changing and growing. It provides a different kind of contextualizing that works to my benefit.

Leonard Jacobs: Because I'm a historian and a dramaturg, I offer a perspective that most theater critics cannot. Most theater critics don't understand all the composite parts of a theater experience. I think that's a problem, and it's a shame. It's a real deficit in not only contemporary theater criticism, but in much of the criticism of previous generations.

Michael Musto: I take a very personal approach to writing about theater. In my column, I can approach theater in a more subjective manner. I'm writing my deeply personal, impulsive reactions to shows—as opposed to writing a sort of measured review, the way you would have to do in the *Times*. It's much more fun to do it my way. I can just go with my impulsive reactions and say outrageous things. Some people say my column is like a blog (even though it came out before there was such a thing as blogging).

Terry Teachout: I've been making different kinds of art since I was born, and I think that makes a difference in how I write. It adds a respect for the craftsmanship of theater. Wilfrid Sheed once said that a critic should appreciate "the simple miracle of getting the curtain up every night." I don't think

I've ever fallen victim to the sterile perfectionism that comes from people who haven't gotten their hands dirty in the process of making art.

Charles Isherwood: A lot of my fellow critics got into the business through musical theater. Not that there's anything wrong with that, but I was not a passionate musical theater person. That's not what sparked my passion and interest in theater. In some ways, I suppose that's a handicap. But in other ways, it makes me more objective.

Richard Ouzounian: When I came to theater criticism, I was already a successful director, writer, and artistic director. If I say a play is badly directed, I know that it was badly directed, and I know why. I have been, for that reason and many others, kind of a contentious critic over the past 15 years.

Rob Weinert-Kendt: I have a broad perspective because I covered theater in L.A. for so long, and I work at *American Theatre* magazine, which covers theater all over the country. I have a broader knowledge of theater and a broader sense of what theater is, beyond just Broadway and Off-Broadway.

Zachary Stewart: I'm considerably younger than most of my colleagues.

John Simon: I have jokingly said that the *Guinness Book of World Records* people should take note that I'm the oldest person writing drama criticism who has done it uninterrupted for so many decades. I also write in a somewhat more learned style. I know certain things. I make allusions to things that mean something to me, but may not mean anything to young people, or even to other reviewers. I make references to things which the usual reviewer doesn't know about, and which people can learn from. Many people have said to me that they don't care much for my opinion, but that they're very grateful for all the new words they've learned by reading me.

Michael Riedel: I'm the last Broadway newspaper columnist. Back when there were a lot of newspapers, they all had Broadway columnists: the *Herald Tribune*, the *New York Times*, the *Journal-American*, the *New York Post*, the *Daily News*, *PM*. They all had theater columnists because Broadway was a big part of entertainment culture and New York City. There's no *New York Times* theater column anymore. The *Daily News* never replaced me after I left. *Newsday* did away with its theater column several years ago. I'm not so sure the *Post* will hire someone else to be a Broadway columnist after I'm gone.

Michael Dale: My complete lack of confidence in my opinions makes me unique.

Perez Hilton: I'm not trying to be a theater critic. I'm just a theater fan sharing my thoughts with fellow theater fans on my blog. I went to NYU and studied acting. I've seen hundreds of shows. That doesn't necessarily make me a theater critic, but it definitely makes me someone with a deep passion and understanding of the world of theater and entertainment.

Richard Zoglin: I feel like I'm more of a populist. I'm usually much more receptive to the Disney musicals and things like that. I'm a little more in tune with the average audience member.

Don Aucoin: I was a reporter, rather than a critic, for most of my career. I still think like a reporter. I still put a huge premium on clarity. That comes from having written about all kinds of subjects for the front page of the newspaper, where you need to make yourself as clear as possible, as quickly as possible.

David Cote: I think I am well-regarded because I have more sympathy for the artistic process than some of my colleagues. I'm told that theater people—playwrights, directors, actors—respect my opinion, so that means something. Having worked for years Off Off Broadway doesn't necessarily prepare me more than my colleagues, but I try to be more sympathetic to experimental theater or playwrights who are trying something different. If I'm distinctive at all, it's been because I'm trying to be more of an advocate, holding big nonprofit theaters' feet to the fire.

MATT WINDMAN: *How have you changed as a critic since you started writing?*

Alexis Soloski: My prose used to be more convoluted, though even now I still use too many adjectives. When I was in my early 20s, I felt like I had something to prove—that I knew a lot or that I "got it." That eased off. If I don't understand something now, I'm comfortable saying so. I'm also comfortable with not always getting things right or admitting that I was wrong.

Michael Dale: I used to try to write about every actor in a show and every element of a production. I don't think that's necessary anymore. If something stands out, I'll write about it.

Linda Winer: I don't think I've changed that much. When I go back and read clips from when I was a zygote, I recognize the voice. I know who she is. I'd like to think I've gotten better. But since I now write such short reviews, it's hard to know for sure.

Leonard Jacobs: For a long time, I was self-consciously clever. Cleverness should be organic and not conscious. In other words, you shouldn't strain to be clever. Younger critics have a tendency to show off their knowledge. I think that my work has evolved to the point where I feel comfortable and secure with my own knowledge. Cultivating your own voice as a writer is a long process. I don't think I reached a place where I felt clear about my voice until the last couple of years.

John Simon: Anyone that reads me regularly is in a much better position to decide how I've changed. To yourself, you're always the same person. You look in the mirror: you have less hair than you used to, and there are lines on your face, but you sort of take all of that for granted. You don't think,

3. Education and Personality

Once upon a time, I was a handsome youth, and now I'm a decrepit cretin. One looks in the mirror and is still the same person. There are some ways in which my writing has gotten better—possibly because it's less authoritarian, less flashy, and less effect-driven. But on the whole, it's still the same person writing. When I read something that I wrote 30 years ago, I don't feel like it was written by a different person.

Michael Schulman: I now write with more ease. I have a more relaxed voice on the page. I'm not analyzing every single sentence. I also have a much better handle on certain writers, certain actors, and certain institutions because I've seen a lot more of their work.

Terry Teachout: I know more simply by virtue of having seen a lot more plays, but I don't think the point of view that I bring to that knowledge has changed very much. I'm middle-aged and have worked as a professional critic for 30 years, so I don't think it's likely that what I do will evolve very much. If anything is changing me, it's the fact that I'm now also working as a theater professional.

Ben Brantley: When I started at the *Times*, I hadn't been a professional theater critic before. Suddenly, I was on one of the most conspicuous platforms in the world in which to be a theater critic. I was very conscious of not wanting to make any kind of mistake. I did a whole lot of research for every single thing. I still do research, but not to the same degree.

Jeremy Gerard: I've learned how to write short. That's slightly facetious, but it's true.

Robert Faires: The younger me seems to have been a little more casual in the way he writes. Maybe I've gotten more formal as I've gotten older. I hope I've become a better writer. I work at being descriptive in a way that connects with a reader, where I can say more about the human condition, or what I've learned as a human being.

Jesse Oxfeld: One thing I became aware of was how much I grew to resent a really bad show. There were some shows that just shouldn't have been put up in the first place. The fact that I had been made to spend three hours sitting through this bad thing would make me angry and resentful. That probably showed up in the writing, which may not have been entirely fair.

Peter Filichia: When I started out in my twenties, I was a terribly severe critic. Just like all the other critics, I was marking incompetence and making fun of names. After a while, that just didn't appeal to me anymore. I realized that it wasn't doing any good. I was very influenced by an article in the *Times* in 1973 about the musical *Seesaw* and all the troubles it had out of town. Michael Bennett had to come in and save it. When Joseph Kipness, its producer, called Bennett up, he said, "Whenever a Broadway musical dies, Broadway dies a little with it." That was profoundly changing for me because I had assumed there were no repercussions when a show closed. Kipness reminded me that every failure leads to less theater.

Roma Torre: I've gotten tougher over the years. I'm not quite as forgiving as I used to be. I used to beat around the bush because I didn't want to hurt anyone's feelings. It was partly because I've been in that position. I did a lot of theater when I was younger. I've been on the rude end of a review, and it stings badly. Over the years, I realized that there's no point in pulling my punches. I used to be a lot more lenient about a performance that wasn't quite as successful as it should have been.

Michael Riedel: My writing has become less nasty and more playful. It's easy when you're young to think everybody's up to no good, and that you're going to expose them, ridicule them, and tear them down. But as you get older, you realize that loads of people in the theater are not trying to put on bad plays. They are doing the best work they can. Sometimes they succeed, and I celebrate it. Sometimes they fail, and I make fun of it. But I don't think it's a crime against humanity to put on a bad play, as I once did when I was young, aggressive, and obnoxious. Also, I make fun of myself more now than it used to. I just don't take myself seriously, and I really don't take the theater that seriously.

Michael Musto: I've become a little more humane. I still have quite an edge and a sharp tongue, but I'm a lot more forgiving now. In the old days, I was ballistic if a show didn't rub me the right way. As you get older, there are more things you can appreciate. Not everything seems old-fogeyish or boring—even if they're doing the eight-millionth version of a Rodgers and Hammerstein musical you first saw as a kid.

Richard Zoglin: I've gotten surer of my opinions. There are certain kinds of plays I just do not like. There's a certain kind of New York relationship play that I see over and over again. I have little patience for it, and I'm now more outspoken in saying that. Earlier on, I would have been more careful about that because most of those plays get good reviews, and I didn't want to look like a dummy. When you start out, you think that there's a right opinion and a wrong opinion. But as you go on, you realize that everybody's opinions are equal. That said, sometimes it still bothers me when I like something that everybody else hates.

Frank Scheck: When I was younger, I was more tempted to be overly sarcastic. As I've gotten older, I've gotten more tempered. But if you're writing for a paper like the *Post*, which likes a certain degree of sauciness, you have to keep them happy as well.

Adam Feldman: I'm probably a bit more mindful now of avoiding unnecessary cruelty. I try to save my fire. There's a bit of violence in some of my earlier writing that now looks a little arrogant in retrospect—not that I don't still indulge in it sometimes.

3. Education and Personality 69

Thom Geier: I've gotten a little kinder. I don't think I have as much cruelty in me anymore. Over time, I've come to realize what a miracle it is to get any production mounted. Even productions that fall short of their ambitions are still achievements.

Peter Marks: I now notice more of the subtlety of what's going on. In some ways, that makes writing harder. I used to give more of a definitive yes or no, and I've learned over time that a lot of things are "maybe" and "sort of," and you have to be able to express that in a way that's clear.

Chris Jones: As I've gotten older, I've become less excited by some things. You might say I've become more cynical. When you're very young and you see something great, you find it peerless. When you're older, you don't find it so peerless. You've been there before, and you have a sense that you will be there again, so you become more sober. I've also come to greatly value truth, which I don't think I fully understood when I was young. When I go to the theater, I want things to feel true in some way, and I find myself very resistant to anything that feels untrue. I want things to be real—to have truth and integrity.

Elysa Gardner: When I got the job, I hadn't written professionally about theater before, so there was a lot of on-the-job learning. The first play I reviewed was Eugene O'Neill's *A Moon for the Misbegotten*, and I thought, Why couldn't they have given me a Neil Simon play? You evolve as a writer in the same way that you evolve as a person: you see more, you learn more, you take in more, you have different experiences, you become familiar with more work, and you become familiar with different interpretations of work.

Howard Shapiro: It doesn't make my criticism any different, but I've become more aware of how the business works. That helps me understand why actors might do a show just to qualify for Equity healthcare.

Robert Feldberg: Over time, you gain the means to compare things from show to show, which is an important part of what a critic does. You get to know the work of individual directors, writers, and actors. You learn what's possible in the theater.

John Lahr: I'm in psychoanalysis. I've changed and gotten deeper as a person, so therefore my criticism has changed.

4

The Theater Community

MATT WINDMAN: Can a critic also work in the theater as an actor, playwright, director, producer, or dramaturg?

Michael Dale: It certainly has been done, and I'm sure that those who do have certain issues to contend with.

Zachary Stewart: Definitely. In fact, it is better if a critic has actually practiced the craft he is criticizing.

John Simon: If a critic writes an occasional play, that's one thing. But if a regular playwright were to become an important critic, that would be a whole other ballgame, and that would not work. If Ben Brantley were also a playwright, his absurdities would be less tolerated. At least now one assumes that he has no special interests that support his critical sense.

Thom Geier: Having personal relationships with people in the industry you're covering complicates how you cover that industry—but that's not to say that it can't be done.

Rob Weinert-Kendt: The *New York Times Book Review* is full of authors reviewing other authors. I don't know if we'll ever have that model, where playwrights are reviewing other playwrights, but I would love to see the walls break down a bit. Of course, criticism is really not a way for a theater professional to get ahead. It can actually be really detrimental to a theater career to write reviews.

Michael Riedel: In the old days, critics also worked in the theater. George S. Kaufman was the theater editor of the *New York Times*, and he was writing Broadway shows at the same time. The ethical lines that people abide by now are relatively new in journalism. Back in the day, people were crossing and jumping over the line all the time.

In this day and age, I don't think you can do only one thing. If you're in the media business, you have to be a writer and a broadcaster, and you have to be comfortable on television and radio. There's a long tradition of theater columnists being media personalities. Dorothy Kilgallen was a panelist on *What's My Line?*. Alexander Woollcott appeared in *The Man Who Came to*

Dinner at the Bucks County Playhouse. It's all part of the fun. I love performing. I'm a total ham. Of course, I have a limited range as an actor. I'm mainly restricted to playing myself—but I do a very good job of playing myself. I do a lot of things. I'm on *Theater Talk*. I have a regular radio gig on *Imus in the Morning*. I do a lot of work for the radio station WABC. I was on the TV series *Smash*. I give lectures. I'm working on a book.

Michael Sommers: It's hard for a critic to be a playwright or do something creative in the theater. If you're doing your job right as a critic, people in the theater will hate you. In any event, I couldn't write a play or even a longer piece of fiction now. My critical sense is so developed that I couldn't really free myself up enough to do that. But in this new world, where you can't make a living as a drama critic anymore, you have to do other things. I just don't know how you can juggle it. I'm no good for anything but this. There's a playwright (who I won't mention by name) who has gotten plays produced and also operates as a critic. They're rather dull plays (if I may say so), but that's his problem.

Roma Torre: I think one can inform the other. Truffaut was both a film critic and a brilliant filmmaker. George Bernard Shaw was a theater critic, and he wrote great plays.

Charles Isherwood: Some people try to pursue both. It used to be easier in the old days when you had George S. Kaufman, who could do both, and Harold Clurman, who was doing everything.

John Lahr: Tom Stoppard began as a critic, and so did William Inge. There are lots of people who start from the outside and work their way in.

Matthew Murray: Walter Kerr and his wife worked in the theater. Terry Teachout is a playwright and his work has been produced in town.

Chris Jones: I haven't figured out how I could do it in a way that would make me comfortable. A critic, to some degree, needs authority. And the moment you do a lousy show yourself, your ability to judge the work of others is compromised. Criticism is a funny business. It is part of the artistic process, but it's also entirely separate from it. It requires you, to some degree, to give up on your own creativity. Some critics, over the years, have found that very hard to do. But the moment you start writing plays yourself, you're in a compromised situation—or at least there's the danger of that.

Ben Brantley: I think you can't. I'm kind of a purist in that sense. If you did that, you'd want to promote what you do in your capacity as a theater person. You wouldn't want to alienate certain people. On the other hand, there are some people who really can do both, who can work with someone on one project and then give them a bad review in another context, and it won't be personal. I'm just very uneasy with that.

Peter Filichia: I think it should be mandatory. It's very healthy for a critic to try to write a play, or work on a show, and see how that works out.

Alexis Soloski: I don't have the stomach for it. To me, it feels too tricky ethically. That said, when Project Shaw puts on a staged reading of a Shaw play with a cast of critics, I'll take part in it. If I get to sit anonymously in the dark and judge people on their performances, it's really only fair to turn the tables every now and then.

Andy Propst: Let's say you're a critic in a theater community where there are only seven professional theaters, and you're also a dramaturg at one of those theaters. If you're reviewing shows at the other six theaters and dismissing everything, it will look like you have an agenda. No critic should have a hidden agenda. Their writing should never be suspect.

Christine Dolen: I know that a lot of critics do both. But because of my background in daily newspaper journalism, I'm quite opposed to it. You walk on one side of the line or the other. You don't straddle. Whether or not there's anything questionable about doing both, it certainly looks questionable.

Leonard Jacobs: I think a critic can and should do professional work in the theater—even if they aren't very good at it. Peter Brook said in *The Empty Space* that a critic should try "putting his hands on the medium and attempting to work it himself." If you've never acted, what right do you have to talk about someone else's acting? Have you ever tried to write dialogue and create a character? Do you know what it's like to direct and move actors around a stage? If you've never done any of that, you can still render a judgment. You can still say whether you liked something. You can even try to say why. But to me, that makes the critic less educated and less legitimate.

Howard Shapiro: I understand why other critics might want to, but I couldn't do it. I want to be an audience member, like the people sitting right beside me. I think being an audience member is the way for me to give the most honest viewpoints. I even have trouble being on panels. If I'm reviewing something and they want me to do a talkback, I say no because that's getting too close.

Scott Brown: Not only is it possible, it can work out quite well. I don't think it's a requirement for being a critic, but it does produce a different kind of criticism that is based on a different perspective. Those critics have a more process-based approach to what they're seeing. It's not that they're going to be categorically easier on a performance, but there's perhaps more of an understanding of how the performance arrived there—that what we're seeing is not just something that just strangely formed in the head of Zeus.

Some of the harshest critics are other performers, who can be absolutely brutal. Part of that is because they understand the process. It produces a certain kind of insight that is useful. That's not to say you need to know exactly how something was made. In the end, it's a critic's responsibility to evaluate the final product, and it doesn't matter if the critic is familiar with the production process or not.

Michael Portantiere: If a theater critic writes a play and a specific actor stars in it, it would be a little dicey if the theater critic later reviewed another play with the same actor in it.

Linda Winer: I can't do both. I have emotional conflicts of interest. I don't really have friends in the theater. For me, there is a drawbridge up over the moat. I learned this about myself in Chicago, back when I was a baby critic. I was writing about people I knew. We all lived in the same neighborhood and went to similar schools. I found that if I can see the face of the artist I'm writing about over the keyboard, I'm in trouble. I would second guess myself. I'd wonder, Am I being nicer to this person because I like him? Am I being tougher on this person than is fair because I want to prove to myself that it's not because I like him? There are layers and layers of that. Because there are so many intangibles, I prefer to simplify the situation as much as I can.

There are people who need to work in the theater—not just financially, but emotionally, psychologically, and intellectually. That's great if they can do it, but I can't. It may have something to do with being a woman who was, you know, raised to please. I struggle with writing about people that I care about. What we say is not polite to society. We're writing things that affect livelihoods and senses of security and senses of self.

John Lahr: Doing professional work in the theater makes you completely different as a critic. If you have actually written a play or a joke, if you've had that experience, it changes the language that you use. It changes how you deal with artistic events because then you understand how much is invested in an endeavor and what it means. A lot of the people dishing it out haven't done it. The critics who are absolutely, outrageously mean are anorexic critics. They can eat, but they can't swallow. Those critics have never made anything. They couldn't make anything and still write that way.

Marilyn Stasio: If a critic wants to write a play in his or her spare time, good luck with that. But if you're a paid reviewer writing for a commercial publication, you cannot pursue producers in order to get your play produced. It's not ethical. You really can't participate in the creative process if it means collaborating with people whose work you might review. My work as a dramaturg was different. It was done more in a teaching capacity. For the most part, I advised young writers. I had no trouble with that.

Hilton Als: It's important to take risks of your own. Write your own plays. Dramaturg some productions.

Jason Zinoman: To be honest, it's a bad idea. I have a stronger position on this than most people. Critical independence is tremendously important, and we shouldn't lose sight of it. The argument for doing work in the theater is that you can gain knowledge about the artistic process. I would argue that you can gain some of that knowledge without sacrificing your independence by being a reporter. Theater criticism is hard. It's like how being an actor or a director is hard. And if you want to be good at it, you need to give it your full attention. It's not as easy as just giving your opinion on a few things. A lot of people in the theater don't realize that.

David Cote: I'm working on a play right now, as well as several opera libretti. It's delicate because it's not like I'm asking New York producers to put on my play. I have a producer, the Gingold Theatrical Group, which commissioned the play and is developing it for a production someday. Still, I don't want to be put in a situation where I owe something to producers. Luckily, there's no money to be made from it. How many American playwrights are living off their playwriting? I'm simply hoping that someday somebody will want to produce it.

Helen Shaw: I stumbled into dramaturgy. My first job in New York was working on a production of Brecht's *The Resistible Rise of Arturo Ui* with Al Pacino, John Goodman, Steve Buscemi, and Paul Giamatti. More recently, I was the dramaturg on the production of *The Tempest* that was done by the Public Theater in Central Park with 200 people. I'll never be able to review anything directed by Lear deBessonet because I worked with her on *The Tempest*. I also feel very uncomfortable reviewing anything at the Public Theater. I think I have to let the statute of limitations expire before I can start writing about the Public Theater critically again. That's the cost of doing business.

Peter Filichia: Years ago, I was asked to play the Narrator and the Mysterious Man in a benefit reading of *Into the Woods* for a theater company. I thought we'd just rehearse the day before, but we ended up rehearsing for a month. I was in way over my head. In any event, it turned out to be a way of seeing how much time, energy, and talent goes into these things, all of which we blithely don't take into consideration.

Robert Faires: Since I started writing theater criticism, I've walked the line of being a theater critic while remaining a practicing theater artist. At the beginning, I wrote for an alternative paper that was fine with me continuing to act and direct at the same time. Then I married an actress, so I am deeply inside of the community that I cover as a critic. Every day, I face the question of whether my criticism is on a solid ethical ground. Are my friendships and relationships with the people I've worked with affecting what I have to say as a critic? I take that very seriously. It's something that I wrestle with and never take for granted. When I, as an editor, bring on a new writer, the first conversation we have is about the ethics of this profession, particularly in a city where the lines between the artists and the people who write about the artists are very porous.

Jesse Green: I personally have to figure out how to deal with the fact that I was involved in the theater at a professional level at the beginning of

4. The Theater Community

my career. I have lots of friends in the theater, some of whom are now very prominent, and that's an issue. But all things considered, I would rather see critics have experience in their field to at least some extent than sit above it all in a tower, not really knowing anything about the work they cover, or the lives of the people who make it.

If (God forbid) my spouse was an actor and got cast in a show, I would not write about that show. But if a friendly acquaintance of mine was in a show, unless I felt that the acquaintanceship prohibited me from being honest, I'd still write about it. I once heard from somebody at the *Times* that to determine whether a relationship is too close and would create (or give the appearance of creating) a conflict of interest, you should use this test: Do you know the names of the person's children? If you do, then the relationship is too close. I think that notion can be debated, especially since a lot of people in the theater don't have children.

Peter Marks: It's a tough thing to navigate, but I see no reason why a critic can't write a play. I've tried my hand at playwriting, and I still have plays in my head that I'd like to work on.

Terry Teachout: Working as a playwright has made me a better theater critic. It has taught me things I couldn't learn any other way. If you're asking whether it's getting in the way of doing my job as a critic, the answer is no. Occasionally, there are shows that I can't cover because I've worked with someone, but that's only happened four or five times. Beyond that, it hasn't made any difference. When it became clear I that my writing was going to be produced professionally, I had to sit down with my editors to figure out how to approach this in terms of a conflicts policy. Because I'm straight with them, we haven't run into any problems, and I don't think that we will.

MATT WINDMAN: Is the critic part of the theater community?

John Simon: This question comes up fairly often. Frankly, it means nothing to me. It's as if you were to ask me whether it makes a difference if a critic takes a daily aspirin or not. Community is a rather suspect term. People who have the same kind of profession, or who live in the same part of town, may be part of a community. I guess anyone who belongs to the Tea Party—God help them, or God help us—may be part of a ghastly community. The term community may apply to theater in some sense. But in terms of thinking about the theater, it has nothing to do with it.

Matthew Murray: Theater is typically centered around the community in which it's created—whether that's New York, Chicago, Seattle, or any other place—and the critic is a part of that community in a way that film critics aren't necessarily.

Michael Dale: I think that's a question for actors, playwrights, directors, and other theater artists to answer.

Ben Brantley: I can only speak for myself, but I'm very much outside of it. I don't hang out with theater people. It's just not my world.

Alexis Soloski: I like to think we're all part of the same community and working towards the same goals. I don't think of myself as an artist, and I leave the art up to them. But during awards season, I do feel like we can be part of the larger community. The *Village Voice* sponsors the Obie Awards, and that's what they are meant to celebrate: the surprising and confounding Off-Broadway and Off Off Broadway theater. I also find it nice to put on a dress and heels and lipstick once a year.

Chris Jones: Outside of it. The theater critic's primary responsibility is to the paying customer and the future of the art.

Christine Dolen: The critic should never be part of the theater community. Once a critic starts forming friendships, whether or not they genuinely compromise his or her ability to be effective, it certainly looks that way. That being said, somebody like myself who's worked in a region for a long time gets to know people. That can be productive because it helps with reporting. Still, it's a slippery slope when critics socialize with the people they're writing about.

Frank Rizzo: I think the critic is—and should be—part of the theater community. I just attended a fiftieth-anniversary gala at the Eugene O'Neill Theater Center in Waterford, Connecticut. The first thing they created after the National Playwrights Conference was the National Critics Institute. They believed that the critic is part of the artistic process, and that there's a contribution from theater criticism. I grew up outside of Boston, and I couldn't wait to read the reviews of the latest out-of-town tryout from Elliot Norton, the "Dean of American Theatre Critics," and Kevin Kelly, who was acerbic and kind of mean but very smart. They were part of the process. They didn't just give a thumbs up-thumbs down review. They wrote as if they were part of the process of shaping the show as it moved forward to Broadway.

David Cote: They are outside of it. They are not involved in the creative process—actively at least. They are on the periphery of it. They are lay people who drop in for a short period of time. They are like unexpected guests who have very little idea how the party came together.

Helen Shaw: I think they are part of the theater community. You would have to be very naïve to believe that the things you write won't hurt people, and that they won't be mad at you. They will be. They will be legitimately mad at you—and that's profoundly their right. You're like the friend who tells everybody that their haircut looks bad. That friend is not too popular. Whether we like it or not, there is some kind of circulatory link. When the criticism is better, the theater is better. And when the theater is better, the criticism is better. Being part of the theater community does not mean blind boosterism, but it does mean thinking about and acknowledging everything that goes into making the work that we are seeing.

Roma Torre: I think you have to remain on the outside. I often get asked to do events, and I mostly say no because I don't want to get too close. There are some performers who regard me as a friend, but I have to keep my distance. It's unfortunate because these are wonderful people. They do great work, and I admire them tremendously, but I can't get too close.

For 17 years, I have done red carpet shows, mostly for the Tony Awards. But this year, I decided it was too compromising for me to continue doing that. I'm always living in fear that one of the people who I reviewed unfavorably is going to throw a pie in my face on the red carpet. It's too much of a professional conflict for me to stand there making nice and joking around with these people, who I may not have said very nice things about in a review. Theater people have thin skin for the most part, and they remember everything you said, including the negative comments. So I thought, I can't do this anymore. It's just too uncomfortable and awkward. I am pulling myself even further away these days. It just has to be that way.

Michael Musto: A critic is definitely part of it, but on the outside. They can't get too pulled into the middle. The role of a critic is to sit back and evaluate. Some residual glitter does fall on your shoulder. You are an exciting part of the theater world, but you always have to remind yourself that you're the person taking it in. You're not center stage. You're fifth row center.

Rob Weinert-Kendt: The critic is part of the theater community, but he is the annoying guy at the party who's telling everybody, "You look like shit." He's the kind of person it might be hard to be friends with all the time, but he's the kind of person you need. You need a truth teller. The problem is in confusing him with an authority. He's not the authority, but he's the one who's going to tell you what he really thinks, and I think there's value in his subjective opinions. He's not objective. He's not standing on some mountain, looking down. He's in the mix of everything. Whether you like him or not, you can trust him to say what he thinks. There's a huge value in that, and the theater community could definitely use more people who will tell the truth.

Zachary Stewart: He's the weird kid sitting by himself at lunch. He has no tribe, but he's in the same physical space, and his observations about everyone else are usually the most on-point because of his outsider status.

Don Aucoin: I see myself as a journalist who's reporting on the theater community, writing reviews, writing think pieces, and generally assessing the work. I didn't see myself as part of the political community when I covered politics. I didn't see myself as part of the TV community when I was a TV critic. That being said, I understand that nobody's doing theater for the money. Theater people often make enormous personal sacrifices to do it.

That matters a lot in terms of my fundamental respect for them, but it doesn't make me a part of the theater community.

Robert Faires: Every critic gets to choose the amount of distance he or she wants between himself and the artists who are working onstage. However, when we think about the ecology of what's taking place, I consider the audience to be a part of the theater community. Without the audience, there's an element missing to the artist's work, and the critic is a part of the audience. In some ways, the critic is the mediator between the audience and the artist. Also, I know for a fact that theater artists are reading me and paying attention to me.

For as long as I've been doing this, there have always been avenues for artists to interact with critics, to be friends with critics, and to become critics themselves. There have been a number of critics who started out as artists, decided to be critics for a while, and then became artists again. You'll find very few critics who erect a barrier between themselves and the artists, and you'll find very few artists who aren't willing to interact directly with critics on a very personal level.

Elysa Gardner: I'm certainly not part of the theater community. You can have a nice repartee with someone, but you don't become buddies with a playwright or actor, no matter how many times you interview them. You can't really be part of the community if you are observing it from the outside, but we are constantly absorbed in the theater, trying to understand it and appreciate it.

Scott Brown: Critics are part of the theater to a certain extent. The critic is always going to be the cranky old man who lives at the end of the community, in a house nobody wants to walk by, but there is a connection there. In some ways, it's a very personal connection. Even people who say they don't read the reviews really do read them because it's irresistible. It's human nature. They get to know the critics not as people but through their work, which gives them a distorted understanding of who the critics are. Likewise, the critic gets to know a distorted version of who an actor, director, or playwright is because they're meeting them through their work. But even with these unusual misunderstandings and misapprehensions, they do get to know each other. There's an intimacy there.

Jason Zinoman: Some people will say that you're a part of the theater community and mean it as a compliment. I appreciate where they're coming from, but I don't think I'm really a part of it. I see myself as a sort of satellite.

Adam Feldman: There are different approaches to this. Some critics make a strong dividing line between them and the entire theater community to protect themselves from contamination, from possible conflicts that might arise, from knowing too much about artists or groups within the theater community. I understand that approach, but I don't happen to share it. I have many friends in the theater world. I try to know as much as I can about what's going on in it, and I try to remain as collegial as possible. I think having greater insight into the creative side makes me a better critic. It makes me smarter about what I'm seeing. It also disinclines me from being simply mean.

Historically, for many people on the creative side, their relationship with critics has been seen as antagonistic, but I try not to think that way. I'm often in social situations with people who are doing work that I have written about, or that I may write about in the future. I trust that they understand the way the game works, and the fact that if I say hello to them at a party, it does not mean I won't write honestly about their work in the future. If I'm close friends with someone, then of course I won't review their work, but I review work all the time of people I've had interactions with, and sometimes I review it negatively. That's my job. I have been unfriended on *Facebook* by people after writing reviews of their work that they were not happy with. I can't blame them. I certainly don't like being criticized in public.

Peter Marks: I am a member of the journalism community, which is separate from the theater community. It just so happens that the people who care most about what I write are the people I'm directing my words to the least: the theater community. Having said that, being able to move within the community as a reporter and a critic is useful. I do think there's a problem with critics who think they're part of the community. Then you're limiting your voice, and the reader can tell the difference at some level. They can discern if your writing seems to be for that group of people. They'll feel like it's not for them. Then you might as well be a dramaturg or a publicist.

Howard Shapiro: The critic is not in the theater community. Rather, the theater critic is *of* the theater community. That's something that I learned from a critic named Clifford A. Ridley, who was the critic for many years of the *National Observer* and then became the theater critic at the *Philadelphia Inquirer*. He was a journalist foremost. I'm aware of the symbiosis between critics and theater artists. But if I walk into a show worrying about the theater's finances or the actors' feelings, I can't do my job. We've all been at opening nights when the house is papered. That papered house includes people who are in the theater community. Critics know that they can disregard almost any reaction that those people have because they're friends with those onstage, and my role isn't to be a friend.

John Lahr: There is a widely-held view that critics should not mix with or know the people who are making the art in any way. I think that is a really retrograde position that enforces ignorance. The only critics who have value are those who involve themselves in the art. I can easily justify that by naming all the people who you might say were really great or significant theater critics: Stark Young, Robert Brustein, Harold Clurman, Eric Bentley, Kenneth Tynan, Bernard Shaw. The people we read decades down the line are those who worked both sides of the street. All the others don't have a smack of the life of the theater, no matter how slickly they write.

Jesse Oxfeld: I like to have a drink and schmooze, and I'm perfectly happy to sit in bars adjacent to theaters and chat up people who may be part of the theater community. I sort of inject myself in that way. But ultimately, a critic is not a part of it. If you accept the distinction of a critic versus a reviewer (where a critic is someone who really is engaged in the art form), then maybe the critic is part of the community, whereas a reviewer takes on himself a certain journalistic impartiality.

Michael Riedel: I'm totally a part of it. The columnists have always been a part of it because we draw attention to it. I don't want to be a theater critic. I have no interest in going to a zillion plays and sitting in the dark and then rushing home to write a book report. I much prefer to be part of the theater world—hanging out with people, gossiping and swapping stories, and finding out what's going on.

Jesse Green: Criticism is a form of writing. It's not a form of theater. A sad delusion that I have often fallen prey to is that writing about the theater makes me a part of the theater and can substitute for having a life in the theater, which is a choice I might have made and didn't. Criticism makes up for that in only a marginal way. You can be part of the discussion, but only from the sidelines.

Peter Filichia: I know that a lot of critics avoid getting to know people who work in the industry. I take my cue from Stephen Sondheim and Frank Rich. Sondheim helped Frank Rich to become a major theater critic because of a review he wrote of *Follies* in the *Harvard Crimson* in 1971. Ten years later, Rich nailed Sondheim to a cross when reviewing *Merrily We Roll Along*. The fact that they were friends had nothing to do with anything. Recently, the artistic director of a New Jersey theater got married and invited me to the wedding. I didn't go because that would be getting a little too close. Still, I found it very interesting that they wanted me there.

Robert Hurwitt: There have always been critics who've gotten too familiar with the people they're covering. George Jean Nathan was famous for his interactions with theater people, both in terms of chasing chorus girls and encouraging playwrights like Tennessee Williams. I think it was Nathan who advised Williams to turn his short story into a play, which became *The Glass Menagerie*. John Lahr carries on that tradition in the way he writes criticism, and he does it very well.

When you're working in a smaller theater community, it's virtually impossible to maintain that kind of distance. Before I began writing criticism, I was managing a theater and acting. My stance as a critic always was, and still is, to have as much of an open door as I possibly can. When people want to sit down and talk, I try to make the time to grab coffee with them.

4. The Theater Community 81

Thom Geier: We're the wallflowers off to the side at the party. We live under the same roof, but we have to be off to the side. If the spotlight is on us, then we're not doing our job as critics. We're not the performers. We can try to elevate criticism to the level of performance, and maybe get some refractory glow off the spotlight, but ultimately, the real performers are the people onstage, the ones whose work we're commenting on.

5

Ethics

MATT WINDMAN: *What constitutes unethical behavior for a theater critic?*

Linda Winer: Oscar Wilde said, "I hear critics can be bought. From the looks of them, they can't be very expensive."

Marilyn Stasio: It's kind of obvious, isn't it? Unethical is unethical. I'm rather hardnosed about that. There's nothing to think about. I know what's right and what's wrong. The important thing is to write with no ulterior motives.

Michael Dale: Anything that keeps critics from writing honest opinions.

Peter Marks: It's actually very hard for a theater critic to be unethical because someone's going to call you on it. You're in a fish bowl. People are watching you all the time. I try to never even close my eyes at the theater because I'm afraid someone is going to accuse me of falling asleep—and I have seen critics fall asleep at the theater. I've seen some fall asleep this year alone. To me, that is more of a breach than some other things.

My code of ethics is what I bring to the theater each time I see a play. I come in as an honest broker. I try to leave any personal feelings I have about people outside the room. It's about me and that production—and that's hard for some people to understand. They think you're bearing grudges, settling scores, and getting even with people. They like to assign those kinds of motives because sometimes that's easier to digest than the thought that a play just isn't very good.

Terry Teachout: Whenever I teach a course on theater criticism, I tell my students that rule number one is to not write about anyone you're having sex with. If you construe that a little bit more widely, that's valuable, too. But if you take it too literally, you become a kind of eunuch who has no contact with the outside world of theater, or whatever medium you happen to be writing about, and I don't think that's a good idea.

The obvious examples of unethical behavior are obvious because they are the right examples. You don't write about people with whom you have outside relationships. It's never a good idea to write about friends for all sorts of reasons, one of which is you usually can't please them. If you have or ever had a professional or fiduciary relationship with someone involved in a production, at the very least, you have an obligation to disclose it to your editors.

Michael Riedel: If we could take bribes, I would have a house in Nantucket and wouldn't have to use my sister's house—though I suppose taking a bribe might not be such a good thing. But back in the day, it was standard procedure. If you look at the history of the Paris Opera House, all of the critics were on the payroll of the various singers. In fact, critics led claques that were paid for by the singers. A singer would pay for a critic to lead a claque. That's where the word comes from. A claque is a group of people who would cheer for who the singer who was paying them and boo the singer who wasn't. Sadly, I don't think they have that kind of money anymore. Maybe Hugh Jackman does, but everybody already likes Hugh Jackman.

Zachary Stewart: Taking money in exchange for positive coverage or allowing personal or business relationships to influence coverage. This includes so-called "sponsored content."

Michael Sommers: You should be the perfect theatergoer. I've seen bad manners among critics. I've seen them come in late. I've seen them come in having had too many cocktails. That's not unethical, but it is bad behavior. The *New York Times* is extremely strict. If I'm dying, I can't accept a glass of water from anybody in the theater.

Howard Shapiro: When I'm addressing a group of audience members, they always ask if I've ever been offered a bribe, but that's never happened.

Robert Feldberg: If you become friends with someone in the theater, you shouldn't be reviewing their work. I wouldn't say I'm friends with the people I've interviewed and chatted with, so I have no compunction about reviewing them. Frank Rich was a very close friend of Wendy Wasserstein, so he never reviewed her plays. Everybody knew that, and it was fine.

Helen Shaw: When I was on the Obies committee, I was told (though I think this was tongue-in-cheek) that the standard for a conflict of interest is whether you slept with the person. Mine is that I can't have been invited to their birthday party. My sister is a sound designer. She works all the time, and I won't review any of her work.

Michael Schulman: When I graduated from Yale, there was this whole sort of Yale theater mafia that I was a part of. For instance, I went to college with Alex Timbers, who's now a major Broadway director. I would never review something that he directed. I even acted in one of his early shows.

Peter Marks: On a couple of occasions, I have reviewed work by people I taught at George Washington University. My relationship with them was not one of friendship, but I always try to disclose if I am writing about somebody I've had in a class because it's a different kind of relationship, and you don't want there to be a perception that the person had a leg up.

David Cote: You shouldn't harp on the looks of actors. I think it's unethical to verbally caricature an actor for being too fat or too thin or homely, or to overpraise them if you find them irresistibly sexy. If you believe the actor is not attractive enough for the role (or young enough, or what have you), you can say that, but it's always said in a subjective capacity, with full understanding that theater is, you know, make believe. There are no rules about this stuff. You must ask yourself, "Is this appropriate?"

John Simon: There was a very famous case at the *Times* in the music field where someone quite well-known reviewed something without having seen it. That is totally unacceptable.

Michael Sommers: There are one or two critics who got into trouble for selling their second press ticket on the street outside the theater. Critics typically get two complimentary tickets to a show from press agents, and those critics hawked and sold their extra tickets for a profit.

Jesse Green: The obvious example is taking any kind of meaningful payment from someone who stands to benefit from a good review. That sounds simple, but it's a big gray area because we're all getting our tickets for free. While I was at the *Times*, there was a brouhaha about the supposed discovery that critics and reporters were taking free theater tickets from press agents. What a scandal! It was pointed out that if they didn't take the free tickets, it would add $10,000 to $20,000 a year to the cost of covering shows for each writer, and then taking the free tickets miraculously became acceptable.

We all live with that inconsistency. We're getting these incredibly valuable free tickets. They're the best seats in the house. That does predispose us to think more positively about shows—not necessarily individual shows, but the whole experience of theatergoing. If the show is bad, you don't feel like you wasted money that you worked really hard to earn. To the extent that we are consumer advocates, that's a problem.

Michael Sommers: Canadian tourism groups offer subsidies for transportation and lodging for critics to go out there and write about the Shaw Festival and the Stratford Festival. I used to accept that, but it didn't impact what I wrote about those shows. It was the same as getting press tickets. It's just the way of doing things.

Gordon Cox: Having an agenda of any kind—like thinking, I don't like this theater company, so I'm going to give their production a bad review.

Hilton Als: Using criticism for your own ends. Some people want to become famous through criticism in order to do other things. I don't think you should use criticism for anything other than what it is.

John Simon: Promoting any kind of cause is unethical. Let's say there's a play about a born-again Christian that's worthless, but you give it a good review anyway because you're a born-again Christian. That would be totally unethical.

Howard Shapiro: It's not kosher to call up a director and ask the director to explain what he or she was trying to do in a particular show. Some critics have done that. The director's intent doesn't matter—it's the outcome that matters. That's why you're there. You don't want to have that kind of inside knowledge when you're making a judgment about a piece. I have also seen what I consider to be bad ethics from theater artists who don't understand that it's wrong to go critic shopping in a city. It's not a good idea to get in front of an audience, point to a critic sitting there, and claim that the critic is ruining the theater in the city. I've seen an instance of that sort of thing in Philly.

Michael Musto: Putting all your weight behind a play just so you can claim that it's your play if it wins the Tony.

Gordon Cox: Giving a production a rave as a sort of power play. Without naming names, one can think of a kind of pissing match between two critics of the same paper vying for a position of dominance in terms of the work that they review.

Michael Schulman: I don't know if this is unethical or just tacky, but there's a tendency for people to wait and see what other people are saying before they crystallize what they think about a show, especially if a deadline allows it. You wait to see what the *Times* thinks, or what other people you respect have to say. You need to avoid letting other people's opinions affect your own.

Chris Jones: I try not to be barbarically mean just for the sake of it. At the paper, we have a policy of not causing intentional distress. That doesn't mean that you shouldn't judge a work harshly if it's a poor work, but you shouldn't cause intentional distress.

Scott Brown: We're all guilty of this, but it is probably malpractice to take too much glee in wrecking something. There is a place for the earth-scorching pan, but I think snark has been retailed so widely and perniciously that it's become this fog of contempt. I don't think you're serving anybody well by living in that cloud. Many critics get a bum rap because on the occasions that they are snarky, it stands out because people love reading those kinds of reviews.

Ben Brantley: Not to name names, but I know some prominent theater critics who've reviewed shows without having seen them. I think that's abominable.

Steven Suskin: I've seen critics walk out of shows. If they admit that they walked out when they write the review, that's fine. But if they don't mention that they walked out, that's probably unethical.

Chris Jones: There is a great tradition of critics like Claudia Cassidy walking out of a show at intermission and declaring it proudly in the review, so maybe it's not so bad to do that, but I never leave.

Alexis Soloski: If I'm reviewing a show, even if it's terrible, I'll see it through. I'll say to my guest, "Please go. I'm obligated to stay, but wouldn't you be much happier if you left?" But if I'm there just for fun, and if I'm not having any fun, I'll leave at intermission.

Frank Scheck: I will walk out on a show and not write about it. But if you're going to write about it, you have an obligation to stay—unless it's like the Bataan Death March, it's eight hours, and it's not going to enhance your appreciation of it.

Michael Musto: I think I've only walked out three times in my life. One of the times was with two of the greatest actors in the world, Ian McKellen and Helen Mirren, in *Dance of Death*. They were positioned on opposite sides of the stage, in some kind of heavy-handed symbolism of their separation. I just thought it was torture. Another time, it was one of those shows where it's like, "I'm an old bag telling you my life story, and nothing is going to be shown or actually happen. I'm just going to tell you my life story."

Perez Hilton: I've walked out of shows. I almost walked out at *Holler If You Hear Me*, the Tupac Shakur musical. I wouldn't review a show if I walked out at intermission, but I'm also not going to be held prisoner by an awful theatergoing experience. I walked out of *We Will Rock You*, perhaps the worst show in the history of musical theater, before intermission. I love Queen and their music, but I literally felt like the show was killing my brain cells. It has the stupidest book ever. It's like *Footloose* set in the future—only worse.

Peter Filichia: I don't think there's ever been a period in my life where I've been less inclined to walk out of a show. I have statistics about this. I walked out a lot when I was married because my wife wanted to leave so often, and we only had one car. Nowadays, I'll walk out if I feel a show is really hopeless, but that only happens about one percent of the time. There are times where I'll see a show and, as time goes by, I get more interested in it.

Michael Riedel: Walking out shows a lack of respect for the people putting on the show. However, I won't go to a show if I know it's going to be a dog—unless it's going to be really horrible and sort of campy, like *Spider-Man* or something like that. Then I'd want to describe how horrible it is in my column. But there's no reason for me to go see something like *The Bridges of Madison County*. There's nothing interesting happening behind the scenes that I can write about. It's also not to my taste. More and more, they are putting on shows that are not for me. I'm not interested in sitting in a room full of little kids through a dopey, stupid, kiddy musical. I'm also not interested in harlequin romance stuff for the middle-aged ladies, and they're the bulk of the theater audience.

Terry Teachout: If I walked out of a New York show, I'd be on "Page

Six" the next morning. I once walked out of a regional production, but I won't tell you what or where it was. I just couldn't take another minute of it. Experience has taught me that you can change your mind about a show after intermission. One play about which I completely changed my mind about after intermission was Martin McDonagh's *The Pillowman*. At intermission, I thought, This just isn't working at all. And if I had left then, I would have given it a bad review.

MATT WINDMAN: *Is it problematic for critics to be paying attention to, writing about, and voting for the various theater awards that are given out each year?*

Zachary Stewart: It can be, especially when attention to those awards overshadows the actual work.

Elysa Gardner: The public gets caught up in the awards, and so does the media.

Richard Zoglin: The focus on the Oscars is ridiculously out of proportion, and the same goes for the Tonys. I'm always suggesting things to review, to which my editors say yes or no, and then they come to me each year and say, "You've got to do something on the Tonys." That means more to them than anything else. As far as the other theater awards, I don't mind that they exist, but there are a lot of them, and they don't mean much to me. I do think the critics should vote for the Tonys. As for the New York Drama Critics' Circle, it's good to have those awards, but the annual meeting where we vote on the awards is not my favorite afternoon of the year.

Helen Shaw: I don't mind the razzle-dazzle. Any attention to the theater is good attention. All theater is a gateway drug for other theater. My favorite show when I was 12 years old was *Phantom of the Opera*. I sang every song at the top of my lungs on every single car trip. Now my taste could not be farther from *Phantom of the Opera*. If people get excited about the Tonys, and if they find the competition thrilling, those things will lead them to other things.

Leonard Jacobs: I totally support critics being involved with any kind of award. Critics have a lousy reputation because we're the bearers of bad news, so it's important for critics to encourage and applaud in a very public way, if they can.

Roma Torre: I hope we don't get too consumed in it. The nominees might take exception to the contest we've created around the awards. A lot of times, we've said, "That nominee might have a better chance if he got with the game and promoted himself better." I don't think critics are as involved in the contest as theater reporters are. To them, it's a real story. For critics, it's a once-a-year guessing game. I make my predictions over who will win, and most of the other critics do the same. I don't think that's as much of an issue as the writers who calculate the odds-on favorites, which is sad. I think that could lead to a change in the outcome because voters may look at the calculations and decide to vote for the underdog. It's a very unhealthy practice.

I think removing journalists as Tony voters was the most ridiculous decision in years. There were many explanations for that. One of the rationales—and this is the most absurd thing to me—was that we couldn't be completely objective. If we can't be objective, who else can be among the voting population? The majority of the voters are in the theater community. Many of them are directly or indirectly involved with the nominated shows. We, in the media, don't have any personal stake in the outcome. So if that was the real reason, I think they made a terrible mistake—and I was absolutely angry about it. And you know what? I think losing a hundred or so journalists as voters has affected the outcome of the major awards.

Michael Dale: Who would be better qualified to vote for theater awards than someone who has seen everything and has nothing to gain from the results?

Note: In July 2009, the Tony Awards Management Committee announced that the critics, reporters, and other journalists on the Broadway League's "First Night Press List" (who made up about 100 of the roughly 800 voters for the Tony Awards) were being removed as voters. Without members of the press, the voters for the Tony Awards would consist almost entirely of people working in the theater industry. An email sent to the journalists who had been voters (including myself) noted that, "The Management Committee took into consideration the fact that certain publications and individual critics have historically pursued a policy of abstaining from voting on entertainment awards in general, to avoid any possible conflicts of interest in fulfilling their primary responsibilities as journalists." The email did not go to on explain how exactly it was a conflict of interest for a critic or any other journalist to vote for the Tony Awards.

Numerous news articles were written about the change, most of which painted the Broadway League and the American Theatre Wing (which together run the Tony Awards) in a negative light. A few months later, the roughly two dozen members of the New York Drama Critics' Circle (which is comprised of many of the most well-known New York theater critics, with the notable exception of the critics from the New York Times) were reinstated as Tony voters. In November 2012, I finally became a member of the New York Drama Critics' Circle, and I once again became a Tony voter. I have also been a voting member of the Drama Desk (which considers Broadway, Off Broadway, and even Off Off Broadway shows in its annual slate of awards) for more than a decade.

Adam Feldman: I don't think it compromises us professionally. We do end up writing about these awards a lot, but it's for purely practical purposes. Readers are interested in it. The Tony Awards is a big story. It's the one time of the year when Broadway becomes a national story, and a lot of people who aren't usually interested in theater perk up and pay attention. And many of us are theater geeks. We enjoy the horse races. We try to handicap them based on our perceived insight into what the dynamics might be, but that's just part of the game. I don't think that compromises the way we write our reviews, and I don't think it affects how we vote for the awards.

Marilyn Stasio: Voting for the awards is a waste of time, but I don't think there's anything terrible about it, so long as you're being truthful and you believe in what you're voting for. It only becomes corrupt if you lie. People do lie, and that drives me nuts. There are angry votes, self-serving votes, vengeful votes, suck-up votes. That kind of thing is awful.

Michael Riedel: The horse race aspect of anything is fun. Everyone's thinking, Who's going to win the Oscar? Who's going to win the Tony? Who's going to win the Grammy? Readers like that. People who care about the business want to know what the so-called experts think, or they want to know what the insiders have to say. If journalists care enough to follow the awards, there's nothing wrong with putting predictions out there. There's nothing wrong with saying, "I think this should win because it's great" or "I think this is going to win because I've talked to a lot of voters and they seem to like it." That's just covering the business.

MATT WINDMAN: *Is it all right, or perhaps even preferable, for a theater critic to also write news, feature articles, and interviews?*

Michael Riedel: The New York Times is unique in the respect that it doesn't believe in its theater critics also being reporters. It has the resources to be able to hire both critics and reporters, but most papers don't have those resources. If you go back and look at the Washington Post when David Richards was there, he would do the Sunday interview with the star of the big new show coming to Washington, and then he'd review the show the following Wednesday. Elliot Norton also did that at the Herald, and so did Kevin Kelly at the Globe. That was always the case. The theater people had to let the critic do the interview because they needed the publicity, and they had to suck it up if the critic gave them a bad review. By the same token, the critic had to realize that just as much as they enjoyed interviewing the actor or playwright or director, if that person's work wasn't very good, they've got to put on a different hat and sock it to them in the review. That's the nature of the job.

Charles Isherwood: It can get compromising to get to know people—even on the level of doing an interview. Once you've met and spent some time with these people, you're susceptible to a certain feeling of community. The next time they come before you as a critic, it can be hard to be as objective as you need to be—but I don't think it's necessarily a problem. It's all about having integrity. If you have integrity, you can interview somebody one week and pan them the next. It's hard, but that's what you need to do. Most theater writers now have to do a little of both. That's only going to be more of the case as the newspaper industry keeps contracting.

Brian Lipton: The good old days of being on only one side of the fence—where a reviewer never spoke to the people in the business for the sake of objectivity—are over. To make a living, I often have to review people who I've interviewed and that I know socially, and I'm not the kind of person who enjoys hurting people's feelings. I believe that my first responsibility is to the reader, so I never want to lie, but sometimes you have to read between the lines of what I write.

Ben Brantley: I admire the critics who do both tremendously. Peter Marks at the *Washington Post* does it brilliantly, and he is able to keep a sense of distance in all cases. I remember when Hedy Weiss at the *Chicago Sun-Times* was doing theater and dance reviews and also writing every feature that the paper ran on the same subjects. To me, that is staggering. Hats off to them.

Alexis Soloski: Sometimes you get into an ethically sticky situation, but I love it doing profiles. I like having the opportunity to speak with people, especially when I'm enthusiastic about their work. Having that hour-long conversation is wonderful. I can just fall in love with the person. The *Voice* has always been a little freewheeling, in the sense that sometimes I was still able to review a show even after I wrote a profile on someone involved in it. The *Times* does not feel that way. I understand their logic because you do have to pull back after having made a personal connection, even at a casual level, but I'm certainly professional enough to do that. I recently did a profile on playwright Will Eno, and I enjoyed my conversation with him tremendously, but that did not prevent me from giving a pretty lukewarm review of his play *Open House*.

Zachary Stewart: It's always better to know more about how the sausage is made, provided the critic can separate any affection he or she develops for the subject of those features from honest criticism.

Chris Jones: Except for a few publications in New York, all of us meet artists. We're not just critics. In some ways, it helps because we get to know more. I don't think I could do my job and never talk to an artist. I recognize and respect people who attempt to not do that, but that doesn't really work for me.

Christine Dolen: Besides the *New York Times* and a couple of other publications, most theater critics (if they're lucky enough to have full-time jobs) are doing all of the above. With the contraction of journalism and shrinking staff sizes, everybody is expected to do more. I write theater news and features, and I have a blog. As a critic, you set all that aside when you see a piece of theater, and you just react to what you see in front of you.

5. Ethics

David Cote: If the publication can't afford to have separate critics, then you have to look at the glass-half-full side of it and hope that critics will be informed by a greater knowledge of the craft. By talking to playwrights, directors, and actors, you get more of a sense of what they are trying to accomplish. But the glass is half empty, and you could become overly compromised in your criticism. It is problematic, but I talk to critics across the country and many of them wear multiple hats. To be perfectly honest, I do much less reporting than I used to. The job has become more about blog posts, lists of things, and getting people to click on links.

Elysa Gardner: Being both a critic and a reporter is the toughest part of the job. I have been in the position of interviewing somebody and then seeing them in a play, or vice versa. Whenever I don't have to do that, I'm grateful. In one of those situations (where you have to put on one hat for one assignment, and a different hat for another), you try to distinguish them as much as you can. There are times when I interviewed people and felt like I got insight into a play or a performance. When I had the great privilege of interviewing August Wilson a few times, I got glimpses of the incredible compassion, humanity, and conviction that informs his work—but I'm not fooling myself into thinking I'm developing real friendships.

Michael Schulman: John Lahr has spearheaded a combination of profiling and critiquing. He's written a bunch of pieces that explore the artists' intentions with criticism. The *Times* certainly doesn't do that. It has very strict ethics rules, and that's probably for the best considering its role in the world.

Adam Feldman: At *Time Out*, there are two of us on staff (David Cote and me) plus freelancers. As a general rule, if we run a feature about a show, we try not to have the person who writes the feature also write the review.

Jason Zinoman: I've always been both a reporter and a critic. I've found that being a reporter can make you a better critic because the first job of a critic is to figure out what a show's artistic intent is, and actually knowing artists helps with figuring that out. There are a lot of critics, especially in television and film, who have done no reporting. If they had reporting experience, they would have a better understanding of the artistic process.

Terry Teachout: It's very problematic, and that's why I don't do it for the *Wall Street Journal*. The problem is obvious: It is not easy to write objective criticism if you're also covering institutions as a reporter. Unfortunately, there's nothing to be done about it in the real world of journalism.

Matthew Murray: It's probably not ideal, but this issue is pretty low on the list of things to be concerned about.

Richard Zoglin: It's doable, but it is a challenge. The minute you meet someone in the theater—and they're usually very charming—you automatically want to like their stuff.

David Sheward: In my experience, it's problematic to do both reporting and reviews. In feature writing, you're letting someone else say, "This is what the show is about." In a review, you're saying, "This is what I think about the show." I want to come to the show as the audience does. The experience has to be self-explanatory. I have to be able to get the show without an explanation from the practitioners.

Rob Weinert-Kendt: When you write previews and features, as I do, you start to feel like a PR person. You're essentially writing PR. You publish it, and it gets people to buy tickets, and you feel like you're part of the publicity team, and you are, but I hope I bring my critical acumen into those pieces.

Howard Shapiro: I've found that doing both is difficult, especially when it's a show that doesn't work. Spending that kind of time with a person makes you a fan. Recently, I was going to review Colin Quinn's one-man show *Unconstitutional*, which he's taken on tour. The radio station that I work for asked me to interview Quinn about how he came up with the show on the air. I said, "I'd be happy to. But if I do that, I don't want to review it, too." Not mixing the advance work on a show with the review is a cleaner way of doing journalism, but I also realize that it's a luxury that a lot of publications and stations can't afford.

Frank Rizzo: Before I started reviewing, it was an ideal situation: I would do the advance pieces, and someone else would write the reviews. Once you start reviewing as well, it becomes more difficult. Sometimes you have this wonderful, charming, fantastic interview with an actor, and then you see the show, and the actor is not very good, or miscast, or whatever. But you have to be honest. At the end of the day, the only thing you have is the trust of your readership that you're telling it straight.

Michael Sommers: I always did features and interviews in addition to reviews for the *Star-Ledger*. I also maintained listings. I even had to cover breaking news. I remember covering various Broadway strikes. I'd be outside in the cold on the street till 2 a.m. I ended up covering the New York City blackout in 2004 for the paper because I happened to be in town at the time. I even got injured doing that. A guy crashed into me, and I took a fall in the dark at 23rd Street and 5th Avenue. When 9/11 happened, if I hadn't been in New Jersey at the time, they probably would have made me go downtown and report on it.

I never had a problem with writing features as a critic. Some of the people I interviewed didn't like the idea, but we all had to make nice. It's the sort of thing that journalists do. You're either in reviewer mode or feature writer mode. I had to write previews about shows and then review them later on. I'd talk to the playwright, the director, the designer, or whoever, and then I'd see the show a couple of days later and say what I thought about it. I've always had a good journalist's manner. I've been very fortunate to interview people like Edward Albee and Arthur Miller.

Frank Scheck: If you interview a writer or a director, and if you really like the person, it can unconsciously affect how you write about them. Whether or not that's such a terrible thing is debatable. But if I really like someone that I interview, and then I really dislike their show, it would produce feelings of discomfort in me that I would prefer to avoid. It's certainly possible to still remain objective, but it's more difficult.

Peter Marks: Does it increase your sympathy towards the show? Yes, and that's a problem. We're human. We can't help it. We're going to feel some additional measure of empathy for what they're going through. If you're a little kinder than you would have been otherwise, you can still communicate your objections to the show. I would say that 90 percent of the time, it doesn't really affect what readers ultimately glean from a review.

Peter Filichia: I had a feature article in the paper every Friday at the *Star-Ledger*. I even decided who the feature would be about. As a result, I'd meet these people. The trick was to not be charmed by them because for the most part (Bebe Neuwirth excluded), they'd want you to like them. They'd typically tell you what they thought the play was about. I've always wondered whether I would have come to the same conclusion had I not heard what this person said. That's why the *Times* has its reviewers only do reviews and its feature writers only do features. It's more expensive that way, but it's the right way to do it.

6

The Writing Process

MATT WINDMAN: *What kind of research, if any, do you perform before seeing a show or writing a review?*

Hilton Als: I almost always do research. This is a literary art, and I like to read.

David Cote: It's different with every show. I may read the script. I may read reviews of the play from the past. I may watch the movie version or listen to the cast album. It all depends on how much time and energy I have.

Andy Propst: I try to do as much research as I can before I see a show. If it's a Shakespeare play, if I don't read it word for word, I will at least scan the text so I can remember how the scenes play out. That way, as I'm watching it, I'll know if something was cut. If it's a classic where cuts normally would not happen (something like *A Streetcar Named Desire*), I'll go back and familiarize myself with it to make sure I'm aware of its arc. If it's a classic I've never seen before, I will read it very carefully.

Frank Rizzo: With the last few new musicals I've reviewed, I've asked for a recording of the music so I can listen to the score after I see the show. It's difficult to write a thoughtful analysis of music after just one hearing. Even if it's a rough rehearsal piano version of the material, I find that tremendously helpful.

To give an example, my husband got the CD of the musical *The Light in the Piazza* when I was at work one day. He called me and said, "It's just terrible." When I called him a couple of hours later, he said, "I listened to it again, and it's pretty good." When I got home that night, he said, "This is the best musical score I've ever heard." He literally went from dismissing the score to thinking it was brilliant after just a couple of additional listens. Writers like Adam Guettel (who wrote *The Light in the Piazza*) and Stephen Sondheim and Jason Robert Brown are writing rich, full, complicated scores and not rinky-dink songs. One quick listen—when you're also trying to take in the story and the acting and everything else—just isn't enough.

Charles Isherwood: For playwrights whose work I'm encountering for the first time, but who have some kind of track record, I will usually look back at the reviews of their previous plays. If it's an important playwright whose work I haven't encountered before, I'll try to read the play. If there's a singular or very important production of the play and the library at Lincoln Center has a video of it, I'll watch it. When it's the first revival of a contemporary play, watching the video of the original production can be very valuable. The original production is what the revival will be judged against in the minds of the audience. With a Shakespeare play, often I will reread it a week or so before reviewing the production.

Howard Shapiro: I try to avoid reading anything about a new play. I understand why other critics read new plays and want to know everything about them before they go in. For me, that's not being an audience member. I want the same luxury of being as surprised as the people sitting beside me. I also never read other people's reviews until I've written my own.

Alexis Soloski: If it's a new play, I try to go in cold and just experience it. Then, after seeing it and thinking it through, I often read the play to separate the naked script from the performance.

Leonard Jacobs: Remember when the Public Theater produced Tony Kushner's version of *Mother Courage and Her Children* in Central Park? Ideally, I would have reread the Brecht. I would have looked at other productions to see how Kushner dealt with it differently. How was it staged differently? How did the presence of Meryl Streep, this huge star playing Mother Courage, affect the production? But ultimately, I didn't do any of that. I didn't have the luxury of time.

Terry Teachout: I don't do any research other than just being aware of what's been written about a production, like if there's some buzz about it. Very often, I won't even look at the program until intermission.

John Simon: I do not do research. It makes a difference if you are someone who has spent hours, or even days, preparing. I think of myself as a reasonably intelligent, reasonably interested theatergoer. That's when I can write the most useful and most uncensored review, and that's the way it should be. Of course, if I'm reviewing something like *Macbeth*, I can't help knowing what it's about.

Christine Dolen: I believe in preparing as much as possible. If it's a world premiere, I might read the script first. If I'm doing a feature, I'll talk to the playwright. When the touring company of the musical *Once* came here, I talked to the creators, read feature articles about it, listened to the cast album, and watched the movie.

Dan Bacalzo: I don't do research for every single review, but it's important for certain shows. One of the functions of a critic is to be the informed voice for the reader who doesn't have the time to read the book, or watch the movie that something was adapted from, or do research about something that winds up being the focal point of a new play. The critic really should be doing that kind of work. I'm not saying I've done that for every show that required it, but the reviews where I actually did that kind of work came out better because of it.

Elisabeth Vincentelli: It can become a problem when you compare something to its source and whether it was faithful or not to the source. A show needs to stand on its own.

Jesse Oxfeld: I didn't tend to do a lot of research beforehand, which was partially a function of being a freelancer who wasn't doing it for a lot of money. I saw and wrote about anywhere from two to six shows in a week while also having a full-time job. If the *Observer* wanted to pay me a full salary instead of a flat weekly fee to be a theater reviewer, I would have approached it very differently. Then I would have been compensated for the time to put in a different level of focus and energy.

Michael Musto: I do research without trying because I read the Broadway message boards and the press releases. I've also seen the original productions of all these plays now being revived, so I have all the research in the little microchip in my brain.

Rob Weinert-Kendt: When I was writing for the *Los Angeles Times*, if I saw a play based on a book, I would read the book without fail. I was writing for the paper of record, and I felt like I couldn't render this big judgment without knowing everything I reasonably could.

Robert Hurwitt: If it's an adaptation of a film, I'll see the film. If it's based on a well-known book, I'll read it. If it's based on a historical event, I'll find out some things about it. Also, when you're dealing with an experimental group, you want to know what the theory is behind its practices.

Ronni Reich: Sometimes I'll read something in another review along the lines of, "Twenty years ago, I saw such-and-such production." As a younger critic, I can't do that. I try to compensate as much as I possibly can. I'm fortunate to have access to everything at the Library for the Performing Arts at Lincoln Center and YouTube videos.

MATT WINDMAN: Do you take any notes during a show?

Alexis Soloski: I do, but my handwriting is pretty horrible. Sometimes I come out of the theater, look at my notebook, and can only make out one word out of three.

Robert Feldberg: I used to write down lines of dialogue. But within the last five years or so, the press agents have been supplying copies of the script to critics.

John Lahr: I think I was the first critic to ask for a copy of the script because I didn't want to have to take notes during the show. This was back in the 1960s. When you're backstage on opening night, you become very aware of the presence of 50 critics. If the critics are taking notes, they're not actually spending a whole lot of time watching the play. Their heads are going up and down. They're not in the moment.

Marilyn Stasio: I never look at my notes, but taking them keeps me focused, and reviewing is very much about staying focused. If you're a play, I'm yours. I am with you. I'm paying every bit of attention to you that I possibly can. That's my job.

Charles Isherwood: When I started writing, I was fanatical about taking notes. I was one of those people who always seem to be scribbling notes throughout the show. That's waned as the years have gone by. I still take notes, but I don't consult them as much. For me, the act of note taking is really about fixing something in my mind.

Chris Jones: I write down more at some shows than others. I write a lot down at Second City, Chicago's famous improv comedy theater. Something at Second City is essentially 40 short plays in one. It's very difficult to remember all of that, so I tend to write down everything that I'm seeing. If I'm watching *Hamlet*, I probably don't write down anything. I just listen and take it all in.

Michael Musto: It's hard to take copious notes during a show because you don't want to distract other people. There's also that awkward moment when a great piece of dialogue is said and every critic is writing it down. And you think, I'm going to have the same review as everyone else.

Peter Filichia: I take an enormous number of notes. It's like electroshock therapy for me. Whenever anything crosses my mind when I'm watching a show, I write it down. You never know what's going to turn out to be important. The next day, I always see something I would have forgotten about had I not written it down. But there is a downside to taking notes. I can't tell you how many times the audience has roared with laughter as I'm writing something, and then I'll look up, and it's too late—I missed the moment.

Jesse Green: In the beginning, I took voluminous notes out of nervousness, worrying what my theme would be, what my kicker would be, what jokes I might make, what insights I might convey. I was looking so hard at the mechanics that I would start to not pay attention to the show properly, so I trained myself to take fewer notes.

Linda Winer: I take a lot of notes in the theater. I write in shorthand, which my mother made me learn. It would be very cool if I was like Claudia Cassidy, who could just sit there and remember everything, but that isn't the way I am. Not only do I read my notes, I do a wacky kind of outline where I write down different kinds of information on different corners of the pad. When I'm writing the review, I can just refer to the part of the page where I know the information that I'm looking for will be.

Matthew Murray: I tend to take very few notes. I don't want anything to get in the way of watching the show. That's why you're there, after all: to see what's onstage and write about it. I have seen some reviewers (who shall remain nameless) spend basically the entire performance looking at their pad and writing, only glancing up at the stage occasionally. To me, that's completely useless and insulting to everyone involved.

Peter Marks: Even if I don't take a lot of notes, I keep a pad and pen in my hand. It's like a crutch. It's also reminds me of the distance between myself and the show.

Michael Sommers: The very few times I go to the theater without a notebook, my hand twitches.

MATT WINDMAN: After attending a show, what is your typical process for writing the review?

Ben Brantley: I'm glad we don't have to file our reviews right after we see a show, which the British critics still do. I like to have at least a little time to digest. By the next morning, I'm usually ready to write. I just sit down at my computer and write the review. How much time it takes varies—probably two and a half hours, but sometimes less.

Leonard Jacobs: I find it very difficult to write a review immediately after seeing a show. But back in the old days, that's what the critics did. They would get out of a show and run to the copy desk. Brooks Atkinson would write the review in long hand, while standing up, and hand it to the copy boy. The *Times* would then have it in print by 2:00 a.m. What you were getting in those days was a very visceral reaction. There's definitely something to be said for that, but I like having some time for perspective.

I've walked out of shows in tears. I've walked out of shows in a fury. And then two days later, or even a day later, I thought, Was that really worth crying over or being angry over? Time tempers your emotions. Highly emotional reviews tend to be more hyperbolic than I would prefer. Walter Kerr called *Gypsy* "the best damn musical I've seen in years." He wrote that in 1959. It was a great money quote. But from a larger point of view, was it really the best musical? Was it better than *The Music Man*? Was it better than *West Side Story*? Time kind of leavens the bread.

Richard Ouzounian: I think the worst thing that ever happened to North American theater was when critics stopped reviewing overnight on deadline. They used to write with the passion and immediacy of the moment. Sometimes the judgments would be faulty. Sometimes the critics would have to express themselves in less than gossamer prose, but it's pretty amazing to read Brooks Atkinson and Walter Kerr and see how well they wrote. I know that Ben Brantley makes a point of attending the first preview he can, and then he has days to think about the show and then write the review, rewrite it, and polish it. I just feel like there's something missing—and I think the audiences miss it, too.

There used to be an excitement when the reviews of seven Broadway critics appeared at once. When they were all high as a kite on the newest exciting show, the papers vibrated. No wonder everyone would rush down to the box office to buy tickets. It was a time of kinetic excitement and energy in the theater. Now it's largely about reviews that have been written days in advance and come out online the minute the curtain comes down, and you buy the tickets online. It's not the same.

I still have really tight deadlines. Unless a show has a very late curtain, my review will be online 45 minutes after the curtain falls. Everybody at the opening night party has their Google alert set to see what I'm going to say. It can wreck a party, or it can be, "Holy fuck, he loved us. We're set." The buzz can spread instantly.

Frank Rizzo: When I get home, I write something called "First Impressions." It's just one paragraph. It evokes the old-time reviewer running up the aisle to meet a deadline and write the whole review. In this case, I'm just writing a gut reaction, something engaging and a bit of a tease, which gives the reader a sense of having just come out of the theater. It goes live as soon as I press the button, without any editors. I write the full review the next morning. Whether it's for *Variety* or the *Hartford Courant*, I usually file the review by the late morning or early afternoon.

Charles Isherwood: I'm glad that we don't have to go through the famous Brooks Atkinson routine, where you're running up the aisle as soon as the show ends. I don't know how people did that. They still do it in London, and I certainly admire them for it. I get up the next morning, and unless something is impeding me for some reason, I'll write the review and get it over with. Usually, you're seeing something else that night, and I hate having things backed up. I get anxious when I have more than one review percolating in my head. After I write it, I let it sit for a day, and then I go back and finish it up.

Everybody struggles with finding the lead. Once you get your lead down, things flow pretty easily. I know people who start a review in the middle, but I can't conceive of that. I like to start at the beginning. Once I have that, things sort of evolve. Whatever you think is the most salient point—the most newsworthy piece of information about a play—is where you want to start. If it's a mediocre play that has a truly exciting performance in it, you should start with that. If it's a revival of a musical that's far better than the original version, you can start with that.

Marilyn Stasio: I could never again do what I did in the old days, when I was writing for the *New York Post*. I would run out of the theater at 11 p.m., jump in a cab, dash downtown to that really creepy office, and bang out a review for the late edition. Nowadays, I see the show, come home, and go to bed. And when I wake up in the morning, I have the lead in my head and a pretty good idea of what I want to write. If it hasn't come to me by the time I wake up, it'll come to me in the shower. Once in a while, it doesn't happen, and it makes me crazy because I'll have to sit down to write without having that firm, assured knowledge of where I'm going.

Michael Dale: I usually see a show three to five days before it opens, but I often have other reviews to write and other shows to see during that time. The only process is to block out time when I can get it done.

Zachary Stewart: Depending on the turnaround, I'll either write a rough draft immediately following the show or the next morning. Then I revise and edit in the afternoon. If I'm reviewing something at the Metropolitan Opera or an Encores! production at City Center, where there are no previews and you attend on opening night, I file my completed review the night of the performance, usually at 1 or 2 a.m.

John Simon: I can write a review quite speedily. A couple of hours will usually do. I don't like to compose on the computer. I almost always write first in longhand. It then takes time to put it into the computer. I believe in weighing every sentence I write as to whether it's worthy of being called literature. I may not succeed, but that's the intention. I want to write something that could be read 50 years from now, even by people who are not that much interested in theater, and read with pleasure, amusement, and enlightenment.

Helen Shaw: To write a review, I have to go to a coffee shop where there is no Internet. Otherwise I will go down terrible wormholes of reading interviews with the show's director until I'm well past my deadline. If it's a longer piece, I tend to write from the middle. If it's a short review, I usually write it in a single burst. The way I get over any writer's block is to write about the set design because I have a background in that. The set design gives me a hook. Those paragraphs don't make it into the final draft, but that's where I start.

Chris Jones: I probably review more shows than anyone else in the country. In a typical week, I review five or six plays. Most often I write the morning after I see a show, but sometimes I'll write the same night because of a deadline at the paper. Usually, I get up and come into the office, or I sit in my hotel room in New York, and write the review. If it comes really quickly, it could take me 90 minutes. If it doesn't, it could take three or four hours. I don't write the middle of the review and then go back to the top. I get my lead down, and then I write it straight through.

Once it's written, the review goes online, and then it runs in the newspaper. I rarely look back at a review because by the time it's published, it's the next day, and I'm on to the next show. Sometimes I write more than one review in a single day. That, of course, is one of the great disconnects with the people you review because they're probably working on just four or five projects a year. Sometimes I won't be able to remember a review that someone confronts me about. It's because we see so much. I move on very quickly. For me, it's just a review. But for the people I review, it might be the only thing they do that year. That's just the way it is.

Christine Dolen: I attend shows on opening night. Most theaters in Florida have either no previews or only one or two previews. If a show is only going to run for a week, they won't bother with previews. I get up the next morning and write the review. Then it's posted online, and it appears in the paper the following day. Back when I was under intense deadline pressure, when I had to file immediately after a show, I could write a review in 45 minutes. Now I usually take several hours. I never liked filing right after the show ended. I felt like it wasn't fair to the artists, the readers, or me. The readers deserve more than having me run backstage to sit in a little office to write the review in 45 minutes.

Andy Propst: I have the script by me as I write. I sit down at the computer, let it fly, and hope that inspiration takes me. I don't know what I really thought about a show until I'm done writing the review. There are certain pieces that fly out because I feel so passionately about them, and there are others where it's like sweating bullets because there's so much to talk about and discern about what was working, what wasn't working, and where things went wrong.

Elisabeth Vincentelli: I like writing at my desk at the *Post* because it keeps me on my toes. I do have to file by a certain time. Sometimes I have to write the review the next morning, and that's kind of annoying. But if I have a few days, I'll do a first draft, let it sit overnight, and then return to it the next day and rewrite it. I'll also print it out and reread it. It's amazing all the things you see when it's printed out, as opposed to on the computer screen. I often make edits on the printout and then rewrite it on the computer.

Frank Scheck: Hopefully, I'll start off the review in such a way that it writes itself. You have to find a way to make it flow. Occasionally, when you go back and read it, you think of something else worth mentioning, and you've got to find a way to put it in. In other cases, you find that you've got to cut something.

Jeremy Gerard: *Variety* wasn't interested in the classic inverted pyramid style of writing. You basically had to spill the beans at the top of the review, both in terms of what you thought about the show and what you thought about its prospects for commercial success. And once you had that, you really had to challenge yourself to keep the reader interested. I learned that you can do that and still say a lot.

Michael Schulman: I usually see things on the weekend, and my reviews are due on Monday, so I can write them on Saturday evening or Sunday afternoon. It takes me about half an hour to write a review. Later on, I might make changes for clarity or to the flow of the language. The *New Yorker* has very detailed fact-checking. My editor sends everything that's factual to the publicist, and then it's copy-edited.

Rob Weinert-Kendt: The process of writing a review is like any other process of writing. I focus a lot on the lead and what my opening will be, and then I move through that and try to come up with a thesis statement, a larger view. I try not to write by a formula. I can tell when some critics do that.

Robert Faires: When I sit down to write, I spend a lot of time digging into my own reactions. I want to know not just what I felt, but *why* I felt it. I will peel away reactions and responses like the layers of an onion until I really understand the core of what my experience was. That's what I want to write about. That's what I find interesting when I read reviews. Once I get down to that level, the performances and the directorial work and design work look very different, and I can write about them with a specificity that doesn't feel like the stereotypical rant or rave.

Roma Torre: I write my reviews while I'm on the anchor desk. It can be supremely frustrating because I'm constantly being interrupted, and it interferes with my thought process, but I've gotten used to those things. I now almost work better if I'm sitting at the anchor desk and being interrupted. It forces me to focus and write more efficiently and quickly, and that's something I didn't do so well in the early days. I used to labor over reviews. They would haunt me right into my sleep.

Steven Suskin: I don't have any kind of specific process in terms of handling a review. I start thinking about it before I write. The hardest part is figuring out how to start it. Once I have my lead, I can move along pretty well. It usually takes as much time as I have. If I see a show tonight and the review has to go online by tomorrow before 3 p.m., then that's how much time I have. If I see a show tonight and it doesn't open for a week, I have a lot more time, so I can write it and then go back and rewrite.

Jesse Green: I generally avoid writing the review until I have to, but that's not a process so much as a peccadillo. The way I actually form the reviews is idiosyncratic. I figure out what the big thing is that I want to say. In the first sentence or two, I want to engage the reader in that theme. In a short review, you really only have space for one major idea. You have to know what that idea is as you start, and you have to stick to it. You only get one chance at your first slice. Then I just write it through. By the time I'm at the end, I know it's the end because it sounds like the end. Then I'll go through the review again—cleaning it up, adding details, making sure the argument tracks. That's usually all that I have time for. Once it's in good enough shape, or when my time runs out, I file it. Sometimes my editor has questions, usually just about little word choices, and occasionally about logic. Once I've dealt with those, the review goes online—perhaps as little as 10 minutes later—

and I'm on to the next show. When the online version is picked up for the print edition, I usually have time to improve it.

John Lahr: I don't just pop out a review. That's typing, not writing. The whole point of criticism is to meet the energy of the artist with an eloquence and elegance of your own. One of the problems with most criticism is that it's written too quickly. There's not enough judiciousness in the analysis. The people we call critics have the luxury of more time to write. I would take three days to write a review for the *New Yorker*.

Linda Winer: My husband says, "Linda does her best work between late and too late." I have editors that say, "Linda is a heat-seeking missile." No matter how much time I have, I'm always pushing the deadline because I need the adrenaline. I think you need to have a gut reaction, and then you can do the analysis. The bad times are when nothing's happening—when you sit there and you're not having any kind of passionate response. The flops are the easiest shows to write about. The hits are the second easiest. The loving and the hating bring out passion. But most shows, like most of life, fall somewhere in between. The hardest part of the job, the challenge of the job, is the mixed review—the "yes, but" and the "no, but." The challenge is to have mixed emotions without sounding confused. We have mixed emotions about almost everything, don't we? I work a lot on finding the middle voice. It's so tempting to write only raves and pans, which are also the things that get the most attention.

Michael Sommers: It takes me about two to three hours to write a 500 to 750-word review. It also depends on what the deadlines are. I don't write a review until at least the morning after I see the show. I could even let it go for two or three days. Sometimes shows stack up. I don't have to tell you what it's like in April, when we're seeing 35 shows in 30 days. Trying to work out when you're going to see each play is like a jigsaw puzzle.

Peter Marks: In D.C., critics attend shows on press night. Some companies in D.C. have used the term opening night to mean the first preview performance, while the critics attend what they call press night, which is held later on. I attend as many press nights as I can. I write the next morning, and then it's posted online by 2 p.m. Except in rare circumstances, there are no embargoes on publishing reviews in D.C. In New York, a critic might attend a preview performance but won't be able to publish the review until three or four days later after its opening night performance.

A straight pan or rave will probably take a couple of hours to write. A more nuanced, mixed review could take another hour. I can't write the next paragraph of a review until the paragraph before it is perfect in my mind, so I'm editing as I go through it. Then I will read and reread and talk the review out loud to myself. I'll read through it at least twice for mistakes and errors. The pace of things has become so insane that there isn't a lot of time for back-and-forth with my editors. Most of the time, my reviews are published pretty much intact. Sometimes the copy desk has a couple of questions, often about spelling. They're rarely about structure and never about point of view, which is ideal.

Robert Feldberg: I like to type out the first sentence or paragraph of the review before I go to sleep. I write the rest the next day or the day after, depending on when my deadline is. While you're waiting, the review sort of marinates. I will typically do a rough draft to get all of my ideas out. It's much easier to go back and rewrite and edit when you already have something on the screen. The most basic thing is just getting all of your thoughts out and not worrying about the writing so much. I'll go over it a second time and put it into shape, and then I'll give it a third and final reading.

Robert Hurwitt: Immediately after seeing a show, I head back to the office. Before I get there, I begin to formulate how I'm going to approach the review. Once I figure out what my lead is, I've pretty much figured out the whole structure of the review. I also try to decide which "Little Man" rating I'm going to give. Once I'm at the office, I see how much space has been allotted to me. Then I go out for a smoke. Because of the space limitations, I have to decide what I'll be able to write about and what I'll have to leave out.

I write the lead, and then I write the last sentence of the review, and then I write the body. I might have to change the last sentence later on. Sometimes when I'm halfway through the review, I'll go back and change the "Little Man" rating because I've talked myself into putting it up or down by one. Once I finish the review, I go back over it and cut the number of lines that have to be cut to adhere to the space restrictions. I usually go over anywhere from two to 30 lines. I check all the names because no one else at the paper is going to pick up on the fact that I misspelled someone's name.

Terry Teachout: Sometimes I write about a regional show a couple of weeks after it opens. I'll write about a Broadway show the morning after I see it, but that's not a matter of preference. It's just what I have to do. It takes three or four hours to write the column. I don't really think in terms of an initial draft, and I don't think most people do anymore in the age of word processors. To me, the editing is a continuous process. At some point, at the end of the process, I hear the click in my head, and I know I'm where I want to be, and I send it in.

Matthew Murray: I generally write in a linear fashion. I have to build reviews from A to Z. My brain just doesn't deal well with jumping all over the place. I start with the first paragraph and end with the last paragraph, whereas some people may start at the end or transcribe their notes and cobble those together into a review. I'll spend as much time as is absolutely necessary getting the first paragraph to say exactly what I want, and sometimes that can be a really long time, and then the rest of it more or less flows for me.

Hilton Als: I write a little sentence before I go to sleep. I dig in the next day. It's really about recalling the experience and finding the language to describe it.

Michael Riedel: In order to write my column, I talk to the people I know in the theater business and just say, "What's going on? What's the latest?" I meet people for drinks, lunch, or dinner. I talk to people on the phone. We text and email a lot now. I try to get a sense of what the industry is thinking and talking about. Whatever I find the most interesting or entertaining is what I use in the column. I write pretty quickly. I could write the column in whatever time you give me. If you give me two hours, I'll take two hours. If you give me 10 minutes, I'll take 10 minutes. That's just the nature of journalism. Work expands or contracts based on the time you're allotted, but the thinking and the talking and the reporting go on all the time. I'm always talking to somebody in the theater about stuff. Most of my friends are in the theater, and most of the people I hang out with are theater people. We're always talking about what's going on in the theater. It's an ongoing conversation about the business.

MATT WINDMAN: *What is your word count for a typical review?*

Alexis Soloski: I've written 210 words. I've written 1,000 words. My standard is 575 words. Writing short reviews is a challenge. It's like finger exercises for the piano. You're distilling ideas and opinions into an incredibly short form.

Hilton Als: My standard review is about 1,500 words.

Zachary Stewart: 750 to 900 words.

Roma Torre: In television, we have a very hard two-minute limit for a review. I get grief for going even a second over that. But a lot of shows are very big and complex, and you can't really do justice to them in just two minutes. Also, I have to write to and coordinate with the images that are provided to me, whether it's video footage or still photos. Often, I don't get the visuals early on, so I'm forced to rewrite the entire review later to match the visuals. On the Internet, I can elaborate and throw more things into the review, but that's twice as much work for me because then I have to reedit the review.

Matthew Murray: I don't have hard-and-fast word count restrictions in the way a lot of the print folks do, but I use soft word caps to keep myself from going on and on and on, as I would otherwise do.

Andy Propst: In my career, I've been asked to do everything from 175 to 1,500 words. I'm comfortable with 1,000 words. I think that is a decent length.

Chris Jones: I write what I write. My typical review is somewhere around 700 to 800 words. I just write it, and they usually find a way to fit it in. Sometimes I go much longer than that, like 1,500 or 2,000 words, but that's rare.

Seven hundred to 800 words is ideal for the life I have, which is seeing a play every day. I don't think I could write more than that every day. It would be different if I was only reviewing eight shows a year. Also, there are a lot of shows that you don't need a lot of space for because they don't merit it. There are other shows that I could go on and on about, but the reality is that people only have the tolerance to read so much. And the longer the review, the harder it is to draw people through it, so I try to write only what I think it needs.

David Cote: The reviews in print are about 200 to 400 words. They are painfully short. We write more for online and then cut for print.

Elisabeth Vincentelli: My reviews are between 350 and 600 words, depending on the show and its star wattage. I'm very good at being on target in terms of word count. The *Times* reviews can be very long. Sometimes it's great to have all that space, and sometimes it's terrible. I have about a third of the space they have, so I have to be economical, and I enjoy that challenge.

Elysa Gardner: Typically, it's around 500 words. It's good in the sense that you can't be self-indulgent. You don't get into the stuff where it's as much about the critic as it is about the production. Obviously, there are times when I want more space, and I negotiate with my editors for that. Would I want to review a major production in two paragraphs? I have not been asked to do that, but I suppose that I could.

Frank Scheck: At the *Post*, if you go over 300 words, you're going to get cut unless it's a major show. That's unfortunate because it restricts your ability to go very deeply into a production. On the other hand, it does enforce a certain discipline that I don't think is bad in a lot of cases. It also depends on the show. If you're reviewing a frothy musical or some silly, commercial piece, 300 words is usually more than enough. If you're reviewing a thoughtful play that delves into a lot of issues, it hurts to be limited in that way.

Rob Weinert-Kendt: If I've got more space, I usually take more time to get to the point. If I've got less space, I have to really get to the point quickly.

Adam Feldman: The reviews at *Time Out* are very short, which is a specific kind of challenge. You have to compress a whole lot of material into a very small space, usually two or three paragraphs, though we can write longer versions online. You want to get in a basic description of the show. You want to give an opinion on the show. You also want to get in some writing of your own to make it entertaining and interesting to read. That can be a real challenge, and so it becomes a miniaturist art. It's about learning ways in which you can fit in as much as possible.

John Lahr: When I began to write for the *New Yorker*, my pieces were 2,500 to 2,700 words long, which is quite a lot of space to fill. By the end, my pieces were 1,400 words, which meant I had to do it in a shorthand that I couldn't handle, though the intention was there.

6. The Writing Process

Linda Winer: I now write my reviews at 375 words. It's very hard to say a lot with little space.

Michael Riedel: There's a feeling among editors that people don't want to read long articles. When I started out, I had a whole page, and the paper was much larger physically. I was writing 1,000 to 1,200-word columns. All of the articles in the paper have since been cut down. Sometimes I find that shorter writing is better. It's punchier. Do you really want to get into something that's important only to you and not to the reader? The only person who knows what didn't get into the article is you. The reader never misses it because the reader didn't know it existed in the first place.

I can't stand long reviews. There's a lot of hot air in theater criticism. I also don't read reviews as closely as I used to because I don't find the critics these days to be all that engaging as writers. These critics, especially at the *Times*, have trouble cutting to the chase. I want to know up front whether it's good or bad, and if it's worth my time or not. Frank Rich was very good at that. You knew within the first paragraph if the show was good or bad. Peter Marks also knows how to cut to the chase because he's a reporter. I hate long leads, and I hate long descriptive passages about the way an actor walked across the stage. I hate all that shit. I was taught by tabloid editors, and I have a tabloid sensibility of rock 'em right away.

Peter Marks: You don't want to write 1,000 words about every show. Sometimes a show is only worth 500 words. Some reviews are too long. With Charles Isherwood and Ben Brantley, it's like their showing how big their balls are by the length of the review. Maybe there will soon be arts-oriented websites that want long-form reviewing.

Terry Teachout: I write on Fridays into a somewhat fixed space. I have 850 to 1,250 words. I also write about more than one show. I try to relate the shows if it seems natural, but I never force it. If they fit, they fit. If they don't, they don't. I can decide the different proportions that I give to each show. You don't really have to write 850 words about every show that you see. A review is like an accordion. You can make it smaller or larger depending on what your editor requires. But no matter what the editor requires, I really do try to say what I have to say as interestingly as I can.

MATT WINDMAN: *Do you use the word "I" in your reviews?*

Michael Dale: Only if I'm making a particular point by doing so.

Zachary Stewart: I use "I," although my editor often removes it. I think it's a bit silly to pretend that there's not an actual person with subjective views and feelings writing the review.

Andy Propst: If you look at the history of theater criticism, it wasn't until the 1960s that the *New York Times* allowed a critic—I think it was Brooks Atkinson—to use an "I" in one of his reviews. That sense of voice has changed.

Because of the Internet, print criticism has become more casual. I think that's true of almost all kinds of journalism. Writing online has a sense of being a one-on-one communication, and that lends itself to a certain kind of informality. If you were to compare the tone of a review from 10 to 15 years ago with one from today, you would find that it's now much less formal, a little less from on high than it once was.

Charles Isherwood: The *Times* is relatively free about using it. If you're going to write about a personal response to a particular moment in a play, I don't think there's a problem with using an "I." Some people use "you" or "we," but I think "I" is more honest and less pretentious. It's also a way of personalizing a review and drawing in a reader. You can overuse it. But used sparingly, it's perfectly fine.

David Rooney: One of the unspoken rules at *Variety* while Peter Bart was editor-in-chief was that you didn't use the first person. The first person is much more commonly used in consumer papers. I'm still ambivalent about it. I was so drilled in not using "I" or "me" that I can't help but use it very sparingly. But when there's a reason for it, I occasionally put myself in the review. It's fun to throw it in here and there, to let people know that this is your personal take on something. But ideally, a balanced theater review should be—I won't say detached—but objective and not completely personal. You should be able to put yourself in the audience's shoes to some degree, even if you're not a part of the core demographic of what you're reviewing.

Elysa Gardner: Having some license with it can enhance your work. There are people who use it really artfully. There are certain cases where you have to say "I." You can't say "one" or "you."

Frank Scheck: I try not to use it too often. But every once in a while, if something strikes a personal note, and if I feel that injecting myself into the review would give it more flavor, I'll use it. It also depends on the publication I'm writing for. The *Christian Science Monitor* didn't go for that style. The *Hollywood Reporter* and the *New York Post* are much freer about allowing it. If you use it too much, it's self-indulgent. If the reviewer is constantly injecting himself into the article, it becomes more about him or her than the show they're writing about.

Leonard Jacobs: Traditionally, it's been frowned upon. I don't have an issue with it, so long as it's not excessive. Using the third-person effectively distances the reader. Of course, you wouldn't want to begin a review with the word "I."

John Lahr: Using "I" is hardly ever useful. The *New Yorker* doesn't like it. They strike the word, and rightly so. It's a vulgarity of newspaper journalism. The review should be about the production, not the critic. The trick to writing profiles or to being a good critic is to surrender to the event or the person. Who you are is of no importance. Besides, that comes through in your style and in your reactions.

Terry Teachout: I use it without hesitation, and I don't think anybody should hesitate to use it. We are the ones who are writing the review. It doesn't reflect someone else's point of view. There are publications that impose a house rule about not using it, but I think they're wrong.

Hilton Als: I don't use it that much because it's already implicit in what you're saying. You don't really need to force that.

MATT WINDMAN: *How do you feel about star rating systems (for example, two out of four stars)?*

Hilton Als: They're terrible, idiotic, reductive, and silly.

John Lahr: They're just appalling.

Howard Shapiro: I hate them. They're particularly awful for live theater since it changes from night to night.

Zachary Stewart: Star rating systems are an excuse to not read the review.

Elysa Gardner: It's hard to assign stars. Who am I to say that a show should have only three out of four stars?

Peter Filichia: I wouldn't have a problem if I had to give star ratings. Ever since I started going to the theater in 1961, I've kept a little notebook. It's a record of everything I've seen, and I have a numbered rating for every show.

John Simon: They're pitiful. They're totally worthless. They're the opposite of what criticism is. They're consumer reports of the grossest kind. They belong in consumer report publications, if there are such things. *Bloomberg* used stars when I was there, but I had full control over the number of stars given out. I can imagine a critic writing what is essentially a two-star review and an editor thinking that isn't good enough and turning it into three stars. But as long as the critic controls the number of stars, and it comes after the critic has written a thoughtful review, then it's plausible.

Alexis Soloski: I certainly understand it. I'm obsessed with British detective shows. And when I'm looking for new ones on Netflix, I'll read the descriptions and glance at the star rankings. If it's something that has only one star, I'll be more reluctant to watch it. I also appreciate the value that star ratings have for the consumer, especially since theater tickets are really expensive. If you're going to pay so much money for a ticket, you want a guarantee that you're going to like it. I just reviewed the musical *Rocky* for the *Guardian*. I thought the first part was worth one and a half stars and the last twenty minutes were worth five stars. How do you average that out? I think I gave it three stars. It's not the most useful metric, but I absolutely understand why a reader would desire it.

Ben Brantley: I don't like it, but I understand why other people do. If you have a star rating system, that's what the eye immediately goes to. Someone will think, Since the show only got one star, why should I even bother to read the review? It shuts the door. I know people who only read the first and last paragraphs of a review if there's no star system. They just want the high points. This is a culture where we just want the high points, and that's kind of a shame. If you read the whole review, you get a sense of the critic's personality. If you just look at stars, you don't get anything else.

Steven Suskin: When some publications use four stars and others use five stars, how can you compare them? Does one star or zero stars mean a show was terrible? Do two stars mean a show was very good or average? Stars have different meaning from one paper to another, and that's why I think they're worthless.

Michael Dale: I always find it amusing when a show advertises that it got four stars from *Time Out New York* because they use a five-star system.

Note: Not so long ago, Time Out New York *used a six-star system. When the Holocaust drama* Irina's Vow *came to Broadway in 2009, it advertised how the Off Broadway production had received four stars from* Time Out New York, *without bothering to mention that it was four out of six stars, and thus not a very impressive rating. I went so far as to write a blog post accusing the show of deceptive advertising.*

Don Aucoin: The *Globe* uses star ratings for the movie reviews and restaurant reviews, but not for theater reviews. I actually have no objection to them. If my editor decided to move to a star system, I'd be okay with it. There can be some value to the stars, as long as they're just supplementary and not replacing the review itself.

Chris Jones: It was imposed on me. For the most part, I don't like it. It's reductive. It fucks up the critic to some degree because the star rating becomes too important in the process. You think to yourself, Is it three stars? Is it three and a half stars? Is it two and a half stars? I'd rather put that energy into writing a really good lead paragraph. Also, you find that the people you review and their publicists obsess over the star rating.

It does have some advantages. If you give a show the top rating, you can drive people to it in a way that you can't without it. There are a lot of people who look for what shows get the highest ratings. If you are judicious and sparing in what you give your highest rating to, you can drive a lot of people to a really wonderful show. On the other hand, it's very difficult to get people to read a two-star or two-and-a-half-star review, so you have to really work at it. They'll read a one-star review. But with a two-and-a-half-star review, it's very easy to turn the page.

Helen Shaw: *Time Out* has a star rating system. It's bad in some ways, but I've found it very clarifying in other ways. When your job as a reviewer is to say whether or not someone else should go see a show, it forces you to be brave about saying yes or no. I don't think saying yes or no is the job of a critic. It's the job of a reviewer, and the stars help with that function.

Michael Schulman: I've never had to do that. I know that when it was imposed on *Time Out New York*, the critics weren't happy about it. Suddenly, they felt like grade school teachers.

Adam Feldman: It can be frustrating. In the case of *Time Out*, I wish they'd let us have half-stars because it would double the degree of subtlety that we can put into the star system. But we don't have them, and that's the magazine's policy around the world. If you look at the stars alone, it can be misleading. You can give something a good rating but have some qualifications. Sometimes it'll look like a non-recommendation based on the number of stars, but you might have some good things to say about the show, and think there could be an audience for it. I hope that people look beyond the stars and read the review.

David Cote: It's just another way to tell the reader, short-handed, what we thought. They are there to help the reader navigate the magazine, but I do think they cheat the reader. If they don't have time to read a two-star review, then fine. They might not have an experience they otherwise might have had.

Jesse Green: I'd be embarrassed to be associated with a star rating system. It's even worse than the awards system in its reductiveness. That being said, I secretly have one. I give every review that I write a star rating—actually, a numerical rating. I keep it on an Excel spreadsheet, which automatically provides a running average. I do this because I want to keep track of my trends, and make sure I'm not going off the deep end by being too negative all the time, or lying down and lapping up whatever's given to me and being too easy. But I wouldn't want anyone else to know my idea of the rating for a particular show. I'd rather let people figure that out for themselves.

Roma Torre: I could be a purist and say that it's terrible to reduce the measure of a play to four or five stars, but I know that it helps. When I read the papers and see the number of stars, it sets the tone for the review, and I know exactly where they're going with it. Newspapers love it because it makes it easier for the reader to figure out what's going on. It's like a shortcut. It's sad that we have to do it, but that's the nature of the beast.

Elisabeth Vincentelli: I wish we didn't have them, but we do. I really don't know any critic who is a fan of them, but you work with the format at your publication.

Frank Scheck: I don't like having to do them, but my paper wants them. Ultimately, they're kind of silly and arbitrary. There are times where I'll write a review and decide on a certain number of stars, and then my editor will say, "That reads more like a three-star review or a two-star review."

Thom Geier: We give letter grades at *Entertainment Weekly*. I don't think I've ever given a show an F, but I've probably given a D to some shows. I've talked to some of my colleagues about their star rating systems, and I think we all go through similar contortions in terms of how we grade a show. Sometimes I know the letter grade I want to give outright. Other times I need to write my way to the letter grade. Writing the review actually helps me clarify what my overall opinion is. I might end up writing something that is kinder or harsher than what I originally intended. The grade can go up or down a little depending on how the writing goes.

The highbrow publications that look askance at the rating systems tend to be the places with writers who view themselves more as critics than as reviewers, but we serve both functions. If people are going to spend $125 a ticket, they want to know if it's worth their money. There's a lot of criticism out there that amounts to a three-handed review, where the writer goes, "On the one hand, it's this. On the other hand, it's this. On the other hand, it's this again," and you don't know what the takeaway is. Having a star system or a letter grade helps clarify for the reader whether the show is actually worth forking over money for.

Linda Winer: Fortunately, I don't have to do a thumbs up or thumbs down or stars or grades. That would be hard for me. Who's on top? Who's winning? Who's losing? There's enough of that in our lives already. Ideally, we go to the arts for something other than deciding winners and losers.

Matthew Murray: I have no problem with stars philosophically, but I like not having to deal with them. I don't use such a system, and I'm glad I don't. That's not really the way I think. I'm not sure I can put into words what would make a four-star play different from a three-and-a-half-star one (or, for that matter, a four-and-a-half-star one), and I'm happy I don't have to think about. If I were forced to go this route, I might want multiple star ratings: one for the acting, one for the production, one for the design, and maybe one for the show overall, so I could at least acknowledge that there's no way to give just one score for every part of the production. There are other ways to do that kind of thing. The *New York Times* has no star ratings, but some shows get a "Critics' Pick" designation that lets you know instantly that the reviewer considers a show to be especially good. I wouldn't mind doing something like that.

Peter Marks: It becomes a crutch for some reviewers because if you have the star system, you don't have to be as precise in your review about how you felt. Let's say you give a show three stars, but your review is all praise. How is that different from a four-star review? I guess I could live with it if I had to, but it's very hard to reduce plays into stars. People can also misinterpret it. Let's say you give two and a half stars to a production of *Hamlet*. You don't want someone to say, "You think *Hamlet* is only a two-and-a-half-star play?"

6. The Writing Process 113

Rob Weinert-Kendt: In San Francisco, they've got that image of the little guy on the seat. He is standing and applauding, sitting down and applauding, sitting and not applauding, or he's gone. Those are the four rankings. People hate that guy.

Robert Hurwitt: I am the latest in a long line of *San Francisco Chronicle* critics, extending back to the 1940s, that have objected to the poor "Little Man" system. The "Little Man" is in some ways more seductive than the star system because he's an icon. He's an identifiable human shape. It's the first thing that people's eyes go to.

The "Little Man" leaping out of his chair is an A. Sitting and applauding is a B. Sitting in the chair is a C or a D. An F is when the "Little Man" is not even in the chair. The "Little Man" just sitting in the chair and not applauding is read by many people as a negative review, but it's not meant to be. It's meant to read as average. People's interpretation of what average means can range from not very good to average quality.

People read the review in the context of the "Little Man." It places a burden on the critic because once you've picked the "Little Man" you're going to use, you have to write to the "Little Man." You think whether it was close to being the kind of show where you tell people to drop everything and see it, which is our top "Little Man" rating. If you give it the second rating, you write to explain why you're giving it the second rating. It's a hassle.

MATT WINDMAN: Do you feel any guilt when writing a very negative review?

Michael Dale: No, but I'm much more careful with the way I write negative things.

Zachary Stewart: I do, but not as guilty as I would feel about lying.

Alexis Soloski: There are two kinds of bad plays: plays that make you sad and plays that make you angry. A play is angry-making when you are furious that two hours of your life (not to mention commuting time) have been taken from you to see a play that's poorly done or simply offensive. In those cases, there is no guilt. And then there are sad plays: plays where they just missed the mark. They were really trying to do something, and they just couldn't get there. You feel compassion for that.

Ben Brantley: I don't love writing pans, but I realized early on it was something I would have to make my peace with. I always hope that whoever I write about doesn't read the review—whether it's a good or bad review. I don't think it would do them any good. Plus, that's not who I'm writing for. No matter how it's perceived, it's never a personal attack on the person.

David Cote: I feel guiltier about writing a mixed review of a show that, after the fact, I feel deserved more enthusiasm. Generally, my negative reviews are for big fish in the sea: Broadway turkeys, plays that are just vanity projects, or mediocre living-room dramas by not-for-profit institutions that should be taking bigger risks.

Chris Jones: I feel people's pain. I recognize that they're disappointed, and I dislike being the cause of that disappointment. I like theater people. I find it painful to say they're not doing well. That doesn't mean I don't do it, but I do feel guilt, tempered by the fact that they're taking people's money as they do it.

Elisabeth Vincentelli: Sometimes I feel bad, especially if there were some good intentions that just went horribly wrong. But then there are some cynical enterprises that are just about moneymaking, total offensive stuff that has to be put in its place. People think it's so much fun to write a pan. It's actually not fun at all, yet sometimes it has to be done.

Christine Dolen: It would be different if I were a movie critic. The people who make a film get reactions from thousands of people all over the country. If I'm writing an extremely negative review of a production in Florida, chances are that the artists involved will read it. Even though they're professionals, it can't be easy to read a negative review. And it can have economic consequences. But all that being said, it's part of the critic's job.

Frank Scheck: You try to write a pan in the same way you break up with someone you've been dating. You try to do it without being mean. You point out what's wrong with the show without being cheap about it. There's no point in being kind for kindness' sake, but there is a way to be negative without being nasty. Of course, some critics enjoy being nasty, and their publications like having a nasty critic, and that's fine.

Roma Torre: I always feel guilty. I empathize because I've been there. I worked as a director. I worked as an actress. I know how it feels. It hurts terribly. At NY1, we have artists come in for interviews. The green room for the guests is directly across from the anchor desk. It's all glass. They can stand there and look at me. I just dread when somebody I panned comes in to do an interview. I don't literally hide, but I try to stay as far away as I can. I feel terrible, you know? I know how it is. And yet, we're all mature enough to know that we can't hit a home run every time we're at bat. I hope they understand that if I panned the person or the show, maybe it wasn't all that good. So yes, I do feel guilty, and it hurts, but it's never stopped me.

John Simon: I feel that it is my duty to tell the truth. There is a teacher-critic who once introduced me at a party to a bunch of people as "a critic who never wrote anything he didn't believe," and that is apparently an achievement. It's hard for me to conceive, but a lot of critics write things that they do not believe. I, on the other hand, am totally sincere. I may be wrong. In fact, I may be totally wrong, but I firmly and honestly believe what I write. And if it's something truly negative, then that's it. I can't make it out to be anything else.

6. The Writing Process

If you write a negative review that is also witty, that somehow cuts deeper than a review that is not witty, and you thereby become a nasty critic. But I don't care about that. If people are going to hate me, let them. That's their privilege. And if that actor is going to be upset, that's too bad. Once you're on the stage, you are exposed, and whatever comes your way comes. You must not expect anything less than that or anything more than that. And if it's negative, if it hurts, that's too bad. Everyone is under such criticism. My own criticism gets criticized by other critics, and sometimes it's very tough, and I accept that. We must have tough skin. I'm always surprised when critics like Stanley Kauffmann (whom I thought well of) get upset by something negative that someone else writes about them. If you dish it out, you should be able to put up with it when it comes your way.

Rob Weinert-Kendt: I think you'd have to be a sociopath not to feel bad in some way, to not feel a little bit of the pain that you're inflicting on the people who might read it. But sometimes you've already felt the pain because they brought it. Sometimes you're striking back at something that was really a painful experience because it was so bad.

Perez Hilton: I don't feel guilt because I always give very specific examples to explain why I didn't like something.

Richard Ouzounian: I got past that very early on. There are people who feel like they have to be nice, but that leads to what I call "boy who cried sheep syndrome." If you go around too often saying, "It was a pretty good show that had a lot of nice things in it," people will stop listening to you. If you lead them to too many stiffs because you didn't want to hurt the lead actor's feelings, you're ultimately hurting the art form. That doesn't mean you have to turn into John Simon and slash and burn until nothing's left, but you have to call it like you see it, and that's ultimately what I do. And if I really hated something, I really say that.

Terry Teachout: I don't feel guilty when I write a stinker about a Hollywood star. If he gives a bad performance, he deserves what he's getting. But in circumstances less clear cut than that, I am very aware of the fact that I can do damage to people's lives. If I wasn't aware of that, I wouldn't be any good at this. There's nothing more terrible than a critic who enjoys writing a bad review.

Steven Suskin: There are some shows that are just really bad. There are other shows where people tried hard to do something difficult that didn't quite succeed. I don't feel guilt that I didn't like the show. I try to be as kind as possible. I say, "This didn't work, and it's a shame, and this is why it didn't work."

Hilton Als: I'm always reluctant to review small companies in a big context unless it's positive. You never want to hit a small company that hard because it'll lose its funding.

Michael Riedel: Theater people, when they're in their self-pitying mode, say, "It's so hard to get a play on. It costs so much money, and the risks are so great, that you really should support us." But if you feel guilt, you can't be a critic.

Peter Filichia: I remember Clive Barnes was asked this question on a panel that we were on. He talked about a review he wrote of a musical called *Smile, Smile, Smile*. It ran one night, partly because of his review. In response to the title *Smile, Smile, Smile*, he wrote, "I didn't, I didn't, I didn't." That was the entire review. He said that he really regretted that review because the people who did the show were entitled to know how they failed.

Peter Marks: I feel bad, but I don't ever regret it. It's like when I taught. Some of my favorite students weren't getting the best grades. They were wonderful kids, but I had to evaluate them as objectively as I could, and it killed me.

Jason Zinoman: To do this job, you can't be somebody who hates being disliked. You should be able to stand by whatever you write.

Adam Feldman: I feel guilty sometimes, which is not the same thing as guilt. Unless I acted in bad faith, I don't feel guilt. I've exercised my professional duty. I've tried to write as fairly as I can. I know that sometimes it hurts people's feelings. I know that it has the potential to hurt people's careers. But when shows are really trashed, there tends to be a reason. Someone's got to say it, and it might as well be me. I take that as a responsibility.

It's important that good work, instead of bad work, gets promoted. That's how the cream rises to the top. It helps push the entire artistic process forward. It helps good actors, writers, and directors be seen, and it helps audiences find them. The world doesn't have unlimited time and resources. People can't see everything. You want to help them find the best and avoid the worst.

Jesse Green: I try to not let all of my meanness (and all my lifetime aggression toward and envy of theater people) out, except on the few occasions when I think it's permissible. When a show is merely bad, I don't do it. When a show is good but cynical, I don't do it. But when it's both bad and cynical, then I feel justified, and I'll let myself be mean. Mostly, though, shows are not both bad and cynical. They're one or the other, so I resist the knockout pan, or I at least feel sorry for it. In any case, I will almost never pan actors. If they're miscast, it's not their fault. If they're in a play in which the character doesn't make any sense, that's not their fault. I'm much more likely to pan the play itself or the direction.

John Lahr: I've taken a show down once or twice. I'm thinking of a terrible production of *The Glass Menagerie* directed by Gordon Edelstein, which originated at the Long Wharf Theatre and transferred Off-Broadway in 2010. Edelstein essentially co-wrote the play. He put things into the play that weren't there. He had Tom walking around with a notepad, writing down things being said by Amanda and Laura. Also, there was a terrible production of

Tennessee Williams' *Camino Real* that I saw at the Goodman Theatre in Chicago in 2012. It was billed as Williams' play, but none of his work was in it. I was astonished and appalled. I remember sticking around afterwards to listen to the audience feedback with the dramaturg. I asked the audience if they thought they had actually seen Williams' play.

Matthew Murray: I'm not sure I feel guilt. My responsibility as a reviewer is to tell people about a show—good or bad. I don't want people to waste their time and money on bad theater, so I don't really have any compunction against telling them not to. You're there to call it as you see it, and you have to be ready to take artists to task when you don't think their work is successful. If you're not, you have no business being a reviewer.

That being said, I hate writing pans. I love the theater, and I want every artist and every production to succeed. I've heard plenty of stories of critics who relish writing negative reviews and really pull out all the stops to show what they're capable of in terms of wordsmithing or just overall nastiness, but pans are really hard for me because I don't want to have to say a show is bad. I know I have to, but it's just not my thing. I try to write them as sensibly and as measured as I can, which can sometimes be tough if a show is really bad, and explain all the ways the show doesn't work to my satisfaction. I much prefer writing an incredibly positive review that expresses the joy I feel at seeing truly great theater

MATT WINDMAN: Is there a particular review that you are proudest of?

Ben Brantley: I'm probably proudest of the mixed reviews, which are the reviews that get the least attention, because they're the hardest to write. When you have a very strong response to something, it's not that hard to translate it into words. When something works on one level but not on another level, that's a more complex process. You're taking it apart and putting it back together, and trying to figure out what works and what doesn't work, but without boring people. Most readers today want an extreme response. They aren't really interested in the middle ground, but the middle ground is what's hardest to plow. When I actually write a mixed review in which I said what I wanted to say, that's when I'm proudest.

Howard Shapiro: Every season, there are a few reviews that really stand out. When I finish them, I think, That's just what I wanted to tell people, and I hope people see this play through my eyes.

Elisabeth Vincentelli: I can't think of anything off the top of my head. One of the things about working at a daily newspaper is that you have to crank out so much that it's hard to keep track.

Charles Isherwood: *Spring Awakening* and *August: Osage County* are two of the most exciting reviews I've written. I wrote about them more than once, which is challenging. Those are good examples of new works I really felt I could have a stake in. Ultimately, it's not about me, but it's so rare to find new talent or new plays that you really think have a chance to cross over from the small group of people who regularly go to the theater to a major audience. I think both of those plays have a lot to say about contemporary America and what it is to be human.

Chris Jones: I like my review of *August: Osage County*, which was the first major review of that play, and helped propel it to all it became. I also like my review of the David Cromer production of *Our Town* that moved Off Broadway. That was an extraordinary production, and I was able to somehow get people to go see it. When a show is that good, you really have to give it up for it to get people to go. There's no point in namby-pambying around if something is unmissable. If you believe that someone will be the poorer for not having gone to the show, you have to write with great passion, and that's very difficult to do without repeating yourself.

Christine Dolen: *Anna in the Tropics* had its world premiere here in a very small theater of about 100 seats. I had reviewed other plays by Nilo Cruz before, and I felt the play raised him and his work to a new level. In the way I wrote about it, I hope I captured his unique style and poetic sensibility. And, of course, it was really gratifying to see it go on to win the Pulitzer Prize.

Michael Dale: When Suzanne Somers brought *The Blonde in the Thunderbird*, her exceedingly self-indulgent solo bio-musical, to Broadway, I called my review "Springtime for Somers: A Gay Romp with Suzanne and the Thighmaster on Broadway," and wrote from the point of view of someone who thought the show must be a satire of bad theater.

David Cote: My *Rabbit Hole* review—even if I was a little unfair in some ways. I used a mildly negative review to scream about how I was sick and tired of these bourgeois, overproduced living-room dramas about the tragedies of Westchester homeowners. A lot of people downtown really celebrated that review.

John Simon: *Private Lives* as played by Richard Burton and Elizabeth Taylor. That is one of my funniest reviews, and I like it for that reason. There also is a review I did of an extremely, violently homosexual movie—I mean really 101 percent homosexual—which I liked enormously, and I gave it a good review. I like the review not because it's all that special, but because it disproves what so many people think about me—that I'm homophobic—which I don't think I am. I don't like uniforms. I don't like a play that makes much of being very Christian, or very Jewish, or very macho, or whatever. For example, I have nothing against Alan Cumming for acting extremely homosexual on the stage as long as it fits the play, and as long as it's well-done.

Michael Musto: I reviewed *The Rocky Horror Show* when it first came to Broadway. I thought it was total trash, and I was proud of my honesty in saying so. I don't think the piece found its stride until the movie version.

Michael Portantiere: I'm proud of the fact that I've had an extremely negative reaction to certain kinds of shows, including almost all of the European pop operas (or whatever you want to call them) and most of the jukebox musicals.

Peter Marks: I was very proud of my review of the musical *If/Then* in D.C. I had many different things to do in that review. The producer was hoisting onto me the tryout run of a $10 million Broadway musical. When you're reviewing a tryout, you have a responsibility. They're asking you, "How do we move this along?" They're not saying, "We want to know if we should bring this to New York." This was already announced for Broadway, so my job was to be as clear as I could about what I thought worked and what didn't work. I thought I did a very successful job at that. I don't think they did a very successful job at solving the problems, but it might have been impossible to do that in three months. They needed to go back to the drawing board.

Frank Rizzo: *Sleep No More* had its world premiere in Cambridge. I was reviewing it for *Variety*, so I had to deal with an industry audience, but also capture what was going on, what that experience was like, what I thought of it, and what it might mean to the marketplace. That was a real challenge.

Adam Feldman: I often go back to my review of the musical *Caroline, or Change*, which opened at the Public Theater in 2003 and moved to Broadway in 2004. It is, in my opinion, the best musical of the past 20 years. It did not get the critical reception that I strongly feel it deserved. There were a few of us that loved it, and it's gotten great reviews pretty much everywhere it's been ever since because the cast album came out and people had time to process it. But when it opened, it was not properly received in New York. I went up to bat for it hard in the magazine and elsewhere. That's an exciting place to be: fighting for something that you think is really terrific and at risk of being overlooked. I'm also proud of my negative reviews. There's a review of a Frank Wildhorn musical called *Wonderland* that people still bring up to me because it was written in verse—some awfully good light verse, if I may say so myself.

John Lahr: I'm currently putting together a collection of reviews that I'm pleased with. When I got the job with the *New Yorker*, I had bounced around long enough to know my good fortune. From day one, I was determined to not waste an hour of my time—and I didn't. I worked like hell. There's no single review I like above the rest.

Richard Zoglin: My writing about Alan Ayckbourn. I think he's the best living playwright. I've written a couple of pieces about him when his stuff wanders through New York, and I feel like I've made a good case for him.

Dan Bacalzo: I'm proud of the review I wrote of *Dogeaters* at the Public Theater for *Theatre Journal*, which is an academic publication. I was able to go into a lot more depth, do a cross-comparison between the novel and the stage adaptation, and talk about some of the political issues in the Philippines. I couldn't do all that in a review that had to come out immediately.

David Sheward: My review of *You're a Good Man, Charlie Brown* on Broadway with Kristin Chenoweth. She was such a talent, and she stood out without overwhelming the show. Recognizing somebody who has gone on to a very big career certainly makes me glad that I could be a part of that. I wasn't the only critic to recognize her, but I was a part of that official voice saying, "She's special."

David Finkle: I wrote a review of a production of Ibsen's *Ghosts* that was done Off-Broadway with Amy Irving and Daniel Gerroll. It was very badly directed. *Ghosts* was such a seminal and shocking play in its time that this director thought he needed to find a way to make it shocking again, so he had the actors deliver their lines without emoting, and I wrote about that. I understood how these actors were doing things they didn't want to do. Within a month, I got a letter from Daniel Gerroll where he said, "It's so helpful to have a critic understand what actors go through."

Zachary Stewart: After I wrote a review of the recent Encores! revival of *Zorba!*, Jack Viertel (the artistic director of Encores!) sent along some very kind words about the review, even though it was not the most glowing assessment of the show. That felt very gratifying.

Terry Teachout: Because I travel, I was the first person in New York to really spot David Cromer and see how good he is. I saw a show of his in Kansas City and reported on it in the *Wall Street Journal*. I'm very proud that I was able to say to the readers of the *Journal*, "This is a very important artist. This is someone whose name you should know."

Michael Riedel: I have a good track record in terms of picking the winners and losers. My stuff on *Spider-Man* was pretty on the mark. Before anyone else had written anything about it, I had a sense that it was going to be the fiasco that it turned out to be. When *The Lion King* came out in Minneapolis, I knew it was going to be really big, and that it would bring people to see really see Disney in a whole new light. I think some of the profiles I've done over the years are quite good. I've become fairly adept at writing a little send off to showbiz people that have died. Because I've been around a long time, I've gotten to know a lot of them, and I have some insights into their personalities. I don't just use the same anecdotes that everybody else recycles from the old clips.

MATT WINDMAN: *If you had the chance, is there any review you would rewrite?*

Hilton Als: All of them. I always get that feeling as a writer.

Michael Riedel: If I said it at the time, I meant it. I don't spend a lot of

6. The Writing Process   121

time sifting through my old stuff. Once it goes to the printing press and hits the stands, I don't dwell on what I wrote yesterday. I barely dwell on what I wrote an hour ago.

Ronni Reich: I'm usually writing with less than 24 hours in which to turn in a review, and I do sometimes feel that I haven't considered a show from every angle. Maybe I dismissed something I shouldn't have, or I was too harsh, or I gave some things the benefit of the doubt when I shouldn't have. Hindsight is 20/20.

Michael Dale: Probably anything I've ever written in April, when there's typically a mad rush of a couple dozen shows racing to open before the award deadlines.

Don Aucoin: I can't think of a review where I felt completely differently 24 hours later. Under the pressure of a deadline, I might overpraise or underpraise a performance or some other aspect of a production. It's important to steer away from categorical language like "greatest," "best-ever," or "worst-ever." That's where you get into trouble.

John Simon: I've written so many reviews in my life that I'll be damned if I can remember whether I've been fair in all of them. There must have been a handful of cases where I underpraised something that deserved a more positive review. I often realize that after a while.

Leonard Jacobs: There are times when I'd like to make a 90-degree turn, but not a 180-degree turn. I don't go from completely loving a show to suddenly hating it.

Steven Suskin: From years of working backstage, I know that a show can play better after it opens, especially if it's experienced a lot of changes during previews, but we can only judge what we see when we see it.

Ben Brantley: Sometimes you come closer to saying what you intended than other times. At the moment you're writing the review, you can only write about what you saw and how you saw it at that time. You might see the same show a month or a year later. By that time, you've changed, but the cast may have also changed. That's one of the great things about theater. It's never the same from night to night. You bring a different perspective to it, and who you're watching brings a different perspective to it, too.

David Finkle: When I was younger and thought sarcasm was so great, I might've gone too far. I remember being unnecessarily cruel about somebody in one review. There's no need for cruelty in a review. You can make your point without being cruel.

Chris Jones: There was a review of an early Sarah Ruhl play, back when no one had heard of her, when she was about 22 years old. I blamed her for something the director had done. And 10 years later, she reminded me of it, and told me how much it had crippled her and hurt her. I was wrong. I attributed it incorrectly, you might say, so I would like to redo that one. There are also some shows I overpraised, and some shows where I was too sparing in my praise, but the Sarah Ruhl play is one where I screwed up. It's the one that sticks out in my mind. It was a choice that the director had forced on the playwright, but there I was blaming her.

Elisabeth Vincentelli: I gave the most recent Broadway revival of *Follies* two and a half stars out of four. I was really harsh on it because I had this Platonic ideal of what the show could be, and I felt the production fell short. I was really kind of nitpicky and harsh. But I kept thinking about the show, so I did something that I rarely do and asked the publicist if I could see it again, and I wrote another review of it on my blog.

Elysa Gardner: I banged out my review of Audra McDonald in *110 in the Shade*, and it was a visceral reaction to the show. It really flowed out, and I felt good about it at first. Then I read some of the feedback, and people who were big fans of Audra seemed to think I had a problem with her. I thought to myself, Yes, maybe I do, but that's relevant to the review. After the fact, I thought that maybe I shouldn't have channeled so much energy into asking why this woman is the bees knees to so many people. I probably went on too much about that when I could have described other aspects of the production.

Howard Shapiro: There are a few plays I wish had more time to think about before writing about them, including a couple by Tom Stoppard. I think I would have done a better job if I had another hour at the keyboard.

Michael Musto: There's nothing I can't live with. I still maintain that *Wonderland* was terrible and *A Chorus Line* was great.

Michael Portantiere: I reviewed *Phantom of the Opera* when it originally opened. In retrospect, I don't think I was as negative as I should have been.

Zachary Stewart: I wrote a very effusive review of the musical *Kinky Boots* when it first debuted. In retrospect, the show is quite safe and predictable. The "be who you want to be" message has become a theatrical cliché, a way to draw in the money of gays and the people who love them. It really doesn't challenge our conventional wisdom. If I had to rewrite the review, I'd mention that, although I think the problem has become even more pronounced in the years following that show's Tony win.

Michael Schulman: There was a musical called *Thrill Me* that I reviewed Off-Broadway at the York Theatre Company. I sort of hammered it. Later, I wondered whether it really deserved that kind of scorn. I wouldn't be softer in my opinion now, but I'd modulate the tone. You should only employ pure, unadulterated snark when it's really deserved—like when you think someone had bad intentions.

Richard Zoglin: I think my review of *The Bridges of Madison County* was too favorable. I didn't like it all that much, but I did like the music and the performances, and I ended up writing a nice review of it.

Roma Torre: Going way back, there was a review I did rewrite. It might have been *Waiting for Godot*. I forget which production it was. I hated it the first time I saw it and wrote a really nasty review, but then I saw it again and got it. It just didn't work for me the first time. At the time, I thought to myself, I know I'm missing something. This is supposed to be a great piece of writing, and I'm just not getting it at all. When I went back to see it, I realized what I was missing.

Adam Feldman: Sometimes you can be harder on good shows than bad ones. If it aims low and succeeds, you sort of give it a pass. If it aims high and doesn't quite make it, you end up writing a review that sounds quite critical. There's a Craig Lucas play called *Small Tragedy* that I still beat myself up for. I ended it with a cheap one-liner, but there was a great deal to admire about the show, and I'm sorry that I ended the review on a note that sounded like I was condemning the whole show.

John Lahr: I got into trouble with my review of *The Book of Mormon*. I gently teased Scott Rudin in print because he was being such a control freak. He wouldn't give me the script prior to seeing the show. I just wanted to write well about the show, but the general view was that I had abused my power— and I suppose that on one level, I did. In retrospect, I'm sorry about it, and I would take it back if I could—not my opinion on the show, just the teasing of Scott Rudin. He banned me from his shows for about a year. I previously had a really good relationship with him. He would call me up or send a note if he liked a review.

Peter Marks: The one I always point to is the musical *Glory Days*, which closed after its opening night on Broadway in 2008. I wrote a very encouraging review when the show premiered at the Signature Theatre in D.C., and some very inexperienced producers took it as a ticket to Broadway. I was trying to be encouraging to a young musical theater writer who had talent. If someone had said to me, "We're thinking of moving this to Broadway," I would have said, "It's not ready." I should have said that the writer's next musical was probably going to be better, so I kick myself for that. It had a real charm at Signature, but maybe it was too sincere for its own good.

Terry Teachout: I'm in an unusual position compared to other critics because I make a point of reviewing regional productions of plays that I previously reviewed in New York, so I do get a second chance to engage with shows that maybe I didn't quite get the first time around. A really good example would be *The History Boys*. I wouldn't say I didn't get it when I reviewed it on Broadway, but I didn't get it as well as when I saw it a second time at the TimeLine Theatre in Chicago. I got a chance to go into it at greater length, and to think more about how the play came across when I was seeing a very different kind of production. I make a real effort to see what I think of new plays after they've been around for a couple of years. Right now, I am looking for an opportunity to review *The 25th Annual Putnam County Spelling Bee.* I'm very curious to see how it will hold up.

Matthew Murray: I think my review of the 2007 Broadway musical *The Pirate Queen* (by, among others, *Les Miz* and *Miss Saigon* writers Claude-Michel Schönberg and Alain Boublil) was too affected by what else was happening in the industry at the time. This was when *Spring Awakening* (which I thought was absolutely terrible) was getting so much attention. I might have come across as more positive than I should have, and my enthusiasm probably should have been tempered a bit. But most of the time, I'm willing to go back and defend pretty much anything I've written.

7

Readers

MATT WINDMAN: *What kind of audience do you see yourself writing for?*

Steven Suskin: Different readerships have different expectations.

Hilton Als: That's a very interesting question—and one that I don't think I can answer. If you have an audience in mind, then you're not really writing. I think you need to just do your writing. Frankly, I've never felt inhibited at the *New Yorker* or the *Village Voice*.

Jesse Green: I don't know who my readers are—and I don't know how I could learn. I guess I have a certain impression, but I fear it's a stereotype because it's based on occasional encounters, rather than on any kind of reliable data. *New York* magazine hosts what it calls the *Vulture* Festival each year, which is kind of like the *New Yorker* Festival, but less stuffy. A lot of readers come to that, so you get a sense of what they're like. My feeling is that they are culturally savvy. They seem to be youngish, but there's also an older generation of New Yorkers who have always read *New York* magazine for its smart tone and cultural coverage. Do they go to the theater more than the readers of the *Village Voice* or the *New York Times*? I have no way of knowing that. In any case, it doesn't influence my writing. The dirty secret of all writing is that you're not writing for an audience—you're writing for yourself.

John Simon: To some extent, you have to play with the expectations of the publication and its mucky-mucks, but essentially I am not influenced by the publication—even ones like the *New Criterion* or the *Weekly Standard*. As a result, I may be a little too much for some people. I can't help it. That means too much to me to skirt.

Robert Faires: The audience is kind of invented in my head. It tends to be somebody who shares my love of theater and who wants to know what's happening out there. I don't have a very clear sense of demographics. When I was in my twenties, I figured that people in their twenties were reading me. Now that I'm in my fifties, I couldn't tell you whether people in their twenties are reading me. I have no idea if my audience is male, female, married, or single. That stuff is kind of a blank for me.

Michael Riedel: To be honest, I'm really writing for myself. First and foremost, what I write has to interest me. If it bores me, it's going to bore anyone reading it. If it amuses me, or if I find it interesting, then I can only assume that people who are reading it will find it interesting.

Chris Jones: I don't want to be arrogant, but I know a lot of plays. On the other hand, I write for a general newspaper, so my job is not to write for specialists. For the most part, I write for ordinary people. Chicago is a no-nonsense kind of city, so it's not like I can write academic theses on these shows.

Ben Brantley: I write for an audience that has some knowledge of theater and is interested in theater to begin with. I'm not starting from scratch with these readers.

Matthew Murray: *TalkinBroadway.com* is a site by and for theater lovers, so I tend to approach each show with that in mind. I'm not coming at things the way reviewers do when they're writing for a broader, more general audience, and I'm fine with that. Our site is most famous (or infamous) for its *All That Chat* discussion board, which since 1997 has been one of the most active and engaged theater chat groups on the Internet. My opinions don't always line up with those of all, or even most, of the posters on *All That Chat*, but I like to think they're at least representative of what you get from them.

Alexis Soloski: When I first started with the *Village Voice*, it was what everyone downtown was reading. The audience was young, fairly well-educated, and interested in going out and taking advantage of New York. I'm not too sure what the audience is now.

Michael Musto: My readership is predominately gay, but it's also predominant of people who care about culture, as seen from my slightly jaundiced but optimistic point of view. I just write what comes naturally to me without limitations, and that tends to find a very savvy audience that includes people who really do care about theater, even if they don't go that often.

Don Aucoin: Newspaper readers are general readers. They're usually intelligent, cultured, and educated, but they're not theater insiders. They're not necessarily subscribers to *American Theatre* magazine. I hope all the readers of the *Globe* are at least occasionally checking out the theater reviews. The core demographic that tends to populate theaters is middle-aged and older. It's just a fact that people in their college years or teenage years are not big theatergoers.

Michael Schulman: I like to think the *New Yorker* audience is adventurous in its theatergoing. They'll go to something at St. Ann's Warehouse or Brooklyn Academy of Music or the Public Theater. They'll go to some more obscure place. I think of them as New Yorkers—not tourists or out-of-towners. One *New Yorker* writer, Michael Specter, once said that he thinks the *New Yorker* reader is someone who's extremely accomplished in a field that has nothing to do with what he's reading about. For instance, the imaginary reader might be an extremely accomplished musician who's reading about a public health issue. If you're writing about theater, you might be writing for a heart surgeon. *New Yorker* readers are intellectually curious generalists.

The people who are reading the theater reviews want to have a good reading experience. The *New Yorker* is known for its writing. It's not a consumer guide for buying tickets. We need to give the readers some sort of literary satisfaction. Hilton Als and John Lahr are both wonderful literary stylists. Even if you have no interest in seeing *Rocky*, you can read Hilton's review of *Rocky* and find some beautiful turn of phrase in it, or some joke in Anthony Lane's movie review of *The Hulk*.

Elysa Gardner: *USA Today* has a varied audience. Obviously, there are a lot of business travelers—people who read the paper at a hotel or on an airplane while en route somewhere. The entertainment section appeals to a slightly younger demographic, but I try to write for everyone. I never think, I have to write for this specific audience. I just try to communicate as clearly and entertainingly as I can for everyone.

Adam Feldman: *Time Out* has an intellectually and culturally engaged readership that wants to see things that are entertaining and smart, and I try to write from that perspective. I'm lucky to write for an audience that, by virtue of the magazine itself, is interested in going out and seeing what New York has to offer. That's a lovely group of people to write for.

Frank Rizzo: You have to know who you're writing for. I'm not writing this for myself. I'm writing for a particular market, and for a particular periodical, and the writing has to be for that specific audience. I write for a general circulation audience at the *Hartford Courant*. I like to think of my aunt picking up the paper and reading it. She doesn't know who Jayne Atkinson is. She might not even know who Henrik Ibsen is, but I want her to be engaged while reading the review. I want her to find it interesting, entertaining, and truthful. I've also done freelance work for the *New York Times*, and that writing is a bit different because its audience is savvier in terms of theater.

Jesse Oxfeld: I always had my parents in mind with the *Observer*. They're the kind of people who spend money to go to the theater a couple of times a month, like your typical New Yorker or suburbanite. They didn't need to be convinced to go to the theater or be told that *The Book of Mormon* was the one thing they needed to see. They were people who go to the theater a certain number of nights each year, and I was telling them which shows they should see.

Richard Ouzounian: They are incredibly varied ethnically. As Toronto started to become the great multicultural capital of the world, the *Star* hired columnists to speak to their concerns and made the paper accessible to them. I don't just have a bunch of old, white, Anglo-Saxon, Protestant people reading me.

Richard Zoglin: I'm writing for an audience at *Time* that is not really hardcore theater buffs. It's a general audience. I try to look at theater from the largest perspective. I don't assume any knowledge on the part of my readers. I'm not comparing a production to one from 10 years ago.

Roma Torre: The NY1 audience is a mix. It changes throughout the day. The morning audience is a little more savvy and sophisticated. Later on, the audience is perhaps more blue-collar—people who don't work nine-to-five jobs, like restaurant workers and cab drivers and mothers at home. I'm not sure who the audience is at night. Generally speaking, it's hardcore New Yorkers who cross all economic classes and cultures, and they're diehard. People will quote things to me that I said a year ago. They really pay attention. We were designed for a New York City audience, and that really is who's watching us.

Linda Winer: I've never changed the way I write to suit the different papers I've written for. But for the most part, I write for a mass audience that might love the theater. I used to think that I was writing for my mother, who was an intelligent, undereducated woman. My instinct is to not overestimate a reader's information or underestimate his or her intelligence. I think I'm writing for someone who is intelligent but is not a specialist. It would be great if what I write is helpful or sounds right to the specialists, but I'm a newspaper journeyman. There's a lot of wonderful writing about theater on the Internet, but it's really meant for other theater people. With a general newspaper, you have the opportunity in your first couple sentences to ensnare, to interest, to seduce someone who may not be interested in reading about the play you're writing about. But if you can do that, you may have turned on a tiny bit of light in somebody for the theater.

Eric Grode: Even though the *Sun* was a right-wing publication, I never felt the slightest pressure about that. I wrote one of the more favorable reviews of *My Name Is Rachel Corrie*. If you assume that the *Sun* was going to adhere to its political stance from top to bottom, it wasn't the kind of review you'd expect to see in that paper.

Peter Marks: I think the *Washington Post* reader ranges from someone who goes very often to the regional theaters in D.C. to someone who goes almost never goes to the theater, and I try to write to the middle of that demographic. I don't want to make it so highfalutin that I lose the people who are only interested in the question of whether or not they should go to the show, and I try to write with enough depth for the people who go to the theater a lot.

I write for a very smart readership. The self-selected readership of theater reviews is automatically very high. They tend to be fairly intelligent people. I'm not saying that everyone who goes to the theater is a genius, but you're dealing with a largely college-educated readership. They're people who value culture and the arts. I have not detected much of a difference in terms of the readership of the *New York Times* and the *Washington Post*.

Robert Feldberg: The readership of the *Record* is very diverse. With any general-interest newspaper, you have people who go to the theater a lot and are familiar with it, and then you have people who never go to the theater. Writers form a sense in their head of the general audience they're writing for. You instinctively use certain words instead of other words. You realize that if you mention a show other than the one you're writing about, maybe you should write a sentence or two explaining what that other show is. You should not leave a hole in the story for the general audience.

Ronni Reich: I think the *Star-Ledger* audience is generally very well-informed about theater and very enthusiastic about it. I get emails and phone calls fairly regularly, and I see full houses at shows. I think they have an appetite for variety and a pretty good understanding of what high production values look like, though they can also appreciate something on a smaller scale. It's an audience that spans generations and media, from the print to the online version.

Terry Teachout: At the *Wall Street Journal*, it's an educated audience of laypeople who are interested in theater, both as something to see and as part of the larger world of art and culture. I don't write for theater professionals. Presumably, some of them read what I write, but they're not my audience, so I avoid inside baseball. As a journalist would say, I write in English. I don't use jargon. I explain what I'm writing. I don't assume that the people who read my column know as much about theater as a theater professional would. I'm not writing about lighting plots—though I will mention lighting if it's material. When you're writing about the artistic impression of a theater production, you're saying things that ideally ought to make the same kind of sense to professionals as to laypeople.

Thom Geier: I think *Entertainment Weekly*'s median age is somewhere in the thirties. It's about 60 percent female and 40 percent male. We hear from our readers, even outside of New York, that they want more theater coverage, which is kind of surprising. We get theater ads for both the online and print editions, so there definitely seems to be a healthy appetite for it.

Jason Zinoman: The *Times* has a broad audience. It's not the same audience I speak to on *Twitter*. At *Time Out*, you could write something and be ignored. With the *Times*, you're speaking to a much larger audience.

David Rooney: The big frustration for anyone who writes for a business paper like *Variety* is the question of whether a consumer audience is reading your work, but there is something gratifying about writing for the industry. You know that every producer, Broadway director, artistic programmer, and senior publicist is reading your article.

Marilyn Stasio: I don't write for a consumer audience. At *Variety*, I'm writing reviews for the guy in Dallas who's running a theater with two stages to book. A vivid review can help him find a show that his subscription audience would like to see. A good trade review can introduce him to a playwright, designer, performer, or director he might want to hire.

Steven Suskin: *Variety* has a certain slant. You're writing for the business, trying to encapsulate what they need to know in terms of a show's business prospects. *Variety* wants a punchy paragraph upfront. You should be able to read the first and last paragraph and get the overall opinion. With the *Huffington Post*, I can take an aspect of the show that I think is important and use that to give an impression of the entire show.

Frank Scheck: The *Hollywood Reporter* is a trade publication geared to the industry. The *New York Post* is more of a general-population newspaper, so your style has to be breezier and more accessible.

Jeremy Gerard: There's a big difference between writing for the industry and general readers. At *Deadline.com*, I'm conscious of writing for the industry, which is a challenge because most of the people who are reading my articles know as much about, or maybe even more about, the subject than I do.

MATT WINDMAN: *To what extent do you direct your reviews towards actors, playwrights, directors, and other theater professionals?*

Michael Dale: Not at all. I'm describing the experience of seeing the show to potential ticket buyers.

Zachary Stewart: I write for the ticket buyer, but I hope that my words can be helpful to theater makers, whether through providing honest feedback or with a professional recommendation.

John Lahr: Reviewers write for their audience. Critics write for the artist. A playwright, generally speaking, doesn't know the meaning of his play. He knows the effects, feelings, or ideas that he's going for, but he can't articulate them. That's what a critic is trying to do.

Robert Faires: I suspect that a large part of my audience at the *Chronicle* is made up of people who make theater. Actors, directors, and designers will be the first ones to comment about something they've read of mine.

Adam Feldman: Critics aren't writing their reviews for the artists. By the time we see the show, it's frozen. Nothing we say, no matter how kind or constructive, is going to help the show. We're not the show's dramaturgs. We're not the show's producers. We're not the show's directors. We are writing for our readers. If the creators want to eavesdrop on that conversation, that's their prerogative. Some of them do, and some of them don't, but they are not specifically part of that conversation. They're not the intended audience for that communication.

David Cote: I like to think that theater professionals read my reviews.

7. Readers   131

Alexis Soloski: I think the critic remains in dialogue with the artists, even though lot of artists have learned not to read reviews, or to have someone they trust read the reviews for them and distill any important information. I don't imagine that Audra McDonald is rushing to the red *Village Voice* box on the sidewalk, desperate to see what I have to say, but I do presume that there's a dialogue.

Elisabeth Vincentelli: I try to write something that's constructive for the creative team, especially if I didn't like the show.

Peter Marks: It drives a lot of people in the theater crazy when I say that I don't write my reviews for theater people.

MATT WINDMAN: *What kind of feedback do you receive from your readers?*

Christine Dolen: Maybe some critics get a ton of feedback, but I rarely get any, and I'm not quite sure why. Occasionally, a reader will be outraged by something and write a letter to the editor. I suspect that the artists feel that this is a long, ongoing relationship, so it's better to say nothing if they are unhappy with something I write. I wish they didn't feel that way, but I think that's the case.

John Simon: I'm always happiest when there is some kind of response. But more often than not, there isn't any. I enjoy the violent attacks as much as praise. Most of the attacks on me are totally illiterate and perfectly good for laughing at.

Zachary Stewart: I rarely receive any feedback, but I'm always delighted when I do—even negative feedback. It shows me that people are reading and emotionally and intellectually engaging with my criticism, which makes the work feel worth it.

Michael Dale: When I do get feedback, it's usually from those who disagree. Often passionately. The worst was getting an email from the mother of Rachel Corrie, the activist who was run over by an Israeli tank, who didn't care for my negative review of *My Name Is Rachel Corrie*.

Howard Shapiro: Readers at the *Inquirer* had no compunction about sitting down and writing nasty stuff to me. A lot of people were nice, too. Unfortunately, it's the nasty ones that I remember more.

Michael Musto: Pieces about Broadway don't tend to burn up the charts. Something about Kyle Dean Massey being the replacement in *Pippin* does fine, but even the show's publicist knows it's not going to set the world on fire. It's a local story. People want something with more of an international flavor to it. If you write about Daniel Radcliffe or James Franco or Denzel Washington, people will take notice.

Ben Brantley: If it's a high-profile review, like if it has a movie star, people respond. I get hate mail. I get love mail. It's almost entirely by email now because people can just click on my byline and send words of cursing or encouragement. If they're really hostile or insane-sounding, I don't linger on them. If they're more measured, I try to answer them, whether they agree with me or not. Some of them are very intelligent and make fascinating points.

Robert Faires: There are communities where the theater critics have enough interaction with the audience that it's a give-and-take conversation, but I rarely hear from my audience. Maybe it's because I'm not a critic who pushes a lot of buttons or says controversial things.

Charles Isherwood: It varies. I can write three or four reviews and get no responses from readers because I'm writing about shows that nobody really cares about. I'll get a much stronger response with other shows. I do go through the emails and respond to the ones that are not just sheer vituperation, but sometimes I'll respond to those, too.

Jesse Green: Occasionally, I'll get a few comments, often from cranks or people who want to point out an error. If you go by the comments on the website, what readers apparently want is for me to disappear, die, or have a stick shoved up my ass. Those are real suggestions that have been made. Rarely does anyone bother to make a positive comment, which is fine.

I do get feedback from the productions themselves, usually through press agents. They will be pretty frank about how the people involved have taken a review. I have been happiest when, after I have panned a show, the press agent tells me how much they loved the review. I find that quite delicious because the press agents are the ones who know what's really going on. They may have to flack something that's bad, but they know if it's bad.

Chris Jones: I get all kinds of feedback. It's all by email, except for the elderly, who often send me long, handwritten letters of contempt or admiration. People love to compare what I thought with what they thought. If they think I got something wrong, they'll tell me about it. The people you review usually don't call and complain, but sometimes they do. There are certain theater people who respond passionately to everything, and that includes your review of their work.

Gordon Cox: You get a lot of "I agree" or "I disagree," and that's about it.

David Cote: I tend to hear more from people who enjoy my work. The people who didn't enjoy it or agree with me probably won't tell me, which is perfectly reasonable. I do post my reviews online, and sometimes there'll be spirited discussions from people who disagree with my opinion. I think that's an important part of the process. A big part of the function we serve now as critics is to start such a conversation and spur people into thinking and articulating their reactions to works of art.

Frank Scheck: Usually, the only people you hear from are disgruntled.

You may hear from someone if you've made some mistake. On rare occasion, I'll get a nasty contact from someone I've panned. I'll also get the occasional thank you note, which is sweet but completely unnecessary.

Elisabeth Vincentelli: I learned the hard way that you have to be really careful when you write about a child actor. Anything even remotely resembling criticism will be interpreted as you being a total child hater. I once wrote about a child performer in *The People in the Picture*, a horrible musical at the Roundabout with Donna Murphy. I wrote something along the lines of, "That child was irritating," and I got a lot of emails about it. Neil LaBute wrote to me a few years ago. He's known for writing to critics. We had a very constructive email exchange. That's not going to make me be any nicer to his next project, or any meaner, but it was very interesting.

Matthew Murray: Writing for a site with an incredibly active chat board full of opinionated people, I can get all sorts of feedback: people who love me, people who hate me, people who think I hate everything, people who think I'm not qualified, people who wish I held a job with more power. Every possible thing I can hear I've heard at one point or another on *All That Chat*.

Peter Marks: The best kind of feedback is when someone likes your review but doesn't necessarily agree with it.

Rob Weinert-Kendt: When I wrote for the *Los Angeles Times* and *Time Out*, I would get pushback from people in the production who wanted to contradict what I said because they were inside of it. In the few productions that I've been involved with, I would read the reviews and think, Those critics didn't get the show at all. That's probably what all artists say when they read a bad review. You tend to get more negative comments than positive ones. The people who are most motivated to comment are the ones who are pissed off that you didn't get something, or they have friends in the show, or they think you're full of shit. Conversely, people will agree with your negative opinion and say that, so the comments tend to be of a negative sort: either they don't like what you said, or they love what you said because it was so harsh. It's an unfortunate commentary on people.

Richard Ouzounian: I don't engage with people who write anonymous comments under my reviews online.

John Lahr: The feedback I've gotten has been superb. In my office in London, there's a framed card from Arthur Miller saying my piece on him was "the best thing about my stuff I have ever read." I've gotten cards from Tom Stoppard, David Mamet, Sarah Ruhl, and the public. When I was out on the road, people would come up and say that my writing meant something to them. That's nice to know that because most of the time, you're working in your own little cave of consciousness.

Terry Teachout: It could be something like "Here's a show you might like," or "Here's a company you may not have heard of." I pay attention to that and take it very seriously. I have gone to shows performed by companies I learned about from people who I trust on social media, and I am very pleased with the results. It's a big country, and I try to know what's going on outside of New York.

8

Evaluation

MATT WINDMAN: *How is reviewing a new play or musical different than reviewing a revival?*

Zachary Stewart: Since there's no precedent for a new play, there's an added responsibility to critique the work of the author or composer. If it's a revival, chances are we already know the show works as a piece of writing. That's never certain with a new play or musical.

Hilton Als: You have more history with a revival. With a new piece, you only have the playwright's previous work.

David Cote: You have to treat each as an experience, even if you bring a lot of experience to the table. With a revival, there's obviously more context. Some theaters look at a classic with fresh eyes, and I love that.

Matthew Murray: They're completely different, and I don't care what anyone else, including other critics, tells you. New York theater (and particularly Broadway) is a heavily revival-based culture. Producers are putting on lots of shows with famous titles specifically because the titles are famous and will get people in the theater. Therefore, the reviewer has to work within the broader framework of how the show has been done before. The producers want the financial and name-recognition benefit of putting on shows that have been done before, but they want reviewers to pretend they never have been? Sorry, it doesn't work that way, and I think other reviewers have a tendency of acting as though it does.

Take the musical *Gypsy*. Since 2001, when I began reviewing, there have been two major productions on Broadway: one starring Bernadette Peters (2003–2004) and one starring Patti LuPone (2008–2009). Producers know this. The people for whom I write know this. And anyone who saw both productions knows that there were major similarities in the concepts, not all of which were endemic merely to the text. Not everyone who saw the production with Patti LuPone also saw the one with Bernadette Peters, but it opened on Broadway less than five years after the previous one closed. I would consider it a dereliction of duty for a reviewer to pretend that the LuPone *Gypsy* existed in a vacuum.

Elysa Gardner: With a revival, you are bringing all these preconceived notions and impressions to the table. With a new work, you are inclined to focus more on the material itself, but that's not to say I can't be completely blown away by a certain performance in an original play or musical, or by the director's vision for it.

Howard Shapiro: If it's a new play, I'm going to want to write at least as much (and probably more) about the content of the play as about the production. I think that's what people are most interested in.

Don Aucoin: More plot summary is needed in a review of a new show. If I'm writing about *Hamlet* or *Death of a Salesman*, I don't need to tell readers much about the plot. With revivals, you want to focus on what's new. What original take did the director or the actor come up with?

Steven Suskin: Revivals are only revivals for the people who have seen the show before. For people who haven't, it's new to them. You're writing a review for the entire audience, and not just for the people who are already familiar with the show. You're not just saying, "It's better than it was last time." In some cases, when the show has recently been revived, you have to talk about that. For the recent *Cabaret* revival, you needed to refer to the last two productions because the audience was likely to have them in mind. If you go to a revival and it's not as electric as the last one, you're not doing anybody a favor by pretending the other revival didn't happen.

Ben Brantley: If you've seen a show before—and you probably have if you've been in this job as long as I have—you want to assess how it was received before and whether it feels dated or suddenly revitalized, which can happen. A new show is scarier, both for the people putting it on and for those writing about it. You're writing about something that hasn't been written about before, and that's exciting. On the other hand, writing about the Globe production of *Twelfth Night* was thrilling. It made you feel like you were seeing the play for the first time.

Marilyn Stasio: Directors are usually behind revivals because they have something new to say, some fresh contribution to make. When you review a revival, you're really looking for that original contribution. What's the need to revisit this subject? What makes this interpretation different? What's the vision? What's fresh about it? Look at those fantastic shows that came in from the London's Globe, and the original way they re-examined *Twelfth Night* and *Richard III*. I've seen many productions of *Twelfth Night*, but never one as enjoyable as that.

Elisabeth Vincentelli: I try to avoid comparing productions of the same play because not everybody is going to have seen all of them, or even two of them. Of course, if there's one that's really great, it's going to be hard to not compare them. There's been a lot of *King Lear* and *Uncle Vanya* lately. At one point, there was a lot of *Twelfth Night*. Sometimes you go into a play that's done a lot with a bit of weariness. I feel like I'm getting impatient with Shakespeare—or maybe just the craven, unimaginative way that Shakespeare plays are staged. He's taking up too much oxygen, to the detriment of the other classic plays that we don't see. I'm Shakespeared out!

Brian Lipton: There are so many revivals now that critics get caught in a weird bind. Sometimes I feel like I've seen too many productions of the same play, and all my memories can get mixed up, or I end up comparing the newest production to earlier productions that my readers haven't seen. Maybe that's wrong, but I do think you need to have a real sense of theater history to be truly useful. When they do the next production of *Forum*, I don't need to read the review of someone who saw Zero Mostel in the 1960s, but I definitely want to read the review of somebody who at least saw Nathan Lane in the 1990s.

Gordon Cox: With a new show, it can be difficult to spot the fingerprints of whoever shaped its elements. Did this element come from the dramaturgical input of the director? Was the theme of the play made clear because of the writing, or did the set designer do something? The production introduces itself to you as the play itself. It can be hard to separate the two and understand how the play is separate from the production. With a revival, chances are that you've read it or seen it before, and you get a clear sense of what choices the director made or what's new about the production. It helps to read the script after you see a new play. Afterwards, you can think about what the director added to it.

Michael Schulman: One question you always have to ask yourself with revivals is whether there is a good reason for it to be revived. You need to figure out where it came from and its historical moment to determine how it's being interpreted. Is it a classical interpretation? Is it a completely wild reimaging?

Richard Ouzounian: If it's a new play or musical, you're writing mostly about the work itself. That's what the major item is. You don't necessarily go into depth about the designers or the actors or the director. You'll mention the other people in passing, but you're there to write about the work itself.

Rob Weinert-Kendt: With a revival, you shouldn't spend too much time talking about previous productions. One of my least favorite things is when critics go, "This isn't as good as the last production," or "It's not as good as the movie version." People are always writing about how a show should be done, or how it was done last time, but your real responsibility is to write about what's actually going on in the room, right then and there.

Jesse Green: With a new show, you don't have many preformed opinions. You may be just as surprised as everybody else in terms of the plot. I feel a greater sense of responsibility if it's new. Critics ganging up on a new show can really destroy it. You can really set back a talented playwright unnecessarily. Sometimes you may have to, but it's something you should take very seriously.

John Lahr: You know more when the play is not new. You know the history of the show, and you have more information to convey. You can think about the time the show was written in and how it speaks to us now. Take, for example, the recent Broadway revival of *The Pajama Game*. It just so happens that I saw the opening night performance of the original production in 1954 because Eddie Foy, Jr., was my godfather. I put that in my review of the revival, and I got a really interesting article out of it.

Michael Sommers: It's always thrilling to write about a new play and discover a new voice. I also love a lot of the old plays, and it's great to see new takes on them, like David Cromer's production of *Our Town*, where the kitchen suddenly materialized on Emily's birthday. After all that stark nothingness, you had the real thing, and you experienced it with Emily. That was a wonderful surprise.

Peter Marks: With a revival, you're rendering a different level of judgment. It's all about the interpretation and what the director is bringing to the work and why. Why are they doing this play? Does it have something to do with events outside the play? Does the director have a personal relationship with the play? Is it something about the audience's love of this play, where they can't seem to get enough of it? It's also about discovering things about the play you haven't seen before.

I think the most recent revival of *A Raisin in the Sun* told me something I didn't know about the play. A lot of people objected to Denzel Washington being too old to play Walter Lee, which was a legitimate concern. Nevertheless, I found the sourness in the production—the way the family members were getting on each other's nerves—to be refreshing. There was a sense of what living in that environment for so long does to people, especially to Walter Lee. At least in my experience of the play, that felt new.

Terry Teachout: With a revival, it's easier to separate the show from the way it's being performed. When I review a show by a regional company that I'm unfamiliar with, I always see a revival of a play that I've seen before because I want to be able to see the company and not the play. The first time you see a play or musical, the work is coming at you in a package that is very difficult to tease apart. You're being hit by a total experience. It's only when you come back to it again that you can start to analyze what you are seeing in a clearer, cooler way.

Thom Geier: Oftentimes, it requires less legwork and fewer mental contortions to review a new show because it's being presented fresh. You have less baggage to bring to it. But there's something kind of exciting about both processes. You don't want to be the guy who got the galley of *Ulysses* in advance and didn't get it.

Chris Jones: For me, whether or not a show is finished is a bigger distinction than a play versus a revival. It's partly the result of working in Chicago, where a lot of shows are having their out-of-town tryouts and are clearly not finished. It could be on its way somewhere else. If that's the case, I try to reflect that.

If you were to hold me underwater to get me to confess to a bias, the one I would most readily admit to is a bias for new work or a radically interesting revival. That's just a result of going to the theater every night. With the Denzel Washington revival of *A Raisin in the Sun*, there was nothing in it that was inherently interesting to me. I always have great respect for a new show, for something made out of whole cloth. There is a great risk there, and there is a great striving. When it is serious—and by serious, I mean it is purported to be about life as it is lived—I have even more respect for it. That doesn't mean I'm going to like it, but I do respect it.

Christine Dolen: It's exciting if a piece is having its world premiere at a theater in your area. If the show lives on, your work will become part of the archives. You don't know exactly what you're going to see. It can be great, or it can be awful, and that's exciting. New plays and musicals still have room for improvement when they get their first productions. You can be a little more pointed in your comments about what works and what doesn't work because that can help the creators. If it's premiering as part of the National New Play Network, that can factor into what the creators do during the show's second or third production. It's not my function to be a dramaturg, but I think I can make some helpful observations.

Frank Rizzo: There's a difference between covering the world premiere of a brand-new show and the umpteenth revival of *Hedda Gabler*. I'm blessed to be able to cover so much new work in Connecticut and New England. The greatest joy of my life is to be among the first to write about something that is terrific. One of the first reviews I wrote for *Variety* was the world premiere of *The 25th Annual Putnam County Spelling Bee* in the Berkshires. It was done in a junior high school gym, and I just let loose with a rave. It was a very thoughtful rave, but a rave nonetheless, essentially saying, "This is terrific, and here is why it's terrific." It's great to be part of the process of discovering new work and feel like you're helping to build and shape a show. Whether they take your advice or not is up to whoever is producing or writing the show.

Charles Isherwood: New plays can be very hard to judge. Some plays reveal themselves over time and ferment in your mind. They offer more food for thought than you might think at first blush. When I saw Suzan-Lori Parks's drama *Topdog/Underdog* Off Broadway, I found serious fault with it. I felt like it was overwritten and didn't really work well onstage. But when it moved to Broadway, I saw a lot more in the play. Sometimes you're a little bit chagrined that you didn't find that the first time. Everyone will have that experience sometime in their career. Critics will respond strongly, whether in a negative or positive way, to a play, and they'll come back to it later on and think, Oh boy, I got that one wrong. I remember a critic admitting he called a Sarah Kane play wrong way back, when he was repulsed by it, and now he sees that it has serious integrity.

MATT WINDMAN: *How do you go about evaluating a new play or musical?*

John Simon: I respond as much as I possibly can intellectually and emotionally. I pay as much attention as I can. And then I write.

Charles Isherwood: You respond to the work onstage. I don't think it's fair to include any sort of prejudgment based on a writer's prior work in your assessment of the new work. It's inevitable that you're going to, and sometimes that works in a playwright's favor. If you don't happen to have liked a playwright's previous work, and you finally come upon a play that you do like, you might be more enthusiastic.

Ben Brantley: Is it consistent on its own terms? You first judge a play by what it aspires to do, and how much it adheres to its own aspirations and follows them through. That's rarer than you think. I give anything points for doing what it sets out to do with some clarity and accessibility. Then you start to measure by degree of ambition. How high has the creator set the bar?

David Sheward: I look for credibility on the piece's own terms. In other words, it can be fantastic and absurd, but it has to be consistent within itself and in its own world.

John Lahr: Anyone who talks about standards is a fool. There is no agreed-upon standard. A standard is an aesthetic or a taste that has evolved over time. That's all it is. John Simon is always going on about his standards. But if you look at the shows he liked and those he didn't like, you'll find that his standards tend to overlook major work and praise a lot of terrible shows. Such are his standards.

Adam Feldman: I don't have a checklist. I don't believe in that kind of approach. If I bring in a set of criteria, I'm not doing my job. I try to look at what is being done in the show and how well it's being done. It's very different from show to show. A big, glitzy, come-have-a-good-time kind of show is trying to do something very different from a nonlinear, downtown, experimental, brainy, Off Off Broadway show.

Alexis Soloski: I like the words to sound like words that the people in the play could indeed speak.

David Cote: The language is the first thing I notice. If it's a strongly visual play or a sound-intensive play, I might notice that first. But generally, you are listening to the dialogue. You are listening to how people speak and who these people are. In terms of standards, you have to see what world it's trying to build around you. Is it realistic? Are they sitting in a coffee shop, speaking lines you can imagine people say to each other? If it's more stylized, if they use highly poetic language, that's exciting. You see how it plays out. Even if a play is dealing with family secrets in a realistic setting, that can still be incredibly gripping and revelatory. On the other hand, there are countless other dysfunctional family dramas that are boring, and I hate watching them.

Steven Suskin: I want to be excited by the material. When I go to the theater, there's nothing I like more than to be surprised and delighted by something unexpected.

Don Aucoin: First and foremost, I look for quality. Second, I look for originality. Related to that, I ask whether it expands any boundaries. I also look for evidence of good faith or bad faith. I recently wrote a scathing review of the Queen jukebox musical *We Will Rock You* because it seemed like its only intent was to make the cash register ring. That sort of thing angers me because it's taking up cultural space that could be devoted to other work.

Zachary Stewart: I begin every review by asking myself two questions: (1) What did I see/hear/smell/touch/taste? (2) How does it make me feel? Then I attempt to go about answering how the artist did that and why it is significant (if it is at all). This last part is the most challenging, but also the most important part. No one cares about your feelings, so you have to wrap them in bacon to make them interesting for the readers.

Elisabeth Vincentelli: It's not like I have a laundry list of things I'm looking for, but it has to say something in a way that keeps me engaged and surprises me. It has to have a point of view. And there has to be a certain kind of urgency. There's got to be something that the playwright is dying to say. I have very little patience with all those super nice and safe plays. I call them "couch plays" because there's always a couch in the middle of the stage.

Frank Rizzo: I'm a blank slate. I want the playwright to take me where he or she wants to go.

Elysa Gardner: There are plays I've been impressed with but didn't love. There have also been plays I loved where I was willing to overlook a lot of flaws. That goes for musicals as well. It can be greater than or less than the sum of its parts. It is the sum, the feeling, the impression that you walk away with. I look for a visceral connection. If something is trying really hard to impress me, I get a little put off by that. In fact, that's my biggest problem with a lot of shows: this self-conscious cleverness, where you feel like the writer is saying, "Get it?" And I just want to say, "I get it. Stop! Engage me emotionally." That's what I look for because that's the hardest thing to do: risk sentimentality and achieve something that transcends it. That, to me, is the highest achievement for an artist.

Helen Shaw: I look for effectiveness, truthfulness, ambition, ferocity, technique, lyricism, control of image, avoidance of cliché, complexity of thinking—but you don't walk in with a set of criteria. You walk in with an alert, rested, open brain. In your criticism, you're just reflecting on what you saw.

Howard Shapiro: The standards have to change depending on the show. I expect one thing on Broadway, and I expect a completely different thing from a theater company with a budget of $40,000, but I expect them both to work within the confines of what they're doing. If I go to the Fringe Festival, I don't expect the kind of production that I'm going to get from Scott Rudin on Broadway. On the other hand, if I go to a Scott Rudin production, I expect it to be really polished. Whatever it is, I expect it to work, and I should be able to point out why it does or doesn't work.

Michael Portantiere: There is good storytelling, and there is bad storytelling. There are certain things that go into that, but it's hard to pinpoint by just making general statements. I can see a specific show and then tell you why I think the storytelling is good or not. Consistency of the characters, consistency of tone, avoidance of vulgarity for vulgarity's sake: those all make for good theater.

Michael Schulman: Everything belongs to a genre. I try to determine what genre a playwright is working in, or responding to, or trying to transcend or undermine. Subversiveness always appeals to me, whether it's aesthetic or political subversiveness. What bothers me most is laziness and using clichés.

Richard Ouzounian: I try to determine what the play is trying to do, and whether it succeeds at what it's trying to do on its own terms. I don't ask, "Is this the kind of play I would have written?" or "Is it the kind of play I enjoy?" Instead, I ask, "What is it trying to do, and how well does it do that?"

Roma Torre: My criteria for determining what's good or not is basically four-fold. A: Did it accomplish what the creators set out to achieve? B: Did it make me feel something? C: Did it enlighten me at all? D: Was I entertained? If you have three out of those four, I would say it's a successful piece of work.

Perez Hilton: I like razzle-dazzle. That doesn't always mean big sets and production values and all that jazz. A show like *Once* has lots of razzle-dazzle, though some could consider it intimate by Broadway standards. *Rocky* had a lot of razzle-dazzle. It entertained me, even if the music was uninspired. I love being excited. There is nothing worse than a by-the-books musical, like the most recent Broadway revival of *Annie*.

Marilyn Stasio: What is it about? What is the playwright after? What is he trying to say? What are we supposed to see? What's the theme? What's the point? It's important to this writer, so it's important that I identify it and figure it out. I'm always hoping to find something of real value. I hope that the playwright is writing something of importance about a significant subject, and that he or she is doing it in an original way. Isn't that what we hope every time we go to the theater?

Michael Riedel: I like them to be good. You know: good score, good script, good acting. I don't want them to be preachy, boring, or self-important. I shouldn't fall asleep 10 minutes into it. Fundamentally, it has to be engaging. It can be an engaging drama, an engaging comedy, an engaging thriller. It's got to create a world that you want to enter. It's got to have characters you want to follow.

Peter Marks: I look for interesting things I've never heard before. I'm looking for a unique way of telling a story. I'm looking for truth expressed in a novel way. I look at the theme of the play and whether it's topical, or if it reveals a topic in a new way. I look at whether a character has been created that I identify with in some way. I look for freshness. Considering how so many plays are muddled, clarity, in and of itself, can be a tremendous selling point.

Ronni Reich: The clarity of the story. The integrity of the structure. How things flow. How cohesive everything is. How well-drawn the characters are. The tone of the play. How the production fits with the text. How the language is used. Whether it makes for a compelling whole. I fully recognize that a lot of these areas, if not all of them, are subjective.

Terry Teachout: I try to come clean when the lights go down. My head empties out, and I'm present for the next two and a half hours and completely receptive. I ask myself, What is the playwright trying to do? Then I ask, Why is the playwright doing this? Above all, I want to experience it in the same way the audience does. At some point in the evening, my feelings come into focus. Moss Hart said that during the first 15 minutes, an audience is receptive and open and expecting to have a good time. After that, the door closes, and they're either with it or not. I've seen it happen a thousand times, where suddenly the door shuts and the audience decides it is not having a good time.

I seldom leave a show unsure of what I've seen. Generally, when I get home, I have a clear sense of how I felt about what I saw. But if I don't have a clear sense of what I've seen, that too is a statement on the work. As far as standards go, the yard stick is whether I had a good time with the work— with good being defined very broadly. Was I never bored? Was I thrilled? Did I cry? Did I think about it after the fact? I can then start asking other questions and dissecting craft.

MATT WINDMAN: *How do you evaluate a piece of avant-garde or experimental theater?*

Charles Isherwood: Some of the hardest theater to write about is non-narrative. You have to find other ways of approaching it. You can talk about it more as an experience. It's good for a writer to have to stretch and see different kinds of theater. Certain critics respond to certain artists more than others. Ben Brantley is a huge fan of Richard Foreman. It's probably better to read Ben's review of a Richard Foreman show than to actually see it.

Note: Avant-garde writer-director-auteur Richard Foreman founded and ran the Ontological-Hysteric Theater in the East Village from 1968 to 2010. I attended about a dozen of his chaotic, performance art-style productions—none of which I understood or enjoyed. However, I am especially thankful to Mr. Foreman because one day in 2004, having just seen a show of his the night before, I pitched an interview with him to an editor I had just met—and that turned out to be my very first article in amNewYork. A few months later, I called up that same editor and inquired about becoming a summer intern at the paper.

David Cote: If it is abstract, nonlinear, or multimedia-based, you have to find new ways to describe it. There is no notational language for avant-garde performance. We have no popular vocabulary or shorthand for deconstruction, intertextuality, or metatheatricality. You can simply describe what is happening, or you can try to interpret it.

Frank Rizzo: I remember when I saw a play by Will Eno for the first time. His use of language is so unusual, beautiful, and quirky, but sometimes it's really hard to fathom. It was a really challenging review to write. I didn't know what to make of it, other than that I loved it. I had to articulate why I thought it was wonderful when I didn't know just yet why it was so wonderful. I really had to think that one through.

Helen Shaw: I find it very helpful to turn deeply inward.

Alexis Soloski: In the case of more experimental work, it can be incredibly stylized, but it should be appropriate to the world of the play. I look for a complete vision of the world, whether it's naturalistic or heavily abstracted. I look for the unity of the effort.

Zachary Stewart: A critic can note the theatrical pedigree of an experimental work (and I often do), but that usually has little bearing on a work's ability to connect with an audience beyond a certain snob appeal.

MATT WINDMAN: *Should ticket price be taken into consideration in a review?*

Charles Isherwood: I don't see how a critic can take ticket price into consideration. Do you start grading on a curve? If a ticket to a play is only $20 and you moderately enjoyed it, do you therefore scale up your enthusiasm because it's cheap? If it's an exceptional case, like when they were charging whatever the hell they were charging for *Young Frankenstein*, you can take note of the ticket price in a reportorial context. I don't think the expense of a ticket has ever influenced my opinion. Your opinion is what it is. The fact is that we don't pay for any of our tickets. Very often, we're not even aware of the ticket price. We just know that Broadway is expensive and Off Broadway is slightly less expensive.

Elisabeth Vincentelli: I try to keep it in mind. I mentioned the ticket price in a review I just filed of *The Muscles in Our Toes*, an Off Broadway production by Labyrinth Theater Company. It wasn't a good show, but there were interesting things about it, there was a really great performance in it, and the tickets were only $20 each. So I thought, Do you want to see a really great performance in a not-very-good show for $20? A show like that could be interesting, especially if the subject speaks to you, so I thought the price was relevant.

Ticket price also becomes a concern when you get into the really expensive stuff. It's like $160 a ticket on Broadway now—and that's just for a regular seat, not even for a premium ticket. I brought the price up when Lincoln Center Festival sold tickets to Genet's *The Maids* with Cate Blanchett for $360.

Frank Scheck: I try not to let price be too influential. But if we're talking a big Broadway musical and it's bad, I might be a little more inclined to warn people against it.

Zachary Stewart: A lot of shows on Broadway are fun, but not $150 worth of fun.

Leonard Jacobs: I don't think ticket price has anything to do with anything. I know that a lot of people don't necessarily agree with me on this point, and they're all wrong. Paying $100 for a ticket probably doesn't mean all that much to someone who's making $250,000 a year. It's different for someone making $30,000 a year as a temp. But who am I to decide whether a show is worth the money or not? Someone making just $30,000 a year may think a particular show is the most amazing thing in the history of the world, and that it's worth eating ramen noodles for weeks to save up the money to see it.

Michael Dale: The creative artists don't determine the ticket price, so their work shouldn't be held responsible for it.

Peter Filichia: Ticket price absolutely should be taken into consideration. Many in our society think, If I'm paying this much, I should get so much entertainment for that money.

Terry Teachout: I have said on occasion, "This really wasn't worth a hundred dollars." But since the price of a ticket is a given, I'm not sure it makes a whole lot of sense to talk about it in a review.

MATT WINDMAN: *What do you look for from actors?*

Hilton Als: Truth, humor, and heart.
Michael Dale: Details, details, details.
Adam Feldman: Acting is very hard to define. It's like the Supreme

Court on pornography: "You know it when you see it." It involves the extent to which the actor can transform himself or herself while also being alert to how that transformation plays out in front of an audience. Some actors make the mistake of being overly interior, of not finding successful ways to communicate their feelings to an audience in a theatrical way. And there are actors who make the other kind of mistake, where it looks too stagey, and you don't get a sense of the investment that will bring you along as an audience member into sharing their world. You only get the exterior signs of that investment.

For me, the most exciting performances tend to be the ones in which the actor is making strong and smart choices that illuminate the character and is taking risks with those choices. Strong choices are risky because if you fail, you fail big. A lot of very bad acting comes from big choices that aren't pulled off. But when a big choice is pulled off, it's genuinely exciting. As an audience member, there's a sense of danger involved. The bigger the risk, the more potentially rewarding it can be.

Marilyn Stasio: How do you judge an actor? You can't see their process, so you look for them in the characters they play. They have to understand their characters so well that it feels natural to be in their skins. I'm thinking of Ian McKellen and Patrick Stewart in *Waiting for Godot*. They were so into those characters. They understood them. They'd been living with them. They loved them. They responded to them. They were not acting the characters. They were thoroughly in their skin. That's the best kind of acting.

John Simon: It is very hard to answer that. It's like asking what you consider poetry—although perhaps it's easier with poetry. There are some obvious things. I like good elocution. That's what's so wonderful about British actors when they do Shakespeare—not so much when they do other work. They have the most beautiful diction. Every syllable comes off crisp and unmistakable. When American actors do Shakespeare, it often gets murmured and mumbled.

It's also important to know how to move. British actors spend a lot of time learning how to move properly. I don't think American actors spend such time. Of course, if an actor is playing a lowdown, Bowery bum, he wouldn't want to move as if he was playing King Lear, but elegant movement is a lovely thing to have.

I also think looks matter a lot, especially for actresses, and even for actors. As you know, this is where I get attacked. You're sort of in love with heterosexual actors or actresses. You want them to be charming or beautiful or delightful in one way or another. They don't necessarily have to be beautiful, although it helps. You want them to have some kind of physical presence which is pleasing. A good-looking person can always play down his or her looks, but a bad-looking person cannot play up his or her bad looks. This gets people riled up, I guess because most people are insecure about their own looks. They somehow think that you, as a critic, are reviewing something that they absolutely don't have, so therefore it should not matter. I would not judge people at a cocktail party the way I do in a play, but that is something they do not understand.

Michael Portantiere: I don't think it's appropriate to comment on an actor's appearance unless it has something to do with the actor's specific role. One should be very careful when suggesting that a person is not attractive enough or too heavy for a role. Early on, I made some mistakes in that way.

Helen Shaw: There are a few things that jump out, like if someone can't project or perform in a big house, but most of the time you are looking at people living in roles.

Zachary Stewart: I look for actors to convey the playwright's work in a clear, compelling, and truthful way.

Chris Jones: I look for truth and vulnerability. Over the years, I've found that the most interesting actors are vulnerable. Many famous actors are incapable of vulnerability. Can you show me how you really are? Can you show me how life really is? In Chicago, ensemble acting is privileged in a big way. I've come to greatly admire the ability to be subsumed by a role and disappear into an ensemble.

Perez Hilton: I look for clear, discernible talent—where you look at a person onstage and say, "Wow, they're so talented."

Ben Brantley: Above all, I look for freshness in acting, no matter what kind of acting it is, and how much it steers away from clichés. If it's a naturalistic play, I look for how much real emotional conviction there is, and how much you feel in the moment with the actor. Of course, a lot of it has to do with casting.

Michael Sommers: I'd like to be able to hear what they're saying and see what they're doing. Besides that, I want clarity.

Alexis Soloski: Acting is flexible. I've seen terrible performances that are incredibly moving. Sometimes there is a great poetry from a bad actor, from the chasm between what the actor performs and what the role requires. You see the role in incredibly stark relief when the actor is failing so miserably. I certainly enjoy when there is a close mimetic relationship between the actor and the character. But when there is no relationship at all, that can be fascinating, too. As a failed actor, I'm very impressed by—and jealous of—actors who have remarkable emotional access.

Christine Dolen: I watch the choices the actor makes and figure out whether they're effective in the context of the play. If it's an actor I've seen over and over again, and they're doing the kind of the same performance they usually do (no matter what the play is), they should be called out on it.

David Cote: I look for spontaneity—somebody who makes you forget that they are speaking lines in a theater. I look for someone who has charisma, who has magnetism, who is mysterious. I like people who are unique and who achieve the greatest effects with the greatest economy of movement and vocal intensity.

David Sheward: In the theater, you need to have this combination of presentation and representation. You have to be believable, but also larger-than-life to a certain extent. You need to have both in balance. It also depends on the role. If it's a musical, broadness is acceptable. The recent *Twelfth Night* and *Richard III* from London's Globe had amazing acting from Mark Rylance. He said the lines as if they had never been said before. All too often with Shakespeare and the other classics that have been done hundreds of times, you feel like the actors are just reciting the lines, particularly the very famous ones, and not really saying them because they are so familiar. But with Mark Rylance, it was like hearing those lines for the first time because of the way he delivered them.

Don Aucoin: Ideally, there should be a sort of reality to the performances. Does this actor really seem to understand his or her character? After seeing a performance, can I envision the character's life before and after he or she took the stage? If an actor or actress is performing Shakespeare, are they speaking Shakespeare's language as if it's everyday language? Does it flow naturally from their mouths, or are they declaiming it in an obviously stagy way?

Elisabeth Vincentelli: It depends on what's appropriate for the material. The acting has to be consistent with what the material requires or the director's vision. Sometimes I like a very naturalistic performance, and sometimes I like a very showy, hammy performance. I didn't care at all for Richard Nelson's *The Apple Family Plays* at the Public Theater. I thought they were completely overrated, but I really liked the super-naturalistic acting in them. At the other end of the spectrum, I can enjoy the acting in a stylized Robert Wilson production.

Michael Musto: I look for immersion in the character from moment to moment, and not just in the lines.

Richard Zoglin: I just want it to be true. Sometimes I feel like I'm watching actors who are more interested in getting a Tony nomination or a standing ovation, and are really overdoing it at the expense of the play. I much prefer good ensemble acting that is in the service of the play instead of the actor.

Rob Weinert-Kendt: I don't want to see acting. You know what I mean? I want to see behavior—and I'm not just talking about super-naturalistic behavior, like watching somebody on their couch. The best forms of acting that I've seen have a life of their own. The actors really look like they just walked into the theater, like that's who they really are. That's not acting—that's being. I'm thinking of Taylor Mac in *Good Person of Szechwan*. There was a reality to that performance that was right down to the bone. It was this crazy, Brechtian musical theater piece, but it was so emotionally true.

I think actors have the hardest job. They're the ones on the line, doing and embodying all those things. They're the ones we're staring at the whole time. I don't mind an actor who can do technically proficient things, like Tony Shalhoub in *Act One* and all of what he did in that performance, but it would all be for nothing if there wasn't an emotional truth behind it. I don't think anyone can fake that.

I think we're living in a golden age of acting, especially in musical theater. When I think about Kelli O'Hara, Sutton Foster, and Audra McDonald, I can't think of better actors in any era or any medium. They are not capable of having a false moment on stage, even if they're in stuff that's not all that great.

Roma Torre: Did the performer disappear into the role? Did I stop looking at the person as an actor, and start seeing that person as the character? They have to immerse themselves in the part. That's why so many of us were raving about Audra McDonald in *Lady Day at Emerson's Bar & Grill*. She totally became Billie Holiday. She morphed into that human being. The standard problem with a novice actor is indicating. But on Broadway, you rarely see that.

Steven Suskin: When you have a performance that grabs you, you're not looking at an actor. You're looking at the character. Take Mark Rylance in *Twelfth Night*. It wasn't just this very good actor playing this role. He was so real that you couldn't even start to analyze what he was doing.

Jesse Green: Are the actors contributing to a coherent vision, as set out by the director? I'm less interested in acting as display or entertainment in and of itself. I'm talking here in terms of a serious dramatic work. If you're reviewing a musical comedy or a one-person show, that's a different story, and the "performative" aspect of the performance—the showbiz, if you will—becomes more central.

With plays, I'm looking at the way the actor is able to contribute to the overall point of view of the text, as interpreted by the director. Second, but equally important, is how convincing they are in creating a character that I believe could exist, and who would behave in the way that the playwright intended. You often get a playwright asking for characters to do things that are not credible. Certain actors can make that work, and those are really exceptional performances. Generally, actors can't do more than the author allows them to do, but they need to do everything that the author allows them to do. I'm looking to see how well they walk that line.

I'm also looking at what everyone else looks at. What are their technical skills? If it's verse, how well do they seem to understand the poetry, as it's expressed in the way they speak it? In comedy, some people have an amazing ear that can split milliseconds and sense the temperature of the audience as it rises and falls to a micro-degree. But the first thing to look for is whether are they helping to tell the story that the playwright and the director want to tell.

John Lahr: You look at the way a performer meets the challenge of the part and expresses the feelings behind it. It also has to do with the boldness of the performer and their willingness to find a kind of vulnerability. When I worked on *Elaine Stritch at Liberty*, Elaine just thought she was being charming, but I knew that she was bringing all this baggage with her. She was being very brassy and funny. But behind all that, you could see this terrible, dark shadow, which is what made her so subliminal and compelling.

Michael Riedel: I look for charismatic people—people who come onstage and you think, Wow, that'd be a great person to hang out with. I don't just mean beautiful people. Nathan Lane is no Hugh Jackman. But when he comes onstage, you don't want to look anywhere else.

Peter Marks: Some actors have a level of presence and magnetism that's innate. They're just right for a part. In the original production of Warren Leight's play *Side Man*, Frank Wood played a very blank man who was kind of unknowable and enigmatic. It was a marvelous distillation of who that man was. I've noticed that in other performances of his. There is a kind of vacant quality that he brings. It's him. He's not a chameleon. Sometimes you find that an actor can transform himself or herself from play to play, and you admire the actor more the second time around because you realize how much work they've done to get to this other character. Sometimes it's also technique. It's a very specific skill to be able to plant yourself on a stage and take in both the audience and the reality you're in, and to make all those things seem natural.

When I saw Julia Roberts in *Three Days of Rain*, I thought she couldn't play a character. She just didn't have the skill set, and it was unfair to make her do it. Then you see someone like Laura Benanti, who knows how to use herself on a stage. I reviewed her back in the late 1990s when she replaced Rebecca Luker in the Broadway revival of *The Sound of Music*. She was a bit raw, but I noticed what was good about her. She's loosened up since then.

Ronni Reich: Is a person believable and captivating within a particular role? Do I have a sense that they are acting, and should I, depending on the type of work it is? Do they have the proper range, the proper qualities for the part, in the way they use their voice and body? What is the particular impression that they make? Some of it is charisma. Some of it is personality.... With Shakespeare, you look at the way the actor approaches the language and the nuances within it.

Terry Teachout: You want to be transported. You can see a certain kind of performance, and be constantly aware of the fact that it's a performance, but still be excited by it. There are other performances where the actor seems to vanish. It's a very mysterious thing. Even having done this for 11 years, and even after becoming involved in the craft of making theater, what I find most amazing and mysterious of all are the actors. They're the ones who put in the hardest labor. They're doing something that I can't do. I did my best when I was young, but I was never a very good actor. I marvel at good acting. I think we're supposed to be astonished by it. I would say that the average level of acting is better than the average level of playwriting.

MATT WINDMAN: *How do you capture an actor's performance in your writing?*

Zachary Stewart: It is difficult because the actor's craft is the most intangible of the theatrical arts, but I often mention a trait that is memorable in the performance (diction, posture, appearance, intensity).

Charles Isherwood: Walter Kerr was famous for being able to give these incredible "you are there" descriptions of performances, and that's something I strive after constantly. My colleague Ben Brantley can do that very well, too. It's about being able to retain the image in your head of a particular moment in an actor's performance. It's something that you keep challenging yourself to do better, knowing all the while that you're going to be defeated. The really exciting performances can't be captured in words. That's why theater can be such a powerful experience. It's only happening live for the people who are in the audience. You just do your best to capture it.

Ben Brantley: Ideally, what a critic wants to communicate is his or her visceral response to an individual performer. We all have very visceral responses to actors. We have visceral responses to people in general. It's almost like a social relationship that you develop over the course of two hours. You feel like you've gotten to know the person. Why are you fascinated by this person? What makes this person unique? What kind of physical sensations does this person produce in you?

David Cote: Sketching the essence of performance—like Al Hirschfeld in words—may be the hardest thing in theater criticism. I guess you can focus on a small detail of the face, body, or voice. I think it's about adjectives and extraordinary detail.

Alexis Soloski: I probably use too many adjectives and overuse words like "visceral," "spirited," and "poignant," but I have a pretty good sense memory from years of actor training. When I'm back at my desk, I try to remember how the performance made me feel, and I work backwards from there.

Frank Scheck: You have to feel your way through a performance and convey what the performance made you feel. It's a good test of your writing ability. You inevitably find yourself relying on stock phrases like "compelling," but sometimes a performance is so unusual that it does enable you to write about it in an interesting way. If there's a performance that's special enough, you try to honor that performance. It also gives you a hook for the review. Nathan Lane, when he was starting out, was a revelation. It was like what you imagine it was like to watch Bert Lahr. When someone excites you on that level, writing about them is fun.

Howard Shapiro: How do you describe the food you're being served and make it leap off the page into somebody's mouth? I often describe the way people act with a part of their body that may not be their voice: their eyes, their posture, what they relate by the way they cock their head, other stuff that strikes me. We are lucky to work in a language that has a really broad range of adjectives. At the end of the theater season, I sometimes sit back and say, "Okay, I've used up all my adjectives. I need a couple weeks off." And then I kind of regenerate.

Michael Schulman: Acting is much harder to talk about analytically than playwriting. Unfortunately, I don't feel like I have the space to do it in a meaningful way.

Peter Filichia: It's very hard to write about actors who aren't particularly distinctive. If they aren't distinctive, how can I write about them distinctively? I remember my girlfriend telling me, "You won't believe how many paragraphs Frank Rich wrote about Robert Lindsay in *Me and My Girl*." When I went to see the musical, I understood perfectly. That was one of the greatest performances I've ever seen in a musical. I would have had no trouble writing a few paragraphs on why he was so spectacular.

Steven Suskin: You can use a lot of words to describe a performance, but simply finding the right phrase is ideal. In my book *The Sound of Broadway Music*, I talk about how composer Jerry Bock played a score for a prospective orchestrator who said, "Well, I kind of hear elephants on tip-toe," and Jerry gave him the job. I try to come up with a picture in words that captures what I want to say.

Terry Teachout: Detail and metaphor. I try to create a word portrait of the actor's appearance. I think this is as close to writing about abstract music as a theater critic gets. There's no formula. It's the part that gives the review its color and life.

MATT WINDMAN: How do you evaluate direction?

Helen Shaw: We all tend to review a director on the basis of his most recent show, rather than the one we're actually looking at. We write the review we meant to write the time before.

Zachary Stewart: Directors coordinate the entire production, so I look for a cohesive vision for the work encompassing performance, design, and text.

Ben Brantley: You shouldn't be thinking about direction while you're watching a play. Direction should be seamless, unless the point is that it's meant to put a frame or quotation marks around things. You look for momentum, a kind of variation in tempo, a play that doesn't lag. You look for a sense that the director has served her or his cast well, that they haven't hung the actors out to dry, that the director steered them from making mistakes, which is sometimes hard when the actors are big stars.

Charles Isherwood: Sometimes the best direction is direction that you don't notice. Obviously, the director is in control of shaping all of the performances onstage to some degree. The adage that "90 percent of directing is good casting" is not wholly true. But even if it is, the director is the one doing the casting. His responsiveness to the text, and his way of communicating what he feels about the text, can be read in all of the performances onstage to some degree.

I'm sure some directors get very frustrated if they don't get enough credit, or if they're blamed for certain things, but critics are not in the rehearsal room. We don't know who made what choice. Something may be an actor's choice, or maybe it was made in collaboration with the director. You don't know, so you try your best. It's easier with classic plays since you've probably seen other productions. Sometimes what a director's trying to do is glaringly apparent, especially if you go to Europe.

Chris Jones: There are directors who are able to create, who catch every detail of a play, who are not lazy, who pay attention to specifics, who have a strong a point of view, who create an arc that makes an evening feel complete (even if the play itself has no apparent arc at all), who get out of the way of their fellow artists.

Christine Dolen: You can tell what the director did from the overall tenor and style of a production. He or she has to sign off on what everyone onstage is doing.

David Cote: I look for a director who zeros in on what the play is about, who works with the play, who brings clarity. I also look for directors who can blow the dust off classics.

David Sheward: Direction is a combination of showmanship, strength of vision, and knowing when to pull back. Sometimes the direction calls attention to itself. Sometimes that works, and sometimes it doesn't. It depends on what's necessary for the play.

Elisabeth Vincentelli: If you were to talk to the director before you review their show about what they're doing, you'd be reviewing their intentions or their private personalities. The director would say, "Well, what I'm really trying to do is this and that," but that's not what you're reviewing. You're reviewing the results onstage. You're not reviewing what's in their head. You're reviewing what they've accomplished, what's onstage. Sometimes it's very clear what they're trying to do and what their aim is. Other times, you have no idea what they're trying to do. You're reviewing something that's confused and aimless, and you are not in the business of trying to read minds.

As a critic, you're not reviewing the creative process. That's not possible. You're reporting on the result. Sometimes that's unfair because they didn't have the money, or they didn't have the time, or someone made them work with a star they didn't want to work with, but that's tough. People don't buy tickets with an asterisk saying, "We really tried, but this is what we ended up with."

My views on direction are very much influenced by having grown up in France. I saw Ingmar Bergman's *King Lear* when I was 19 or 20 years old in Paris, and it was a shock to my system. I tend to really enjoy a European-style production. I am very pro-director. I think directors need to be very hands-on and creative. I really think the director is as important as the author. In the United States, critics tend to side with the author. The respect of the author takes precedence here, and directors tend to be a little too reverent of the material. I like to see directors go at a text very forcefully, and I think that's a European approach. I often think American directors don't go far enough in tackling a classic text. I wish they would be a little bit more inventive. British directors can be quite inventive. But at the same time, I am very unimpressed by the Anglophilia that runs rampant in New York theater circles. It's insane.

What's very important are pure aesthetics. A show has to look good. I like directors who are aware of the spatial relationship on the stage and play with that. Very often, American directors are terrible at that, and have no eye for spatial composition. That's very important because the director controls the audience's attention. They have to direct us. We have to be total puppets in the director's hands. It's not just about putting a bunch of people onstage and blocking them. They have to completely control us. The directors that I admire are the ones that completely control both our gaze and our thought process.

When Ingmar Bergman did a show, he never wanted to have surtitles. He insisted on having simultaneous translations into English. You'd get those headphones with a person speaking the translation in your ear from the Swedish in monotone, without any inflections. Bergman didn't want us to look at surtitles. He wanted to control the audience's gaze the entire time, so the lesser evil for him was the headphones.

Howard Shapiro: Pacing is important. I think of a director as the conductor of a train. The director is moving something at the speed that he sees fit. The director also holds the keys to interpretation. A performance may be wonderful, but the interpretation, the way the story's going to be told, has to be approved by the director.

John Simon: What you want is for the play come as alive as it possibly can, by whatever means. In some cases, it means enabling the actors to come across as human beings. In other cases, when it's something like *Macbeth*, it's getting the best kind of diction out of the actors, the best kind of movement, the most elevated style. In comedy, it can mean helping the actors get the most possible laughs. In tragedy, it might be getting the most possible tears—not actual tears, but a kind of mental tears. It's doing the utmost for to keep the play alive.

It also means not losing the sympathy of the actors whom you're directing. The demanding, arrogant, dictatorial director doesn't really care about how the actors feel about him or her. That's not a good thing. Alfred Hitchcock didn't give a damn about what actors thought of him, but it truly works better if it's a happy family.

Michael Musto: I look for the vision of the director, and whether it's an appropriate way to interpret the material, like if some new light was brought to familiar material, but not in a way that just arbitrarily reimagines it. I feel like too many critics automatically applaud anything that's reimagined.

Michael Schulman: Critics often say things like "ably-directed" or "well-directed" or "capably-directed," but what does that mean? Sometimes direction is an invisible art. I would say that the way to analyze whether a director is successful is to determine whether something coheres—whether there is stylistic coherence. Are all of the actors in the same play?

Rob Weinert-Kendt: The director has the job of keeping and guiding our attention. I feel like the director is directing the audience. They're directing where our attention goes, like whether our attention should be on the set, or the performances, or something outside the theater that we need to be thinking about.

Roma Torre: Did I notice the direction? If I noticed the direction, then it didn't work. As soon as I start fidgeting in my seat, I'm aware of the direction. If I can sit through a play without looking at my watch, looking around, thinking about where I am, or losing interest in the thing, then I know the direction worked. But there's a caveat to all that. Some shows feature bravura direction that does stand out, but in a way that enhances the experience. I'm thinking of shows like *Once*, *The Curious Incident of the Dog in the Night-Time* and *Peter and the Starcatcher*.

Steven Suskin: I don't look for anything from direction. I think that a good director is invisible. If you're paying attention to what the director does, you're missing the show. If all the elements—the text, the performances, the design—work exceptionally well, then credit the director.

Adam Feldman: I look for smart choices. It's certainly easier when you're watching a revival because you have something to compare the production to, so the director's choices—in the physical staging, the character relationships, and the dynamics and shape of the play—are easier to evaluate. In comparing the roles of the director and actor, I have a rule of thumb: If the actor's choice is wrong (if the actor is doing a good job in communicating an interpretation, but the interpretation itself is misguided), then it's the director's fault. On the other hand, if the choice or interpretation is right but the actor isn't pulling it off, then it's the actor's fault.

John Lahr: What you're looking for is innovation, energy, and critical intelligence. There's such a difference when you see a play directed by someone like Mike Nichols. Whether it's a comedy or a drama, there's a sharpness to the decisions that the actors make moment to moment, and in the way they interact. You know you're in the presence of a very intelligent guy. The same goes for someone like Michael Mayer or George C. Wolfe. You can see it. You're looking at a kind of geometry.

Matthew Murray: What is the relationship of the staging to the script? Is it in harmony with it, or is something off? Does it seem like the director is trying to fix the script or make the director the star, or is the director truly trying to tell the story of the script in the best way possible? Are all the various elements of the show of a single, cohesive piece? Are the actors all doing the same show? If not, why aren't they? It's almost never because there's something wrong with the actors.

In some cases, it's really easy to see what the director imposes on the piece. Take a look at the musical stagings of John Doyle, and you'll see a director who is dictatorial in assuring that everything molds to his vision—regardless of whether or not it's appropriate for the score and libretto. Almost no one else working today is that easy. But with time, experience, and exposure to lots of work, you can get to the point where you can generally discern where the director's responsibility ends and the other contributors' responsibility begins.

Marilyn Stasio: The director has so many things to do. They're responsible for everything. For example, the Broadway production of the musical *Violet* had a terrible set. You can blame the set designer for that, but I blame the director because the director let that happen. Everything is the director's job. It's a hell of a job.

Peter Marks: First of all, I look at the visual sense. Some directors are very good visually. When I see a production of theirs, I know they're going to have a really interesting visual concept.

Ronni Reich: I pay attention to the overall effectiveness of a production: whether the pacing feels right, whether the characterizations are convincing, whether the styles in which the actors portray the characters are a part of a cohesive whole. If it's a revival, I consider whether the liberties that have been taken make sense or add something fresh or vital to the production. What kind of creativity or imagination are we seeing from this director? Do the performers seem inspired?

Terry Teachout: If the work itself is good, I want the director to serve the work and not get in the way of it. There are a lot of different ways to serve the work. I think that David Cromer's great genius—and I use that word very deliberately—is that his productions are transparent. They come through clearly, yet they have a poetic and personal stamp that's very unusual. Interventional directors can be exciting, and I'm always willing to like the show that I'm seeing rather than see another show. But all things being equal, I prefer the transparent director to the interventional director.

Thom Geier: Bad direction stands out more easily. But if you are enjoying something and loving the pace of it, you can assume that the director had a hand in honing it into a clockwork production. If something is lethargic and slow, and if all the actors are lined up like elementary school children at a pageant and being shuffled about in the most awkward way, you can probably assume that the director did not effectively block it.

MATT WINDMAN: How do you evaluate design elements like scenery, costumes, and lighting?

Alexis Soloski: It's all about achieving the world that the playwright and the director dream up.

Michael Dale: I'll almost always give a description of the set because the visual usually gives the quickest indication of what the playwright and director have in mind. The other design elements (and I'd include orchestrations here) get a mention if they stand out in a way that interprets the material.

Zachary Stewart: Every design element is a deliberate choice. Does it further the story the playwright is telling? Does it add to the mood the director is fostering? Unlike acting, this can be achieved through tangible examples of physical craft.

Charles Isherwood: I don't write a lot about the technical aspects of a show. You try to describe the lighting, the sets, and the costumes in pretty straightforward terms. Hopefully, you can make an intelligent comment on how they add to the effectiveness of the play.

Chris Jones: Design is very interesting because it varies more than anything else. It's the most driven by budgetary concerns and physical concerns. I look for revealing, multilayered designs that keep revealing more over the course of the evening. I was at a play the other day that had a simple design. It was set in an elementary school classroom. At the end of the show I didn't leave. I just looked again at the set because I was seeing things in the design that were explications of things in the play that I missed. You know the Rococo idea of a painting that's in motion constantly? I think the best designs, even the ones that don't move at all, are constantly in motion and revealing things about the play. They can be very simple and still do that.

Elysa Gardner: If you're reviewing a show that is essentially a spectacle, you have to talk about the sets and costumes. But if you're reviewing a production of *Who's Afraid of Virginia Woolf?* and you only have 450 words, you're not going to want to spend an awful lot of time talking about the costumes and scenery, although they could be relevant.

Frank Scheck: If something strikes you in a particular way, you should acknowledge it, but you shouldn't pretend to be an expert either. My knowledge of design is essentially that of a layperson. I don't have technical knowledge in any of those fields.

Terry Teachout: They're relevant when they're salient. They should be mentioned when they stand out, but there are productions in which everything comes together into such an organic whole that you really can't tease the elements apart, especially with lighting. This is particularly true of naturalistic drama. I find that most critics don't write often enough, or well enough, about incidental music. They tend not to notice how lighting contributes to the effect of a performance. Scenery is the easiest to write about, though critics often make the mistake of assuming that the responsibilities of the director and the set designer are separate. That's usually not the way it works.

Thom Geier: If the design calls attention to itself, it had better serve the overall function and message of the production. It does not need to call attention to itself in order to be effective.

MATT WINDMAN: How do you determine who from a production deserves praise or blame?

Chris Jones: One of the hardest critical jobs is the correct appropriation of praise and blame. Did this actor do this? Was it a directing choice? Did this flow from the play? Was the director absolutely doing that? A critic does not see the production process. To some degree, the critic is trying to imbue the process. Experience helps because you get to know what people can do. If you've seen an actor do lousy work for the last five years, and suddenly he turns in a brilliant performance, the director probably had something to do with it. Similarly, if you see a very capable actor at sea, you can pretty much discern that he was misdirected. If you've seen a play five times before, and have seen it done brilliantly at least once, you know what the play can be. Experience and the ability to have comparatives are the only ways to really get at that, unless you follow gossip, which I mostly don't, though occasionally some reaches my ears.

Helen Shaw: As theater critics, we'll be sitting there, looking at something, trying to figure out what the director did and what is on the page, and that's really guesswork. However, the more experience you have watching shows being constructed, the more those guesses tend to land.

Don Aucoin: If an actor does something that's jarring and makes no sense, you find yourself thinking, Was that the director's decision? Was the actor going rogue? What happened there? If I'm not sure, I'll write in my review that "an actor has either chosen or been directed to do such-and-such." In the interest of fairness, you have to air on the side of caution. You might blame the director for a certain bit of business and later learn that the script has stage directions that called for it.

Zachary Stewart: It's usually easy to tell which element of a production is jumping out and demanding attention. Whether or not that attention is adding or detracting from a production is also fairly obvious.

David Cote: Critics see a show one night. They have no knowledge of the chain of events leading up to that one night. We don't know who made what decision. You don't know who had the "muscle" in the rehearsal room. When I see a critic try to mind-read while reviewing a show, I think it's overreaching. Assigning motives is really tricky stuff. It helps to read the script. That way, you can see if they followed it. If you feel the director fumbled the play, you need to explain why they fumbled it in an articulate way. If you make an argument, you have to get to the bottom of it. A good review always has an argument behind it.

Michael Portantiere: I think that I can, to a large degree, separate the text from the direction while the play is happening. Separating the direction from the acting can be much more difficult. But overall, if a show doesn't seem to be well-directed in terms of blocking or focus, or if the performances are widely variable in quality, those would seem to be faults of the director.

Elysa Gardner: When considering acting and directing separately, it's a big challenge to determine where the director came into it. In the last production of *Gypsy*, you very clearly felt the presence of Arthur Laurents as the director. It was impossible not to talk about him. That was very much his vision and his production.

John Lahr: In the *New York Times*, you'll see a scenic designer get criticized for a set, but the critic doesn't understand that the set that they're criticizing is an agreement between the director and the set designer. The set designer doesn't go off and say, "Here's your set. Stuff it." They don't know how the things that they're writing about were arrived at.

Peter Marks: I think that we underestimate the contributions of the director and overstress the writer, especially with new plays. It's almost an unfair pressure we put on writers because directors can ruin a new play. Very often, we get it wrong. As writers, our default is to blame the writer. Writing is the easiest for us to understand. It's the process that is the most like our own.

Sometimes we miss what the director is doing. It takes a lot of analysis. Sometimes you just don't have the time to figure out where the gap is between what the words are and how they were expressed. If you talk to directors, they'll say that 90 percent of their job is in the casting. If you take them at their word, you could say that part of the reason a play didn't work is because there was no chemistry between the actors.

There's a lot of guesswork involved. I've had situations where I've praised the choreography of a show, and then the director will then write to me and say, "I did that." And I'll say, "Well, how am I supposed to know that if there's a choreographer? They were dancing. Why did you have a choreographer then?"

Howard Shapiro: That's very hard to do, though I think that there are ways to finesse it. For instance, I didn't like Jude Law's interpretation of Hamlet. I thought his Hamlet was more of a high school boy than a college boy, but he followed that interpretation through the whole production. He gave a really good performance within that interpretation. For me, that was a problem of direction, but I wouldn't call up the director to ask where the interpretation came from, as much as I might want to out of curiosity. That's not what I'm supposed to be doing. I'm supposed to say how it seemed to me. I think it's enough to say that without pointing at someone and saying, "It was that person's idea."

Michael Dale: It's easier when an actor simply doesn't display mastery of the craft, which is often evident when you see a celebrity with limited stage acting experience. I tend to give actors the benefit of the doubt as far as interpretations go. If I'm seeing a cast full of professionals who are giving questionable performances, I will blame the director for that.

Leonard Jacobs: You can never truly know whether a bit of staging or an actor's choice came from the director's instruction or suggestion, or if it originated with the actor. Criticism is, at best, an educated guess as to what went on prior to the performance. Hopefully, that educated guess is informed by perception, observation, and previous experience.

Roma Torre: People often ask me how I separate direction from playwriting. It's very hard to do that. My husband is a playwright, and he did a play Off Broadway a few years ago. There was a review—I think it was in the *Daily News*—that praised the director for something that really was attributable to the playwright, and I was really annoyed by that.

Adam Feldman: It's easier to evaluate the direction of a movie because the director has such a permanent presence. Literally everything that you see in a movie was the director's choice. You have no agency as an audience member to look elsewhere. You're only seeing what the director wants you to see. You're seeing the version that he or she has chosen from available options. It's different with theater. The actors have more agency onstage. The writer has more power behind the scenes. The director has much less power over what the audience actually sees.

You don't want to say it's a great play if it's actually an ordinary play that happens to be lifted by a tremendously gifted cast or director, nor do you want to blame the writing for the failures of the production, but they can be very hard to separate. Sometimes you can have a perfectly good line that ends up sounding terrible because it's badly delivered. Or, you can have a line that is not particularly interesting that an actor makes fascinating. Sometimes it's useful to just look at the play on the page and imagine how else it might have been done, for better or worse.

Terry Teachout: Understanding what a director does is a critic's hardest job. Direction is the thing you don't see onstage. When you go to the New York Philharmonic, you see the conductor up there waiving his hands. But when you see a play, you don't see the director up there directing. If you've been doing this for a long time, and if you know previous work by the director or the playwright or the actors, you may be able to make educated guesses. But when you talk to actors and directors, you find out how wrong you can be. That's just the way it is. You do the best you can, and you should not be presumptuous about your knowledge.

9

Crisis

MATT WINDMAN: Is theater criticism currently in a state of crisis?

Ben Brantley: I think theater critics could vanish altogether, at least as we know them now. What still makes a theater critic special? It's now so easy to go online and log into a forum or a chat room, where everyone's giving their opinions.

Michael Musto: Everyone today is a critic. Everyone has an opinion. Everyone has a venue where they can send out to the world their own opinion on a Broadway show. Everyone can get an audience.

Steven Suskin: Nobody seems to want to pay for theater criticism anymore.

Jason Zinoman: The biggest obstacle is the business model of theater criticism. If you look over the last hundred years, people have always said, "Theater criticism is dying." And 99 percent of the time, it was just the usual kind of delightful hyperbole of the theater world, but this time is different for structural reasons.

Theater criticism doesn't seem like a blue-collar profession. The public image of the theater critic remains someone who's dapper and well-dressed, right out of *All About Eve*. But in reality, the profession has been completely wiped out for the people who have lost work, and the people who are working can barely make a living. I know critics who are homeless, who have to sell their furniture to get by. It's become a brutal job. It's no longer a sustainable profession even though, ironically, more people are viewing cultural things online than ever before.

Being a theater critic is an incredible job, and people should be grateful to have a position like that. But at the same time, it is a job. Critics are workers. They need the dignity of a steady salary to do their jobs well. I can name the number of theater critics who have health care on one hand.

The first people that got hit by the thinning out of the journalistic ranks were the editors. When I started at the *Times* and *Time Out*, I had a lot of really smart editors who beat up my prose. I learned how to write through tough editors. There are still great editors out there, but not many of them. I would argue that there's less room to fail now. As with artists, it's important for critics to fail in order to learn how to succeed.

We now have a better sense than ever of what people are reading by measuring clicks—how often articles are viewed online. What we've learned is that theater criticism gets a lot less clicks than articles about television and movies. That seems obvious, but now we know it with more precision than before. There's a lot of pressure on editors and publishers to focus on things that get read more often, and that's never going to be an Off-Broadway play. We're depending on editors to think there's something about the cultural value of theater criticism that matters and merits support.

Michael Sommers: We're a passing breed. We're passing right in front of your eyes. Everybody's a drama critic now because everybody's got a blog. Everybody's on *Facebook*. Everybody's on *All That Chat*. Paying jobs for drama critics don't exist anymore because everybody's giving it away for free. Traditional print journalism is not covering the arts anymore. *Backstage* doesn't even carry reviews anymore. When times were good, I was making over $100,000. That's a decent job. You can get by in New York on that. It wasn't huge money, but it was good enough.

Terry Teachout: The outlets for professional theater criticism are continuing to dry up, and I don't see that trend reversing. When I was first going to the theater, every big-city newspaper had a full-time staff theater critic, often more than one. The major national news magazines all covered theater routinely. Beyond that, theater was something discussed on network television. It was much more a part of the national conversation that it is now.

The hardest thing for theater critics is finding a place to write that will pay, so it can be either a full-time job or a significant source of income. That problem is so overwhelming that it overshadows every other problem. The next generation of people who might have become drama critics won't even consider it as a possible line of work. They're perfectly aware that you can't make a living doing it. It's hard enough making a living as a writer in any capacity. The days of writing specifically about theater as a critic—which, in the old days meant you weren't also writing features—are largely gone.

I am lucky that I write for the nation's largest newspaper, and have been going about things in the way that critics were half a century ago. I have so far been insulated from the problems I'm describing. But outside of me, the people at the *New York Times*, and a very small number of other newspapers, everybody is in trouble.

I don't know if there's anything that theater critics can do. It doesn't have anything to do with their work. It has to do with the institutions themselves. There are things that arts journalists can do to increase their value to their institutions. But if the institutions themselves don't place too high a value on the arts, it really doesn't matter how good the critics are. Eventually, those institutions will look at the critics and say, "You are superfluous."

Chris Jones: There are fewer and fewer outlets for serious arts criticism. There's more pressure to write shorter, to write with video, to become partners with the people you review, and all this other bullshit. The great and noble tradition of the critic just showing up and writing his or her response is becoming rarer. It's not just a problem. It's a crisis. So much arts journalism has become an adjunct to the promotional campaigns of the people you're writing about. Independence is becoming harder to preserve at many outlets across the country.

Peter Marks: The challenges include the declining tolerance for nuanced points of view, the intense financial pressure on large news organizations, and a ratcheting up of theater marketing, which is diminishing the voices that are out there from having an impact. They tend to suggest that because there are so many voices out there to listen to, none can be listened to.

What's not a problem—at least in Washington, D.C.—are the shows. They're more challenging than ever. They're not dumbed down in the way that Broadway shows so often feel. There's a meaningful community of people who want to walk into a theater and be challenged, and that's gratifying.

Layoffs are always a threat. I serve at the pleasure of the owner and the editor. Right now, the *Washington Post* is slightly unique in the sense that Jeff Bezos just bought it and is investing in it. The paper's staff is actually growing. It's a mini-golden age moment for the *Post*. He's trying to support the enterprise and see what's possible. And in a moment of possibility, you can breathe. I don't feel like my job is under threat at the moment—though that might change tomorrow.

Charles Isherwood: Theater criticism performs a valuable function that certain people will always value, but it's hard to tell. The journalism world is shrinking by the minute, and arts coverage is getting drastically cut all over the place. There are fewer jobs, and there's less space.

Michael Riedel: Once upon a time, newspapers were licenses for printing money because they had a monopoly on advertising. If you wanted to sell anything—be it a used car, a house in the Hamptons, or a Broadway play—you could only do it in the newspaper. The *New York Times* could charge $150,000 for a one-page ad in the "Arts and Leisure" section. But nowadays, you can sell things on the Internet. You can do direct mail or e-mail blasts. You can go to *Broadway.com*, funnel all your tickets through them, and pay much less in advertising dollars than you used to at the newspapers when they were the only game in town.

There's a feeling on the part of all the newspapers that Broadway is not as important to the culture as movies and television. And because of that, they don't need to hire someone to cover it regularly. But at the same time,

Broadway's never been bigger. It's a mega-multi-billion dollar global business and an enormous part of the New York City economy. I think you could make the case that now is the time for newspapers to have more Broadway coverage. More and more people are going to see the shows, which are full of big movie stars, but editors don't see it that way. That's why they're doing away with theater critics and theater columnists.

David Rooney: The number of outlets where you can actually make a living as a critic keeps shrinking. When the recession hit in 2008, it really hurt print media advertising. At that point, the migration from print to online publication was already under way. And as print started to become obsolete, the idea that arts critics had to be salaried positions went away. When other aspects of the media and the ad market improved as the economy picked up, criticism didn't bounce back. The notion of salaried arts critic positions has kind of had its day, and that's very sad.

Look at places around the country. Seattle used to have four major daily newspapers. Each of those four papers probably had a music critic, fine arts critic, dance critic, classical music critic, pop music critic, theater critic, and film critic. Many of those jobs have disappeared or gone to freelancers. A lot of papers are owned by umbrella companies that are now centralizing those positions among multiple publications. They might have one staffed position instead of several. One staffer can supply film reviews for three or four different papers around the country.

The idea of what a review is has been bastardized by the continuing evolution of the Internet and social media, to the point where you're invited to write a review of the toaster that you just bought online. Everything is perceived as a review now, so the distinction between a professional critical opinion and a less-informed consumer response has become blurred.

I know people who work at film and television schools, and they're astonished by the fact that film students no longer read reviews. Back when I was first getting interested in critical writing, they would have all been reading Pauline Kael or Vincent Canby or one of the other big-name critics. There is a whole generation coming up that is not being schooled to look to reviews for opinion. They look to one another, or to social media, for opinion. They don't really care what the critics have to say. They circulate opinion among themselves by text, email, *Twitter, Instagram, Facebook*. All of that has encroached on what was traditionally the reviewer's turf. It doesn't mean that reviewers don't have authority anymore, but it does make it harder for them to stake a claim.

Every year, I go to the New York Drama Critics' Circle and see that more jobs have fallen through the cracks. One day, *Bloomberg* suddenly decided it didn't want arts coverage anymore. What's that about? It's happened all over the place. Jobs are disappearing.

It makes more sense for media corporations to just hire freelancers. That way, they don't have to deal with vacation pay, health insurance, retirement plans, and benefits. I don't know if readers notice the difference. I don't think it necessarily changes the quality of the writing because there are some pretty fantastic part-time theater reviewers. Being full-time or part-time does not in any way distinguish a talented writer from an untalented writer, or a perceptive critic from an unperceptive critic, but I do think it is part of a steady erosion of the profession. The more those voices are eliminated from full-time staff (whether it's a trade paper like *Variety*, or a consumer publication, or a wire service like *Bloomberg*), the less authoritative the critical voice becomes. It means that anybody stepping in to fill that breach really has to work harder to define themselves—to establish a style that fits with that of the publication and still have some kind of personal voice.

If you want to work in arts criticism these days, it almost always has to be a sideline to a paying job, or you have to be incredibly ambitious and energized and have endless stamina to push and push and push and pitch and get your coverage in as many outlets as possible.

Alexis Soloski: When I started out, this seemed like a reasonable career choice for a young middle-class woman. There were, if not legions of opportunities, at least a number of them. There are so many fewer positions now. I'm very glad I teach and do other things. I don't know what the critical landscape will look like in another 10 or 20 years. There'll always be someone at the *Times*. Theater is a big enough industry in New York that we'll need that. We'll always have professional theater criticism, but I imagine we'll see a lot less of it going forward.

Elisabeth Vincentelli: I'm living through the extinction of the dinosaurs. Going forward, only very few outlets will be able to have full-time paid critics. It's not just us. It's music critics and movie critics, too. We may still have critics who review one or two shows a week, or who write a review every other week, but the critic for a daily newspaper who sees everything, who goes through that exhausting grind, is going to disappear.

Practically speaking, holding a day job and writing on the side is really difficult, and I know because I did that for years. With theater, unlike a book or a CD, you have to be at the shows, and they're in the evening. That means you don't have enough time to think about the show. Being a full-time professional critic gives you the freedom to write what you need to write and not fear that a publicist is going to blacklist you.

A full-time critic becomes a familiar figure, and that creates a benchmark. You find critics you trust, whose tastes you understand, or who articulate their analysis of a show forcefully and in a stylistically satisfying manner. With that disappearing, it's very depressing.

John Simon: Print publications are gravely threatened. They are having a terrible time, and a lot of people are getting fired. There is a great plague killing off critics across the whole land. I don't know when exactly it started, but it's a relatively recent development. And if they have to save money and cut down on things, theater criticism one of the most expendable things as far as they're concerned. Any day, theater critics may be sacked, and there's nothing much they can do about it.

It doesn't even have to do with the positive or negative reviews they write. They might get fired for no good reason at all. Or, in some cases, half a good reason, which is almost as bad as no good reason. If you're a severe and tough critic, and suddenly you don't have a job anymore and are looking for a new job, then the fact that you have been a very severe critic becomes a serious danger. It results in being turned down by 75 publications, as I recently was. There's the danger of somehow prostituting yourself, or feeling obliged to be more positive when you really don't want to be, and trying to make sure you're staying in the good graces of your readers and editors.

Also, there is a general kind of stupidification in the land. People who should know things and be able to do their jobs properly do it poorly and inadequately in every way, and that extends to everything from plumbing to drama criticism.

Rob Weinert-Kendt: Apathy and not being read are the things that frighten me the most about the future of theater criticism. Even the people who are passionate about theater don't read criticism or care about it. That is also true of criticism in other fields.

When *Backstage* cut theater reviews altogether, it was a horrifying wakeup call. *Backstage* had a mandate to cover every show it possibly could, more than any other place as far as I know in New York and L.A. It was a service to the community. But who was reading those reviews? Who was the audience for them? It's related to the challenges a lot of theaters are experiencing all over the country. Who's their audience? Who's going to be their audience next year or 10 years from now?

The number of people who have full-time employment and are receiving health coverage to cover theater is probably under 10. There's Peter Marks in D.C., Chris Jones in Chicago, the two guys at the *Times*, Charles McNulty in L.A., Robert Hurwitt in San Francisco. There's a really small list of people who get paid to mainly do criticism. That trend has been going on since I've been in the business. Often, there is a main critic, and everyone else is freelance, and the freelancers either work at the paper already or have a day job. It's reflective of how theater is economically. No one goes into theater for the money, and no one goes into theater criticism for the money. That's not a joke. It's not even remotely funny. There's just no money in the coverage of theater.

Robert Faires: Theater critics are an endangered species. We get less space than we used to. We're expected to speak in the vernacular, the shorthand of the day. It's got to be short and sweet and no more than a tweet. It's very hard to pack a lot of critical insight into 140 characters. Over the last 15 years, my space has been contracting. I find it harder to generate the same critical impact that I used to. A lot of my writing is devoted to telling people, "This really is important, and you need to pay attention."

Helen Shaw: There aren't any theater critic jobs. That's a problem because professionalization has a real value. There used to be 30 theater critic jobs in New York, and now there are maybe 15 jobs. There are five jobs at the *Times*, a few jobs at *Time Out*, one and a half jobs at the *Voice*, one job at *New York* magazine, one job at the *Wall Street Journal*. There's the *Post*. There's the *Daily News*. I think you can get to 15. Some of those are not full-time jobs. They're opportunities where you need to have another job on top of that to support yourself. We're losing good critics because we don't have enough places to put them.

Roma Torre: All of the television networks used to have theater reviewers: Jeffrey Lyons on Channel 4, Dennis Cunningham on Channel 2, Stewart Klein on Channel 5, Joel Siegel on Channel 7. About 10 years ago, there was a critic at one of the major TV channels (none of the above mentioned) who sat behind me at *Our Town* with Paul Newman. She said to me, "What do you think of *Our Town*?" I gave her some thoughts, and she said, "I can't write this review. It's such a stupid play." And this was their designated theater critic. I thought, Oh my God. They might as well not have anybody. That person didn't last long, and nobody replaced her. That was the end of theater criticism at that particular channel.

With the dumbing down of television, there's a sense that theater is only for the elite, and that the average New Yorker doesn't care that much about theater, at least not enough to warrant paying a critic. That doesn't make sense to me because whoever does the film reviews can also do the theater reviews. They just don't think it's necessary anymore. But theater is so integral to New York City. How many people come to New York because of Broadway? So many of the local news channels are run by non–New Yorkers who really don't appreciate what New York is all about. One nice thing about NY1 is that everybody at the top of our management grew up in New York City. They understand what New Yorkers appreciate and what they don't.

David Cote: The readership of criticism is shrinking in favor of social media or corporate-controlled opinion channels. How many critics have lost their jobs in recent years? People seem to have less and less time and interest in theater criticism. It's all very depressing. I guess the biggest challenge is finding a way or a platform to be honest and feel useful and to attract and keep loyal readers.

9. Crisis 169

Jesse Green: The *New York Times* will always have a theater critic, probably two critics plus a lot of stringers. I don't think *New York* magazine will ever stop covering theater. I don't think the major tabloids will completely stop. But the fewer people that have full-time jobs to do this, the narrower the coverage will be. You'll still get coverage of Hugh Jackman coming to Broadway, but you're going to have a hard time getting coverage of a new play by a young author in a basement in SoHo. I don't even cover that, but somebody does. But for how much longer?

There's also a general lack of interest in the theater, or at least a lack of ability to discover and maintain an interest in theater because of its cost. Put that up against the immediacy and availability of other forms of entertainment and the long-reputed decline of literacy. At this point in our civilization, people may not want to read 1,100 words about *Titus Andronicus*. The theater world has not done enough to show new audiences why they should part with their money. I have a niece and a nephew in their twenties who will drop $150 on a concert. So when we talk about how horrible the ticket prices are on Broadway, it's still the kind of money that kids are willing to spend if they're convinced there's a reason to. Part of what I want to do is convince people to go to good theater, though I don't want them to have to pay full price. That's the biggest systemic threat.

Jeremy Gerard: There's an insidious belief among publishers that entertainment writing and criticism should go hand-in-hand with advertising dollars. So if it's not something that generates advertising, like a friendly feature, why rock the boat? It's not just in theater criticism. Look at the crisis for reviewers of classical music, or the almost nonexistent profession of dance criticism. Things that don't generate advertising revenue are facing tremendous challenges.

Richard Zoglin: Newspapers and magazines want to seem hip. They're all going for younger audiences, while theater is perceived as being for an older audience.

Ronni Reich: We're all now very much aware of online traffic and how many page views we're getting. That has an impact on advertising and on your value to a news organization.

Marilyn Stasio: We're losing our strength because everybody's a reviewer these days. There are too many of us. When the field is overrun with people, it devalues it. We're in an age in which everybody thinks they know everything. So the impulse is to say, "What does the reviewer know? I could do that myself."

David Finkle: Theater is not revered in the way that it was, and that's reflected in the shrinking of theater coverage in many places and the loss of jobs. Look at what happened at the *Observer*. They let their theater critic go. Here's a paper that says, "We're interested in New York City, and in everything that makes New York City interesting," and it dropped its theater critic. What does that say?

Richard Ouzounian: Papers have less space because they're selling less advertising. Although we can always write online reviews, I'm very wary of what I call the "online ghetto." J. Kelly Nestruck at the *Globe* is currently writing 700-word reviews online. But in the paper, they get squished down to 200 words.

I keep desperately trying to keep newspapers alive. I think that if you take away the newspapers, there'll be nothing left. There has to be a place where you have to write within the restrictions of taste, space, money, and time, and where you get paid well for doing it. What we have to do is fight for it. I'm already having a dialogue at my paper about this. I don't want to retire, and they don't want me to retire, but I'm getting to that age, and they're already saying, "Can't you bring along a few more people, so we have some choices when you go?" My paper still thinks that there should be a theater critic in a theater department.

Christine Dolen: I'm probably only going to be working for a few more years. I would like to think that someone will replace me, but I'm doubtful. The newspaper has to prioritize and use its resources in new and different ways, but perhaps I'll be proven wrong.

Zachary Stewart: Criticism is in a state of transition. As the wall between sales and editorial becomes increasingly nonexistent (partly due to the move online), financial pressure to promote advertising clients will increasingly fall on critics, just as pressure to bury negative stories will fall on reporters. But readers are smart and they know when they're being bullshitted. Eventually, the stupid publications will trade away their credibility for short-term revenue, and they will lose the readership that advertisers crave. This crisis of credibility can be seen in nearly every industry, from financial ratings agencies to fast food chains. There will always be a need for truthful, informed, and entertaining criticism. Publishers need only to offer a financial shield for it. Eventually, the smart publishers will find a viable way to do this in a digital landscape.

MATT WINDMAN: *Some of you have lost or left your positions as theater critics recently. If you don't mind, can you talk about what happened?*

Jesse Oxfeld: I wrote for the *Observer* just shy of five years before I was let go. It's a newspaper that is not financially robust, and where things are always changing. During the time that I wrote there, I think I wrote for five different editors-in-chief and four different cultural editors. It was a broadsheet, and then a tabloid, and then a broadsheet again, and then a tabloid again.

Being let go wasn't astonishing news to me. It ties in with what's happening at every publication, where revenues and budgets are shrinking. The *Observer* was losing money for years. Why does Michael Feingold no longer write for the *Village Voice*? I'm sure he was relatively expensive by the salary scale of the *Voice*. He'd been there for years and had some seniority that I'm sure was worth something. If you have freelancers writing things instead, you don't have to pay them as much. Why was David Rooney let go from *Variety*? Because *Variety* decided they'd rather have freelancers writing the reviews. It wasn't worth the additional cost in benefits on top of a salary to have a chief theater critic. As it happens, *Variety*'s current critic, Marilyn Stasio, is a fairly regular freelancer, so they still have a serious person doing it, and David Rooney has ended up as the lead reviewer for the *Hollywood Reporter*, but as a freelancer, not as an employee. Michael Sommers was the theater critic for the *Star-Ledger* and got a very nice buyout offer.

There's certainly an idea that this is an expendable position. To some extent, you have to live in the world as it is. I've also worked as an editor and have been involved in running publications. Let's say, for example, that I'm an editor at the *Star-Ledger*, and I have an *Associated Press* subscription. If I can run *Associated Press* reviews for free or a marginal cost, it doesn't make sense to pay a salary and benefits to Michael Sommers. I only have so much money because the circulation is shrinking and advertising is going away. I'd rather spend that money on an enterprising political reporter in Newark than on a theater critic. All of these publications are losing money, or at least not making the money they used to, and are looking for things to cut.

To some degree, I feel like being a theater critic was a fun thing that I did for five years, and whatever I do next will be different. Theater criticism is not the entirety of my career or my expertise. I enjoyed doing it and being a part of that world. I do miss it now. But on a practical level, it's difficult for me to imagine another situation where I'll have that opportunity again.

Peter Filichia: I held my position as the New Jersey theater critic at the *Star-Ledger* for 19 years until I took a buyout. They said it was a one-time offer. At the time, I had this idea for a play, there were books I wanted to write, and the idea of staying home and not having to go to New Jersey every day was tempting. Sometimes I traveled as far out as Cape May, which is two hours away. Not that long ago, 167 people were laid off at the *Star-Ledger*, and they got nothing. I don't have any hard feelings about it at all. They gave me a year's salary and health insurance for life. Since then, I've written four books. I currently have four Internet columns. I work mostly for Music Theatre International. I write a column for them every Friday, for which I am paid pretty much what I got when I was at the *Star-Ledger*.

Alexis Soloski: I was with the *Village Voice* for 16 years. I saw nearly all of my friends leave or get fired. I saw the paper shrink to a quarter of its size. It's very sad. It's a paper I really fell in love with as a teenager. In some ways,

I still love it and what it can be, but the resources have become so limited that it's not the same paper anymore. When I moved to the *New York Times*, I didn't make an announcement. I don't really go in for big gestures. At the *Times*, I'm doing reviews as well as features, profiles, and listings.

David Rooney: One of the few upsides of being pushed out of *Variety*, my professional home of almost 20 years, was the incredible outpouring of support I received from the industry. The very first note I got was a sort of "What the fuck?" email from Scott Rudin. All sorts of people like Andre Bishop, Oskar Eustis, and Todd Haimes followed. That was a great source of comfort. I know that sense of injustice did filter back to *Variety*, though I don't know whether or not they actually said, "We made a mistake" with regards to film critic Todd McCarthy and me or anyone else. There was a sense in the industry that *Variety* was getting rid of one of the things that made it strong and identifiable: critical voices that people know and trust.

When I was suddenly without a professional home, it was very good to have a window of exposure at the *New York Times*. They were extremely generous in reaching out to me. They offered me a steady stream of reviews and feature assignments. It was a very good way for me to maintain visibility while I looked for something closer to full-time employment.

I got a call from the *Hollywood Reporter* the day the announcement was made that *Variety* was cutting me and Todd McCarthy. It was from Elizabeth Guider, who at that time was the editor-in-chief. She was also an ex-*Variety* colleague. She said, "I would be nuts not to reach out to you. You have knowledge across theater and film and television. It would be great to get you onboard in some way." I said, "Let me think about it because I'm still catching my breath." But we kept talking.

My title at the *Hollywood Reporter* is film and theater critic. I spend my year juggling theater coverage with film festivals, most of which conveniently coincide with the downtime of the Broadway season. If something is opening when I'm at a festival, my colleague Frank Scheck steps in and covers it. My background was in film before I started covering theater, so I actually welcomed the opportunity to get back into film and spread myself between the two mediums. Film festivals are hard work. At Sundance, I'm usually sitting up in my hotel room surviving on room service, writing reviews until four in the morning, and then getting up to see more films each day.

It's been interesting to shift my writing style in my post–*Variety* life. *Variety* has a very identifiable style, with its own industry "slanguage." It was great to work with the editors at the *Times*, which has very particular style rules. They're endless. You're learning them all the time. After so many years at *Variety*, it was interesting to adapt to that. At the *Hollywood Reporter*, the house style is much more elastic. I have the freedom there to put my own stamp on my reviews.

9. Crisis

Howard Shapiro: The features editor of the *Philadelphia Inquirer* came to me on October 1, 2012, and told me the paper was going to have several job shifts because they needed people to do specific things. I was going to be sent to New Jersey to cover townships, and I had three weeks to move to New Jersey. After I learned that, I was actually preparing to go. Three decades earlier, I had been the deputy New Jersey editor, so I thought I could do it, but then I realized that I didn't particularly want to do it. If I did, I would no longer be a theater critic. I'd be out of the business. People wouldn't think of me in that way when they thought of my journalism. Then they offered me a buyout. And by the end of the month, I was gone.

There were almost a dozen staff moves. Some people believed that because they were older and making more money, they were somehow being driven out. I took the management at face value. I knew they needed reporters in New Jersey. There were a couple days in a row where the paper had a "New Jersey" section without much Jersey news in it. Some of the people who stayed went to the Newspaper Guild, which represents them, and got their old jobs back after arbitration, but I was done. I had a terrific ride at the *Inquirer* and a great career, but it was time to move on.

I'm now reviewing on the radio. Before I left the *Inquirer* building, I called WHYY. Like so many big NPR stations, WHYY is building its own local news team. Because newspapers have fewer resources to cover news, public media sees an opportunity there. They were building a staff of very smart, mostly young people. I'm not a full-timer. My title is theater blogger, or at least that's what they call me on the radio, but essentially I'm the theater critic.

Jeremy Gerard: I was thrown out of *Bloomberg News*. The world of culture and the arts was shocked when *Bloomberg* decided to discontinue our section, which was called "Muse." Virtually all of the critics and editors were fired or relieved of their duties, or whatever you want to call it. *Bloomberg* stopped its regular coverage of the arts, with the exception of the work done primarily by Manuela Hoelterhoff, who had been our boss. The rest of us were out on the street.

We were all shocked because Michael Bloomberg himself is such an advocate for the arts. It seemed impossible that the news organization he built would suddenly say, "We're not doing this anymore." From a practical standpoint, you can't be shocked by it. We were hardly central to the core business of *Bloomberg News*. Had it been a different owner, perhaps it would have not been so shocking—although it's hard to imagine *Reuters*, the *Wall Street Journal*, or certainly the *New York Times* saying, "Those aren't our core readers, so we're not going to cover culture anymore."

I very fortunately landed a new job at *Deadline.com*, where I'm working with my old *Variety* pal Mike Fleming, who runs it. I'm sort of holding down the New York office. My career has followed the world: from the days of very old media, where I was literally cutting and pasting copy that came off a printer at *Our Town*; to the first days of the computer era at the *Dallas Morning News*; to classic mainstream media at the *New York Times*, *Variety*, and *New York* magazine; to electronic media at *Bloomberg*, which didn't put out its own hard copy but was published in many newspapers around the world; and now *Deadline*, where I'm completely online and never see my name in print, except when somebody's catching up with a story I've broken.

John Simon: Adam Moss, who took over *New York* magazine in 2004, obviously didn't like me, or agree with me, or whatever. That caused my departure. It was a surprise because I had three or four other editors-in-chief who seemed to be perfectly willing to keep me on, and then suddenly this guy who was hated at the *Times* (and whose departure was celebrated by the *Times* people with joy) was hired by Bruce Wasserstein, Wendy Wasserstein's brother, who had purchased *New York* magazine. I guess Wendy had it in for me, even though we had been friends. She seemed to have told her brother to get rid of me, and he told Adam Moss. Anyhow, that's how I was kicked out.

After that, I was hired by *Bloomberg*, and it was okay for five years. Then something must have happened. Manuela Hoelterhoff, who was in charge of all the arts at *Bloomberg*, turned against me, as she has against all kinds of other people, too. They were also trying to save money at *Bloomberg*. And since they had Jeremy Gerard as an editor, they promoted him to critic since they were already paying him a salary, and therefore he'd cost nothing, whereas I cost them money. So it was a good time to get rid of me.

When *Bloomberg* let me go, my wife contacted 75 magazines, newspapers, colleges, and universities to find a writing or teaching position for me. But out of 75 attempts, only one single thing, the *Westchester Guardian*, accepted me. It is kind of peculiar because, at least among people who know something about theater, I have a certain standing. You'd think there'd be more than this one small, obscure publication. Nevertheless, I am very grateful for the *Westchester Guardian* because it saved me in a sense. Only it responded. By now, I think a whole lot of magazines, newspapers, and whatnot have young people working for them, and they either don't know who I am or don't care. And if they do, it means that if they hired me, they'd have to pay me a living wage. Whereas if they hired some fresh young kid out of college, he or she will be grateful to work for practically nothing. That's the kind of people they want.

The good thing about writing for a publication like the *Westchester Guardian* is that I can write about whatever I want. I also have a blog called *Uncensored John Simon*. I write a new blog post every two or three weeks. I can write about anything I please. In my opinion, I'm doing some of the best writing I've ever done in that niche. But unfortunately, very few people are even aware of it. I also do freelance work here and there—in fact, as much as I can. I write quite a bit for the *Weekly Standard*. I also write for the *New Criterion* and the *New York Times Book Review*. Every once in a while, something else comes along, but not too often, I must say.

Leonard Jacobs: I blame what happened at *Backstage* on the colossal, shocking ineptitude of its owners. I was with the paper for 10 years. I was hired as an associate editor, and I later became the national editor for theater. In 2006, the publisher was given a mandate by the owners to extract a couple more million dollars in gross revenue out of the business. It wasn't really clear how they were going to do. I was part of a small working group that came up with a business plan that involved reorganizing, rebranding, rethinking, and ultimately relaunching.

However, the powers-that-be did two things. For one, they never foresaw the Great Recession or the changes in the media that were starting to happen before the Great Recession and were then exacerbated by it. Second, six months after they put money into the business, they wanted it back. They couldn't extract their investment in just a couple of months. It takes more time than that, particularly in publishing, which has small margins to begin with.

In 2006, they started cutting from the bottom of the masthead. They got rid of excess people and excess jobs. When I was promoted to national theater editor, I had a very healthy five-figure budget for my writers in New York, L.A., and regionally. Over a period of about a year and a half, all of that went away. Eventually, they started cutting from the top of the masthead, which was when I was downsized. I knew it was coming. I was just waiting for it to happen. At this point, nobody is left at *Backstage* from my time there. There was a national editor-in-chief—she was let go. There was a managing editor on the East Coast—he was let go. There was a managing editor on the West Coast—she was let go.

A book of mine, which was a celebration of the collection at the Billy Rose Theatre Division of the New York Public Library for the Performing Arts, came out about two weeks after I left *Backstage*. I spent some time promoting the book. I was also still writing reviews for the *New York Press* and freelancing, so it wasn't so terrible. Around that time, I was introduced to the idea of blogging. I wasn't desperate for another platform, but I created a blog called the *Clyde Fitch Report*, which reflected my longtime interest in this late-nineteenth/early-twentieth-century American playwright. I slowly figured out that I could use the blog to write about arts funding, the economic impact of the arts, unions and management, and similar topics. I was encouraged by a colleague to try and make money from the blog. He came up with a five-year plan to go from making no money, to making a little money off of it, to finally making a respectable living.

I only got about two and a half years into that plan. I made about $15,000 or $20,000 off the blog. People would call me up and say, "I want to advertise on your site," and I didn't know what to charge them. I'm a content guy—not an advertising guy. I also did a lot of freelance work that had nothing to do with theater. *Crain's* did an article on me, so it was kind of an exciting time. But there comes to a point where papa needs new shoes, you know? In 2010, I noticed a job listing for a director position at the New York City Department of Cultural Affairs. I had never worked in government before. Heather Hitchens, who I had become friendly with (and who is now the executive director of the American Theatre Wing), encouraged me to apply, and I got the job.

Michael Musto: I was really surprised by what happened at the *Village Voice*. The paper was dwindling. It was turning into a very slow operation without the ability to pay real, full salaries. But on the other hand, everyone kept telling me how I was an institution, and that without me, the *Voice* wouldn't be much of anything. Maybe what's happened since then has proven that to be true. I was extremely dedicated to the *Voice*. I gave it my heart and soul for all those years. When the rumor got out that I was being laid off, Aaron Hicklin, who's the editor of *Out*, reached out to me and said, "If it does happen, I would like you to come aboard." I had written for *Out* in the past, so I was delighted at the opportunity. Everything I write has an LGBT text to it (not just a subtext), so it made perfect sense. I'm now pretty much romping around, just as I did with my *Voice* column. There's not much difference. I'm exploring different topics and covering a lot of Broadway and Off-Broadway shows.

Michael Sommers: I took a buyout from the *Star-Ledger*. At that point, the Newhouse chain had disbanded its syndicate. They closed their Washington bureau, which was where all the national stuff went through. At the same time, the people at the *Star-Ledger* said, "We're going to have to let a certain number of employees go, and we're offering the following terms." I could see the writing on the wall. The arts writers were going to be the first to go. They said something to me along the lines of, "Maybe you can cover the crime beat in Newark," and I wasn't about to do that. So I walked the plank and took the buyout. I was one of the first staffers to go. A lot of other people who stayed were sorry because the terms that were offered later on were not nearly as good as what I got. Even now, the *Ledger* still might not make it. They sold their main building. They're down to a skeletal staff, which is apparently getting paid bupkis.

The *New York Times* contacted me four years ago and asked if I would write reviews of New Jersey productions, which was very flattering. I'm also writing for the website *New Jersey Newsroom*. I'm still seeing shows from the best seats. I'm not making as much money as I used to, but I love doing this.

9. Crisis

Sometimes I do wish I had become an expert in another field. Maybe I'd still have a steady job if I stayed a sports writer. But the way I see it, you only get so many dreams in life. And for me, one of those dreams was to live in New York, see all the shows, and make a living as a writer.

MATT WINDMAN: *If there are fewer professional theater critics going forward, will that have an effect on the theater itself, or might it make no difference at all?*

Peter Marks: I would argue yes. There has to be a watchdog—a conscience to make sure that what's being produced isn't appealing only to the lowest-common-denominator, and to make sure some other work gets through.

Zachary Stewart: It will be harder for the casual theatergoer to hear about shows and put them in context.

John Simon: If there weren't critics, people would have to depend on advertising. And advertising, by definition, almost always lies, and that could make a difference. But who knows what would happen if there was nothing but publicity that was mendaciously favorable and not critical? If everything was written by advertisers and not reviewers, it would make a difference, but I don't know what that difference would be. First of all, people might suspect that kind of thing of being too good to be true. Second of all, if people fell for it and believed all the good publicity, and then they went and were burned, they would probably get pretty sour and bitter and stop going to the theater.

Terry Teachout: It depends on how good you think criticism is for the theater. I suppose that if it's a choice between really bad criticism and no criticism at all, none is the better choice. But in general, having reasonably good criticism is good for the theater. Most of the well-known critics who have covered theater in the last three-quarters of a century were people who specialized in it, spent a lot of time thinking about it, and in a few cases had professional experience in the theater. That kind of professional commentary is valuable.

If you have no one offering independent, expert commentary on the theater, then theater companies are inevitably going to enter a kind of drift where the only thing that influences their activities is the box office. There'd be no voice in play other than how many tickets are being sold. If you're a serious artist, you have priorities other than selling the largest number of tickets possible. Good arts journalism can help educate the public. In the absence of that kind of educating influence, all of the arts are going to drift more in the direction of the box office. I'm not saying the public is always wrong, but it's important to have other voices in the mix.

Ben Brantley: I guess the theater could go back to playing immediately to the people. Like in *Mr. Burns, a Post-Electric Play*, maybe we'll fall into a neo–Dark Ages in which it's all thrown together from memory and put on for the people to look at and approve or not. Good art finds its own way, and maybe not during the creator's lifetime.... I don't think criticism is an initiator. It doesn't pose questions. It answers them. Of course, there have been some activist critics over the years, like Kenneth Tynan. I don't think Shaw really changed anything as a critic. He had to become a playwright to do that. In film, there may have been a few critics who actually made an immediate difference, like Pauline Kael and maybe Andrew Sarris.

John Lahr: The demise of criticism will affect the theater because people need to be guided and opened up. Criticism is a minor art form. But when it is an art form, it gives people a different lens through which to view the theater. They can shed light on it. It's the light against the darkness that matters. You could say that critics are in the illumination business. If you can illuminate something in the theater, it makes it more fun and desirable.

Rob Weinert-Kendt: Critics are often holding institutions' feet to the fire to do more new work—even though when the theaters actually do produce new work, the critics' verdicts are often mixed. That's a constant drumbeat: Where are the new plays? Where is the new voice? I think that's one area where critics have a real value. They're going to review new work honestly, but they are continually looking for the new, the fresh. That's why they go to the theater. They don't want to see the same old thing. And they can make and support little discoveries. I think that critics have a role in keeping the industry—I hate to say honest—but in reminding them of what they're doing it for: to support living writers and living artists.

David Sheward: There will more and more lowest-common-denominator shows. It will be more and more difficult to get challenging shows done. They'll get done, but there won't be voices to champion them and get people in to see them.

Howard Shapiro: Whether it's good or bad, criticism gives a kind of publicity to a show that people pay attention to. People need to be reminded that there's a show to see.

Gordon Cox: One could argue that plays have become less adventurous because critics have less weight with audiences and, therefore, have less opportunity to argue in favor of a project that is not as immediately appealing as a big, splashy musical. Fewer people take the time to pay attention to the critics that might steer them toward something that is more adventurous or boundary-pushing. One of the reasons that a play will try to get a big star is to get people to come and buy tickets and kind of critic-proof a production. The revival of Harold Pinter's *Betrayal* with Daniel Craig was not particularly well-reviewed, but that didn't matter. Lots of people went to go see Daniel Craig. That is, in part, a response to the power of critics.

Ronni Reich: A lack of theater criticism is a major issue in New Jersey.

I regularly get emails from theater companies saying, "No one's reviewing us." I am one of few critics in the state working for a mainstream, large publication. Some theaters are now using volunteer bloggers, who are the only other voices out there, and what they write ends up in emails that the theater sends out to its customer base.

10

Economics

MATT WINDMAN: *Is it disconcerting that so many theater critics are now writing without getting paid for their work?*

Hilton Als: I wrote without pay for a very long time, and I don't think it did any harm. Writers will get there if they put their writing first, if they believe that their writing is important, and if they have a voice. You should never feel that it's an unpaid position. You're being paid by learning.

Andy Propst: Writing for free is disconcerting. But at the same time, it's a survival tactic. I'll point to myself. I have grown to love the process of reviewing. And at this juncture, in absence of a forum that is paying me, I have a well-established platform at *American Theater Web* where I can self-publish. I don't know what that means for me in the future. I've lucked out with my newest professional gig, and that could be what keeps a roof over my head while I do criticism on the side.

There is a value to anyone's writing, and we have entered an era in which writing and the dissemination of information can be done for free. I'm not by any means diminishing the thoughtful work that may go into a post on *All That Chat*, or one by a very good blogger, but there is something to be said about someone who is in the trenches, being edited, and being vetted. That process requires some kind of compensation.

There are actors who are willing to work for free or a small stipend. This is what they want to do for a living, and they hope that they will reach a point where they can move to increasingly high-paying jobs. Just because you can put something up online, why should that shut the door on ever being able to earn a living at it?

Charles Isherwood: It's a very dispiriting sign of the times. Part of you thinks, Why are these writers giving away for free what they deserve to be paid for? But the truth is that having a voice in the market is a form of currency in and of itself. That means you get free tickets. And if you're somebody who loves theater, you want free tickets. And perhaps you think, I'll do this for free for now. But when a job opens up somewhere down the road, if I've proven myself worthy, I will be hired. But I haven't heard of any people going from writing for free to writing for pay. I've only heard about it going in the other direction.

Christine Dolen: I think it's good that there are many people writing about theater, but how do they put food on their table if they're not being paid?

David Cote: I don't think that being paid is the be-all and end-all, but I don't know how long someone can sustain going to the theater and writing reviews without getting paid for it. Some bloggers do it for free tickets, and that is certainly an incentive, but I think the larger question is whether anyone is editing them. If they can't be paid, then I would assume that no one is being paid to edit their work, so the quality of their writing might be terrible. I need to be edited. If the freelance critic isn't being paid, and the editor isn't being paid, then you are pumping a poorly written opinion into the cultural atmosphere, and I don't know if that helps anyone.

David Rooney: One of the most outrageous things that happened to me since becoming a freelancer was getting a very long proposal email from CNN to write a piece for their website about Julie Taymor being fired from *Spider-Man: Turn Off the Dark*. It was like, "We would love you to write 3,000 words by tomorrow." It was the night when word got out that Julie Taymor was being pushed out of *Spider-Man*. I had been following the situation and writing various stories about it for the *Hollywood Reporter*. They offered me an editorial spot on the home page of CNN.

It was apparently a column space that had been taken in the past by Denzel Washington, Teresa Heinz Kerry, and Ariel Dorfman. Every person named in this email that had written a guest editorial for this spot either had gazillions in movie money, obscene amounts of personal wealth, or a stream of arts grants. At the very end of this email, they wrote, "Unfortunately, this is an unpaid assignment." They went on to explain that it would be great exposure, and that I'd be free to link to any blog or other project I was working on. They reminded me that the site reached 40 million readers a month, and that the piece would be on the CNN homepage for three or four days.

I declined—and not very politely. I think it's outrageous that CNN is putting out feelers to freelance journalists, essentially saying, "Give us your expertise, your knowledge, and your insight into this situation. Write a compelling narrative that consumers will want to read. But we can't pay you for it, even though we have 40 million readers a month." If you have 40 million readers a month, you have advertising revenue.

I understand the challenges of monetizing content on the Internet, and I understand from experience at different publications how hard it is to translate those old print dollars into Web dollars. But it doesn't help anyone that this Arianna Huffington/Tina Brown mentality of not providing adequate compensation for content has taken hold. I think that is the biggest threat to the survival of the theater critic and any other arts critic.

Alec Baldwin can write as many editorials for the *Huffington Post* as he wants. He has buckets of *30 Rock* cash. We don't all have that. And I think it's extremely rude that publications think that it's fine to reach out to freelancers and offer zero compensation or insultingly low fees. Likewise, we are asked to talk on panels and moderate events and things like that, and it's shocking how many organizations expect you to do that for free, without an honorarium of any kind.

We have worked and studied and toiled away to build up a body of knowledge. We should be compensated in some way to share that. It's also up to theater critics to grow a pair and demand payment. They should stop accepting unpaid work. It's fine for people to think that they've got to keep your names out there and keep their bylines visible. And if doing gratis work for the *Huffington Post* is the only way to do that, then fine. I guess there's logic to it. But I also think it's damaging in the long run. People who have worked hard to build a reputation and gain the trust of their readership should place value on their work. I don't think giving up your writing for free is a way to place value on it.

Zachary Stewart: This is not very different from what is going on in other branches of the arts and media. If one has to commit to two years of slave labor (i.e. internship) to get a job at a professional theater or newspaper, our theater and journalism will only come from the children of the very wealthy, who can afford to survive without working for a living. As a result, the perspective of the theater (and the criticism around it) will be increasingly limited.

Don Aucoin: Any way that you can get your voice out there is legitimate, but the broader question is whether I'm bothered by the number of writers who are expected to work for free. That is pernicious. Writers should be paid for their work. But in terms of launching their careers, these days, young writers have to bring readers with them. They need to have a strong presence on social media. That way, they can go to a publication and say, "If you hire me, I will bring these readers with me." That's a big change. It used to be that you got readers by climbing aboard the mother ship.

Elisabeth Vincentelli: Writing for the *Huffington Post* is pure exploitation. I find it a little presumptuous and ridiculous to ask someone to write for free. How am I going to pay my rent? Nobody wants to work for free. You work and you get paid. That's a basic tenet of capitalism. I find it sadly ironic to see how working for free has become such a key element of the new economy: more for the few, less for the many.

Gordon Cox: I think there's something healthy and good about people who pay enough attention to the theater that they want to write about it for free.

Helen Shaw: You can't make a living as a freelance writer. And even if you are writing for money, those prices are going down because there are people that will do it for free. It's just a product of reality. It darkens the landscape. But I would never tell somebody who's writing on a blog or contributing to the *Huffington Post* that they should not be doing it, partially because you have to write so much to become good at this. I've been writing for a decade, and I don't know if I'm any good at it. But I wouldn't write for free. I know that about myself.

Jeremy Gerard: I deeply believe in journalism that people have to pay for. I hope nobody takes seriously the adage that "information wants to be free."

Jesse Oxfeld: I don't think it's problematic. If they want to do it for free, and if they can afford to do it for free, good for them. I'm not interested in writing reviews for free just so I can write reviews. Samuel Johnson said, "No man but a blockhead ever wrote, except for money." It's a job, and I don't feel the need to do it for free for the *Huffington Post*.

Leonard Jacobs: It's very disconcerting that people are writing for free. When the *Huffington Post* gets bought by AOL for $300 million, but the thousands of people who wrote for Arianna Huffington for free get nothing, it goes beyond a level of disconcerting to nauseating, appalling, saddening, disappointing, and infuriating. It's not ethical. It's not moral. It's not right. But from an economic point of view, it's understandable. There is so much supply and far too little demand. Therefore, the price comes down.

Michael Musto: Hiring writers without paying them subverts the whole industry. A lot of people unknowingly become scabs in a way that makes it easier for paid critics to be either fired or diminished in some way. To me, that's a very bittersweet development. Who knew that there was a whole population of people that would gladly write for nothing? A lot of them are really decent writers, too. It's a wrench in the whole business of being a critic, and I don't see any way to slow that down.

Peter Filichia: My feeling about money is that I am like the American Museum of Natural History: pay what you wish, but you must pay something. I will not write for nothing, but I will write for almost nothing because I like to write and get my opinions out there.

Richard Ouzounian: Being a theater critic is a job, and you should get paid for it. My paper pays its freelancers very decently. I recently heard that a paper was using an intern over the summer to write reviews for free, and it's a big, reputable paper. I don't think that's right.

Richard Zoglin: I guess you have to do what you have to do to stay in the field. I am getting less money now than I did before because they're cutting back, but I wouldn't write for free.

Roma Torre: Why do people take issue with that? Do they think it's making it difficult for other people to make a living at it? We're all poorly paid. But some pay versus no pay? I think they're being taken advantage of, but I have nothing against critics who are doing it without pay. My complaint would be with the employers who don't see fit to give them a decent wage.

Steven Suskin: I hope most of our group is still getting paid. Critics who love the theater want to keep going to shows, but there are some critics who can't afford to do it without getting paid. If they have another job, which a lot of critics do, they can keep going.

Adam Feldman: It's terribly disconcerting. I think it leads to a deprofessionalization of the profession. It creates a circumstance in which fewer of the best people are going to want to go into it because it does not pay. It will only attract people who are doing it as a labor of love. There's nothing wrong with that, but that's somewhat different from the job of a professional critic, and it usually means less editorial oversight and fewer ethical guidelines.

John Lahr: It's the way of the world. A critic is a person who has a job. And if you don't have a job, you're not a critic. So if you have to, you make your own job. If people really want to go to the theater every night and write what they think, that's great. I wish everybody could get paid a living wage for it, but there's nothing I can do about it. A few of my friends are writing without pay. I'm lucky to have other strings to my bow. To have had the *New Yorker* job for 21 years was an amazing gift, for which I am terrifically grateful. But when it's over, it's over. The caravan moves on.

Marilyn Stasio: We live in a commercial world. If you're paid to write, it means you're valued. We deal in money. If you work for free, you're not valued. I remember when a friend of mine, who was a really good critic for an important publication, got fired. The *Huffington Post* people asked if he wanted to write for them. He said, "Sure, what's the deal?" They said, "No deal. We're just giving you an outlet." Excuse me? It's humiliating to think that you're expected to write for nothing.

Michael Riedel: No one is entitled to a living. There's no law that everyone should be paid for doing what they want to do. And if they want to write reviews for free, there are places like the *Huffington Post* that'll happily take them. Personally, I would never write a word without being paid for it, but that's just the generation I'm from. I'd much rather be doing other things than writing for the *Huffington Post* for no money. A lot of people writing for places like the *Huffington Post* are doing it for payment of a sort. They're doing it because they want the free tickets. They don't want to pay for their tickets, so they're complicit in this.

David Finkle: I have mixed feelings over this, and I thought about it when I started to write for the *Huffington Post*. I don't like the idea that people are writing without being paid, but I weighed that against the site's readership and where I am in my life. I've reached a point where I can afford to do it. I worked for a long time to get to this point. I do think they're taking advantage of people, and I hold out the hope that they will change their policy. When I used to appear in comedy clubs as part of an act, the clubs didn't pay, but now they do, so it's possible that things will change.

Robert Feldberg: There have always been people who love the theater so much that they'll do things for very little pay or no pay at all. You have to pay somebody to cover a city council meeting because nobody's going to do that for pleasure. It's just the nature of things.

Ronni Reich: It can cheapen the craft when people do all of this work without compensation. I'll see job postings that say "free tickets as payment." That's not payment. That needs to be understood and taken seriously.

Terry Teachout: Amateur writing about theater—and I don't use the word amateur pejoratively—can be of the highest possible quality. I'm not knocking it in any way. But if you want to do anything really well, you have to do it a lot. If it can't be your job, if that's not an option, you're not going to be able to make the commitment of time and energy that makes for a more informed critic. It doesn't mean we're not going to have good theater criticism, but it does put a tremendous obstacle in the road to having good criticism, particularly out in the regions and medium-sized cities where criticism has always been a little dicey. There is no good substitute for being able to work full-time, immerse yourself in the theater world, and practice seeing shows and writing about them.

Jason Zinoman: On a macro level, it is a problem, but I have trouble judging people on that. You can't control the macroeconomic situation. You need to look out for yourself. When you start your career, you have to get published. I reached a point fairly early in my career where I said, "I'm not going to write for free." But I don't want to sound like some old codger. The reality is that times have changed. There are far fewer places that pay. It's true that I've done some jobs that pay less money, or that pay almost nothing, in order to reach more people, and that's essentially the same kind of decision that young people are making. I would put the responsibility on the shoulders of the institutions, and not the people struggling inside of them.

Robert Feldberg: About 20 years ago, I went to a couple of American Theatre Critics Association conventions. Even at that point, there were very few people who were full-time critics. There was a woman from Anchorage, Alaska who was also the police reporter. Other people taught. Some did it on a freelance basis. Some got paid and some didn't.

MATT WINDMAN: *Can a new business model be created for theater criticism that will allow more critics to get paid for their work?*

Gordon Cox: We haven't figured out how to create a model that is sustainable. It doesn't seem like an impossible goal, but it's a hard nut to crack.

Howard Shapiro: I've often wondered about that. I don't know what the model would be. I'm sure that one can be set up because people want to read critics.

Robert Faires: If I knew where the money was coming from, I'd have a better way to answer the question. I see our paper struggling to find revenue for what we publish online, which is where so many people want to get information these days. Maybe it's in creating your own media outlet, blog, or website and finding advertisers or some other way of bankrolling it.

Alexis Soloski: I'm sure there's someone who can organize it, but it's not me. I never took a single economics class.

Ben Brantley: I hope so, but don't ask me what it is. If I solved it, I'd be doing it. But I can't speculate about that. I have no business sense at all. The Web is still such a frontier, even though it's becoming the dominant form of media. No one's really worked out an efficient and sustained way to make money on the Web. It's kind of unnerving, but also exciting.

David Rooney: I recently moderated a panel for the Broadway Association, which is connected to Broadway in terms of businesses, restaurants, shops, hotels, and things like that. I prefaced my opening by talking about the financial results of the 2013–14 season, which grossed $1.27 billion. When I first started covering theater in 2004 in New York, that $1 billion threshold was a pipe dream. Every year, the box office would get close, but it would never crack $1 billion. Now, for the past four or five years, it's cracked $1 billion every year. Attendance has not grown correspondingly, so obviously a lot of that is attributable to premium seating and staggered pricing. Everyone talks about Broadway as the "fabulous invalid," and how we have to keep her on her feet, but Broadway is a very lucrative industry. No one ever talks that way about theater critics, who are quickly becoming the not-so-fabulous invalids.

I'm not saying we should be subsidized by the Broadway industry (although it's a thought!) because we couldn't possibly be objective that way, but I do think that someone needs to take a look at arts criticism as an endangered species, and find a way to foster it and help it grow.

Michael Portantiere: I don't know if a new economic model can be created specifically for theater criticism. People have made attempts to monetize content on the Web in one way or another in order to allow the people who contribute to websites to be paid. If efforts continue to be made, maybe new ideas for monetizing content will arrive.

Michael Schulman: It really depends on the media in general. I don't think theater criticism could do it in a bubble. Every newspaper and magazine is struggling financially, and how it all turns out in the end will determine how theater criticism is practiced.

Michael Sommers: I haven't been able to figure out a model for myself to make a better living at this. I don't know what younger people are going to do unless they're able to cultivate their own personal websites, or whatever a website will be in 20 years, and gain some sort of revenue from it. It was suggested at some point that I do something like that, but I just didn't see myself being able to run that whole kind of operation. I'm Michael Sommers, not Elyse Sommer (who runs *CurtainUp.com*).

Robert Feldberg: I don't see how you can use criticism to make money, other than saying, "Look, we run editorial matter on theater, so this is a good place to advertise." A lot of newspapers run fall and spring theater preview sections to draw advertising. In that sense, they're using the work of critics to sell ads.

Jeremy Gerard: I don't think there's any new economic model. Journalists have to make a living, just like everyone else, and they should be paid for what they do. Do I think there's a possibility that journalism will be publicly or privately subsidized, in the way some other undertakings are? Maybe, but that's not going to change the model, which is that people have to earn a living, and journalists are among those people.

Jesse Oxfeld: The Internet isn't an economic model. It's just a venue. Is there a way to monetize it? If someone wants to endow something like the *Guardian* in London, which is a not-for-profit owned by a trust created by its founders, or a foundation that runs a publication with theater reviews, more power to them. If a producer like David Stone wants to do that with all of his *Wicked* money, that would be lovely, but it's hard to see that happening. Perhaps I'm not a creative enough thinker.

Theater critic jobs have always existed within publications, and publications are now having a hard time figuring out how to make money. We'll always have theater criticism in some form because there are some publications that believe theater criticism is integral to what they do. We're talking about the *New York Times*, *New York* magazine, the *New Yorker*, and *Time Out New York*. When Linda Winer retires, do you think *Newsday* is going to hire a new full-time theater critic? I doubt it. Do you think *amNewYork* would ever turn its theater critic position into a full-time gig, where they're paying someone a real salary to do it? I doubt it. That's the reality of media economics today.

Leonard Jacobs: I don't think there's any profit to be made just from criticism. Nowadays, consumers have such a tremendous variety of choices that I don't know why they would pay for criticism. However, I do think that there is profit to be made from arts journalism. Reviews combined with other kinds of arts coverage could be valuable. *TheaterMania*, which I worked for many years ago, is a good example of an Internet product that deals only with live performance and has figured out how to generate a profit—not from reviews per se, but from club memberships, advertising, and marketing partnerships.

Robert Hurwitt: I don't think you could do it on the weekly newspaper model that's supported by advertising. I've lived in the Bay Area since 1964. During those years, there have been many attempts to create a weekly or monthly arts paper, but every one of them has gone belly up. Not one of them was able to establish the advertising base to keep it going. Most of them never even had enough to be able to pay writers enough to allow them to scratch out a living, even by doing a lot of freelancing.

Terry Teachout: The whole model of newspaper writing is broken beyond repair. We're lurching through a transitional period into a very new kind of newspaper journalism with a different model, different modes of distribution, and different kinds of content, which will arise organically from the ways in which those institutions are being shaped. Theater criticism will evolve as the nature of professional journalism evolves. The whole business is going to look very different 10 years from now.

When I first started blogging, which was more than a decade ago, many people thought it would be possible for bloggers to develop income streams to support themselves as writers, but that hasn't happened. Only very few bloggers who write about specific subjects of extremely wide interest can support themselves. I don't see independent theater critics being able to launch websites that bring in revenues sufficient to allow them to run their sites full-time.

You can't look at theater criticism in isolation. You have to look at the problem of what newspapers will be like in five or 10 years. Will they be supported by billionaires (like how the *Washington Post* was bought), who will run them as a way of providing ancillary advantage to their larger enterprises? I don't know. We still have major newspapers in every city. I wonder if that'll be true in five or six years. Most of us in the business have been looking at certain cities (Detroit is the most obvious example) where the city will no longer be able to economically support a daily newspaper.

The next biggest change will be the move away from print. Over the next decade, I think we will see major newspapers shut down or curtail their print sides. They will be distributed only electronically, but that's a problem. The electronic model has not been as productive in providing revenue from advertising.

Jason Zinoman: If there is a model, it's clearly online. There needs to be an online business model that will both get a huge amount of traffic and do serious work. There's a lot of creative work being done right now in new online journalistic models—places like *Vox*, *Grantland*, and *Slate*. There's a huge opportunity to build a kind of *Politico* for theater.

You would need a few big investors, but I think there's room for optimism. Theater in New York is built on huge investments in shows that will likely lose money, but people invest money anyway because they think it's important or because it's fun. There are people in the city who give millions of dollars every year to support the arts. Magazines like the *New Republic* and the *Nation* have lost a lot of money. They've been run by people who care about ideas and politics and influencing the culture. What you need is somebody who understands this art and believes that it should be covered with all the principles that make for good journalism. It would not be easy, but it would be less hard than it seems. I think it'll happen in the next 10 years. Someone will build a really dynamic online site for theater criticism. That's the solution. That's the future.

Don Aucoin: Newspapers have taken steps toward a solution, with paywalls on websites and whatnot. I hope the next step is to find sustainable livelihoods for talented writers who are currently expected to work for free. Writing is hard work, and people shouldn't be expected to do it for free. But writing is also about self-expression, and I understand the impulse to write and publish and be heard.

Andy Propst: We've entered an era in which an arts journalist needs to be as shrewd a self-promoter and entrepreneur as any working artist and keep his or her fingers on the pulse of what the newest technologies are. In that regard, I think that an arts journalist can attract a career that will keep a roof over his or her head. It won't look like the career of a critic or arts journalist from 50 years ago, where someone was hired by a paper and that was a term for life. But I do think that we are at a juncture where inventiveness combined with talent, respect, and taste can allow an arts journalist to excel and earn a living. At this juncture, there are very few critics who earn their living as critics. In many regards, critics are becoming more like those artists that have to keep a day job in order to do what they love by night.

Charles Isherwood: I recently heard about an experiment being undertaken in Los Angeles. A plan was to put out for a website where the theaters would have to pay in order to have critics from the website review their shows. The critics would be paid a certain fee, and the website would keep a percentage of the money. I find it startling that there are so few publications running reviews in Los Angeles that theaters would be willing to pay to have their shows covered, even with no guarantee of getting a good review on this website. That idea is problematic on a number of levels. The major theaters would probably not be interested in engaging in that because their shows are already going to be reviewed. It would only be the small-fry theaters that would pay to have their shows reviewed, and that wouldn't necessarily draw a lot of readership to the website.

I don't know of any other models being proposed. I know many websites with reviews have been established. Some have been going on for many years, but I don't know if they've provided a living wage to many, or any, theater critics.

Michael Musto: Maybe someone can start a site where they hire different kinds of critics and give them all a home in one place. They can all review the same show and offer different points of view. I don't know where they'd get the money, but there's a lot of advertising money from Broadway.

Peter Marks: I imagine there's an audience for something between *BroadwayWorld.com* and the *New York Times*—something a little more high-tone that also has a consumer component. Maybe a reviewing website can be created that has all the performing arts and isn't just about aggregating content. It's got to feel like a long-term investment. What if five of the best-known theater critics, from the *Times* to the *New Yorker*, created a website in which their reviews on the same shows were posted side by side? Would it find an audience, or would it just die out?

Jesse Green: I suppose we could convince producers to pay critics directly for positive reviews, and then we'd all be rich! Short of that, I don't know. I'm not much of a futurist. I have heard people say that criticism, in its current form, will disappear and completely atomize into the kinds of discussions and bits of information you find in chat rooms, blogs, and things like that. I guess I'm too old to really believe that.

I think we'll stabilize at some point. There will be different kinds of buyers' spheres offering different kinds of criticism. In any case, there's not going to be a lot of money in it for writers. Of course, there's never been a lot of money in criticism for writers. We're basing our sad ideas of where theater journalism stands today on an imagined golden age of Walter Kerr living in an eight-bedroom house in the suburbs that may not have ever existed. I'm not sure if these reviewing jobs ever provided a middle-class income.

Christine Dolen: There are different models that can be experimented with and created, but I think it has to be through a foundation. For instance, the Knight Foundation, which is based in Florida, has a program to hire dance critics to review things.

David Cote: My dream is to come up with a model to subsidize theater criticism. Who will subsidize it? Will theaters want to put money into a company for people to review their shows? I don't know. Theater critics face the same problems as theater companies: a shrinking audience, people who are less and less willing to spend $50 to $60 on a play by a new playwright. Likewise, critics have to find a way to develop an audience to read our stuff. There is also an increasing cultural illiteracy of the media itself, and editors and media owners who don't give a damn about theater. We need to keep fighting for visibility.

Frank Rizzo: If nonprofit theaters support the critics, what happens when those theaters don't like what certain critics are writing? Will they apply pressure to get rid of a reviewer? I've always liked the for-profit model because at the end of the day, quality wins out, and not the pressure of individual theaters. There could be a business model based on readership metrics. If you can prove that you're attracting the readership of a certain type of audience, maybe you can get advertisers, but that's not my specialty. I'm a writer, not a marketer or a business executive.

Thom Geier: I really don't know how that would work. Would the critics be sponsored by an institute for criticism? I'm all in favor of finding as many ways as possible to have writers, journalists, and critics make a living for themselves in this new media culture. More power to anyone who can find a way to make it work.

Elisabeth Vincentelli: I think the nonprofit model is potentially workable. A dream scenario would be to have a nonprofit foundation that would fund critics in New York and other cities. I'm sure there's some billionaire somewhere with deep pockets who would be willing to do that.

Helen Shaw: I don't know what happens when you divorce arts criticism from newspapers, magazines, and cross-interest publications. That's when you start segregating your audience really intensely. That's when you view your metric and see that only 15 people read your review, which you took 15 hours to write, and that's depressing. Publicly subsidizing a news organization is a good first step. There is some great arts coverage through the BBC.

Howard Shapiro: There is a new economic model being set up for the theater criticism that I'm currently doing, which is underwriting for public media. I'm talking about memberships, donations, and private foundations, which are the very same things that support the arts. While that may not be a new model for public media in general, it's a fairly new model for criticism.

Eric Grode: If you're looking at economic models, you'd have to make sure that whoever is subsidizing the critics doesn't color or affect their opinions. It would be great if we can find people with deep pockets who just want theater criticism to be written.

Richard Ouzounian: Universities could be a salvation to a certain degree, but who's going to monitor it? Who's going to be the conduit? Is it going to come through the English department? Is it going to come through the creative writing department? Is it going to come through the journalism department? It's tough to figure that out.

Rob Weinert-Kendt: The people who'd be most interested in there continuing to be theater coverage and theater criticism are the theater makers. But if they were to fund theater criticism, there would be an issue of independence. The White House wouldn't fund an independent journalist to investigate what it's doing.

You'd need to have people behind it who are interested in either the art form or disinterested criticism. A lot of the foundations that could fund things like that tend to be about supporting theaters, productions, and writers, but that shouldn't be at odds with criticism. Theater makers, when you talk to them, recognize the value and role of critics in the abstract, but they've always taken it for granted that the critics are paid by someone else. If you came to them with a bill and said, "Would you like to pay and support theater criticism?" I don't know what would happen.

The economic model that has worked for newspapers is selling ads, and that supports whatever they want to do with that money. There isn't a direct return for international investigative reporting, and there isn't a one-to-one return for every ad dollar for theater criticism. The papers have always covered what they think is best, but that has changed now with the online culture of something being clickable.

I feel like theater writers can still be part of a larger entity. We don't have to go off and just write about theater for theater fans. There is a model directed specifically at theater fans, but you'll find that in a lot of markets, people who are into theater also go to the symphony, the opera, and the movies. They're patrons of the arts. So to have something only be about theater is kind of self-defeating. Maybe we could have something that bands together all of the arts and culture. If theater critics could band together with other critics, maybe something could come of that. You think theater critics have it hard? What about dance critics? What about fine art critics?

Adam Feldman: I think that some kind of independently subsidized theater criticism, separate from newspaper or magazine criticism, could actually change criticism for the better. Compared to the thumbs-up, thumbs-down type of criticism, where you are just doing drive-by evaluations, those reviews could be a little more considered and evenly balanced. But who would want to read them? If reviews were never cheap and shallow, or even a little nasty or crazy, would people enjoy them as much?

Matthew Murray: I'm not sure what the value of theater criticism would be from a nonprofit standpoint, unless you mean actual criticism of the kind that would typically occur at the journal or university level. As far as reviewing, I don't think that can be justified at all. There's a way to make money doing anything if you want it badly enough. If you want to review plays for a living, no one's stopping you from figuring out a way to make it pay. But I have no idea why there would ever be a nonprofit component to it. As much as I love theater and writing about it, I can't see why anyone should consider it that important.

11

Online

MATT WINDMAN: How has the Internet changed theater criticism?

Ben Brantley: In some ways, it's made theater criticism looser, jazzier, more gossipy, and more conversational. Online, a review can have embedded video of the show. You can have a link to buy tickets to the show. It's a one-stop-shop to get an opinion and also get tickets. The Internet has also allowed some publications to have longer criticism online. I can tell people in print to read an extended version of the review online. Those are all positive aspects.

Brian Lipton: You can quickly post things on the Internet, which means you don't have to worry about deadlines in the same way that you do with print, where you have to get it in 24 hours in advance. I can literally send something in to an editor at 9:30 p.m., and it can be up at 10 p.m. or even 9:35 p.m. The Internet is also positive in that, depending on the site, you don't have the same constraints with word count as you sometimes do with print. When I wrote for the *New York Post*, I think my word count was 250 words. Now I can write 500 or 600 words when I feel like it.

Andy Propst: I started the website *American Theater Web* around the same time that Elyse Sommer started *Curtain Up*. I don't think Martin Denton had started *NYTheatre.com* yet. I was breaking a lot of ground in terms of online criticism. I was the first Internet critic at the O'Neill, and the first one accepted into the American Theatre Critics Association. The Drama Desk had not yet formulated how it was going to deal with online critics. There are obviously a lot more online theater critics now.

Elisabeth Vincentelli: The weird thing about the Internet is that it hasn't killed theater itself. There's more theater than ever. The paradox is that the reporting on it and the reviewing of it are completely collapsing. It's just nuts.

Steven Suskin: In the old days, a newspaper was printed in the morning; and by the evening, the review was obsolete. You could see the quotes in advertisements, but the actual review was gone. On the Internet, that's not the case. You can just type in the name of a show and the reviews will come up, even if the show opened years ago. That means theatergoers can read our opinions indefinitely. Before that, you had to go to the library to find the reviews.

Richard Ouzounian: The bad thing about writing exclusively online is that it generates a lot of bad habits. You tend to run off at the mouth. I will occasionally say very cutting and scathing things, but I've also been trained in the art of what constitutes libel and character defamation.

I believe in the critic as a print writer. I worry very much about online writing. I make sure my reviews are online properly and promptly, and that they look good online, but I'm really writing for print. I still believe in the generation of people who leaf through the paper in the morning at the breakfast table, or on the subway, on the train, or wherever. My fantasy is that they flip by the entertainment section and a really attractive picture, or a really grabby headline, or four stars at the top of a review catches their eye and they read the review and say, "Let's go see this."

My colleague on the other major paper in Toronto, J. Kelly Nestruck of the *Globe and Mail*, has been known to say, "I do not care what my reviews look like in the tree edition of the newspaper." He's all about online, *Twitter*, *Facebook*. I think those things can be very important, especially in keeping a national profile and having people outside the city know what you're writing, but I think in terms of the old era. How does it look on the page? How many inches of copy did you get?

Eric Grode: People have gotten accustomed to getting their news for free. Not enough newspapers put up pay walls in the beginning. Now those newspapers have a lot less money and a lot less advertising. The pages are getting smaller, and there isn't as much physical or financial room as there used to be to support writers.

Terry Teachout: By and large, the Internet has been a net positive throughout the arts, even though one of its effects has been to dry up the market for newspapers. It's opening up criticism to a much wider range of people, some of whom know more about it than the people who write about it professionally. It also gives the theater professional an opportunity to get into the conversation, which is something I feel is very important. I believe devoutly in what I call "practitioner critics," insofar as artistic professionals feel comfortable writing criticism. Even if they don't want to write about other people, they should be writing about themselves.

Charles Isherwood: I'm troubled by the fact that a reader can go on a website, read a critic's review, and then write his or her own review in the comment section. That doesn't create an equation between the critic's voice and the reader's voice, but it says that the critic's opinion isn't the only one. The value of our work is being cheapened. Everything gets sort of equalized. I'm sure that sounds elitist, but I don't really care. I guess I am an elitist, in the sense that I do think certain people are good at their jobs for a reason and should be rewarded for that.

MATT WINDMAN: *Are chat room and message board users usurping the theater critic's role, especially since they can often attend an early preview and write a show before the critics get a chance?*

Michael Musto: One of the interesting twists of the new technology is that by the time a show has opened and the reviews have come in from the opening night critics, you've already read on the Broadway boards everything that's right and wrong with the show. So by the time your own review comes out, it doesn't seem quite as special as it used to be. Why are these people wasting their time posting on a website for no money? I'll never figure it out. It's scary that anonymous people out there in the dark are usurping our jobs.

John Lahr: I don't take all that in. One of the things you have to do as a critic is stay sane and keep your mind free of that nattering buzz, all of which means nothing.

Richard Zoglin: When I review something, I'm not obsessively tracking the chat rooms or *All That Chat*. Let the people chat. I don't pay attention to them.

Peter Marks: There's nothing like *All That Chat* in Washington, D.C. There's no communal site where everyone writes about shows before the critics go to see them. Most of the shows in Washington have only two or three preview performances, so there's no chance for other people to get ahead of the reviewers. Some shows here are starting to have longer preview periods, and that's something I get complaints about.

Organizations should invest in branding their critics and making them stand out from everybody else. This is a big, tough job. It's a burden. Not everyone can do it. I guess that's why so many people fall by the wayside. You have to work your ass off at it. You have to establish a voice that rises above the conversation. It's also about credibility. If people who write comments on the chat sites don't put their own name on what they write, they don't have any real investment in their credibility. It makes their judgment suspect.

Adam Feldman: There has always been word of mouth about shows. People have always told their friends what they thought. Now it's just being written down and shared in a more active way. The people who see things during previews represent a certain part of the community. There have been times when the wisdom of the chatterati turned out to be very different from the critical reaction or the audience reaction in the long term.

Terry Teachout: The chat rooms simply accelerate the buzz that has always been an intrinsic part of theater, especially in a city like New York. It just speeds up what already existed. In my experience, buzz is almost always true if it's pronounced in one direction or another. Ninety-five times out of a hundred, if you've heard that a musical is going to be awful, it will be. There's nothing wrong with knowing that. It's always good to avoid punishment.

John Simon: Too much attention is being paid to the chat rooms. While everybody should have his own critical standards, it doesn't mean that they should bother us or other people with their opinions.

Charles Isherwood: The people who are going on these chat sites and reading these first reports from non-professional critics are a very small subset of the theatergoing population. They're the truly obsessive theatergoers. The public may be aware that a show is playing, but they won't know what the responses are until the reviews come out.

I don't go on those sites because reading numerous opinions of a show when it's in early previews creates a bit of a clutter in your head when you finally go to see it. It's hard to get those voices out of your head when you sit down to write the review. When I was at the office at *Variety*, I would kill time by going on *All That Chat*. But now that I'm not tethered to a desk, I don't do that as much.

Also, now that I'm at the *Times*, those crazy queens on *All That Chat* are always tearing into me and Ben Brantley, so it's not enjoyable to look at the site. I guess it's par for the course. George Jean Nathan said, "A man in the brick-throwing business must expect occasionally to be hit by a brick," but I don't go out of my way to hear the awful things people are saying about me. Life is hard enough already.

Eric Grode: If Jesse21 on *All That Chat* does a better job at writing about a show in a chat room than a critic for a sanctioned professional medium, there's no reason why readers should feel duty-bound to read the critic over Jesse21. I'm okay with the idea that the best writing out there should get the most readers.

Jesse Green: I look at those sites, and I enjoy them. They're somewhere between a coffee klatch and a mud fight. Some of the people that write posts are clearly quite knowledgeable about the business or the art of theater. That's great, but it's not criticism. Even the posts that label themselves as reviews are not really professional reviews, as is easily demonstrated if you compare any of them to a professional review. To the extent that we believe that the theater or any other art form is still worthy of serious attention by writers who have a background in the art form, we need professional theater critics.

This is not to say that the presence of those communities is a negative. They support excitement and interest in the theater, but in a different way. It's like the difference between a community theater production, which could be very good, and an Equity production. What you see at an Equity theater may vary in quality, but there's at least going to be some seasoning to it.

Jesse Oxfeld: The overwhelming majority of ticket purchasers have no idea what *All That Chat* is.

Leonard Jacobs: I look at *All That Chat* once or twice a day. It seems to be a group of, at most, a couple hundred people, not all of whom are in New York. I think their influence is limited, and that's to say nothing about their taste. They only influence the other people in the chat rooms.

Terry Teachout: I snoop around once in a while in the chat rooms, but what I find out tends to not be useful. It's the commentary of agitated fans. Sometimes it can be interesting, but there is no substitute for a good review, least of all a 140-character tweet. In the *Journal*, I have 850 to 1,100 words at my disposal, to use in whatever way I want, and I have time to write those pieces.

Alexis Soloski: I don't think citizen journalism does the same job or demands the same rigor. It's great that there are venues that allow people to voice their opinions. I read it, and I value it, but I don't confuse it with professional theater criticism.

Ben Brantley: I think that having a job or a title gives you a feeling of responsibility. If you're in a chat room, you can much more instinctive. It's like tweeting—you write before you think. I think that's the danger of the Web in many ways, especially if you're a person with a low impulse control or who drinks a lot. I'd rather read a reasoned argument than a quick, orgasmic yelp.

David Sheward: It's gossip, not a review. There's nothing wrong with it, but it's not the same as an informed review of the final product. They're saying, "I saw a preview, and this is what I thought."

Elisabeth Vincentelli: It's background chatter. I see a lot more shows than most of those chatters. I see about 215 shows a year. I doubt that many of them can do that. And it's not just a matter of "I see more shows than you, so I know more." We see the show when it's been deemed to be ready. We see what's meant to be the final version. It's good to have a professional assessment of the final version of a show.

I have a lot of friends who like going to the theater but don't work in the theater, and none of them go to the chat rooms. They read reviews, and that's how they pick their shows. They're not insiders. The people in the chat rooms have an inflated sense of how important they are. It's a very tiny group of people, and they're read only by insiders and not the general audience. It's a distorting mirror.

Jeremy Gerard: Those sites create more of a need for professional critics. Anyone who is involved in the performing arts knows that 99 percent of what is put out online in the chat rooms is meaningless. There are some smart people who write smart blogs, but it's hard to find them.

Robert Feldberg: Most of the chat rooms I've seen are pretty amateurish.

They're full of free-floating enthusiasm and opinions that aren't backed up by anything. They're very personal in a bad way. They write, "I went to the theater last night. I saw this. I saw that. I love this actor." It's like somebody's diary.

Thom Geier: If you go on some of those chat rooms on the opening night of a new show, someone will often post a roundup of all the reviews from the professional critics, so it seems like even they care about our opinions.

Michael Riedel: I know for a fact that a lot of the people on *All That Chat* are press agents or producers using fake names to promote their own shows. The nice thing about having critics is that you know who they are. You know where they're coming from. You know they're being paid by their publication, and not by the people that they're writing about.

MATT WINDMAN: Do you use social media as a theater critic?

Rob Weinert-Kendt: Social media is a tool. Some of my favorite film critics engage with readers on *Twitter*. That must be exhausting to do. Peter Marks does it in D.C. I know that Brantley reads a lot of stuff online, but I don't think he involves himself in commenting. In the arts journalism programs that I know about, people are being trained to use social media. A lot of the job listings that I see now are for people to manage social media and file posts every day. The whole business is changing. People are aggregating content and tweeting for a brand or magazine. I'm not sure where criticism is going to fit into that.

Jesse Oxfeld: It's what's happening across the journalism business: engaging with readers online and trying to build an audience in that way. You do end up seeing some interesting conversations between writers and creators on *Twitter*. You also see a lot of conversations happening among critics, which are sometimes amusing and sometimes tedious. What's more interesting is when a debate flares up. Mike Daisey is such an active *Twitter* user. He can be bullying and angry on *Twitter*, but he can also be really smart and insightful. I don't tend to get into those conversations, but they're interesting to watch as they're happening.

Hilton Als: Our editor, David Remnick, doesn't press you into that stuff at all. He's great that way.

Michael Schulman: Every journalist has to have a *Twitter* account now—and I don't think that's a bad thing. It's how you reach people. Jason Zinoman is a very provocative, insightful critic on *Twitter*. John Lahr just joined *Twitter* two days ago. I love watching critics disagree with each other on *Twitter* and hash out arguments about whatever is on their minds.

Terry Teachout: A professional writer uses social media to strengthen the brand that is himself. I use *Twitter* and my blog to point people to my reviews, comment about the theater and the arts in general, communicate with people, and make myself more present. As far as I know, I was the first national arts journalist to start a blog about the arts. It was only by a couple of weeks, but it was me. That was also the year I became the theater critic of the *Wall Street Journal*. In 2003, I realized that blogging was going to become a very important thing. I said to myself, I better come to terms with this now. I did the same with *Twitter* and *Facebook* when they came along. I just see them as part of my daily work, and I enjoy using them, too.

Helen Shaw: I read my Facebook feed, but I very rarely write on Facebook or tweet. I feel like I'm five years too old to really adapt to it correctly. It's something I feel guilty about daily.

Perez Hilton: I use *Twitter, Facebook, Tumblr,* and *Instagram* for all of my reviews.

Ben Brantley: I don't use social media at all. I have a *Twitter* account only because there was someone impersonating me on *Twitter,* and the only way to get this guy to stop was to open my own account. I'm not on *Facebook*. The *Times* would like us all to use social media because it's the direction of things. I'm just naturally a private person. Self-promotion, which social media is largely about, is something I feel incredibly uncomfortable with.

Christine Dolen: I'm *Facebook* friends with tons of theater people in the community, so I learn about things through *Facebook*. I also hear from a lot of professionals on *Facebook* after my reviews get posted.

Peter Filichia: I talk about my theater columns on *Facebook*. Getting the word out is perfectly fine. I'm not above doing that. Even though I'm an old-timer when it comes to traditional theater, I like the fact that all this new technology can help us spread the word.

Charles Isherwood: The industry has changed for all journalists in various ways. The job used to be to see a show and write a review, and that was the end of the process. Now, with the increasing importance of social media, there's a lot more pressure to continue the process: to open yourself up to *Twitter, Facebook,* and reader comments. We're supposed to be much more engaged with our readers now. It's supposed to be more of a conversation, as opposed to, "Here's the official take of the *New York Times*. End of story."

I am not terribly active on social media, but I am increasingly seeing that it's inevitable, especially for the next generation of critics. Even for old fogies like myself, I feel like it's time to start learning those tools. I am somewhat of a *Facebook* phantom. I am not on *Twitter* at all. I follow a few people on *Instagram,* but I am not generating any content. I don't embrace the idea of self-promotion. I feel like a lot of it is, "Here's my review. Read my review." To me, that is an act of narcissism.

It's a challenge for all of us because it's a lot more work. In addition to writing reviews (which takes a considerable amount of thought and research), you have to think about ways of promoting your work and connecting with readers. For people just starting out in journalism, these things come quite easily to them. For people who have been working in more traditional models for many years, it's a whole new ballgame—and one that many of us don't really want to play.

David Cote: I use it for self-promotion—to post links to my reviews and distribute my work. As far as sharing my life on social media, I'm not interested in that. I'm too busy writing. If I'm not writing for *Time Out*, I'm working on my own art. I see people incessantly tweeting about this and that, and I'm not that eager to share my life with strangers.

Richard Zoglin: I do a little tweeting—not very much, usually just a link to a story. I've toyed with the idea of tweeting about shows that I can't review. I really loved the Alan Ayckbourn play I just saw, but *Time* couldn't accommodate a review. I've written about Ayckbourn before, but in this time of picking and choosing, the magazine passed on publishing a review. I did a quick tweet on the show because I was so impressed. I don't know if that was good or bad.

Richard Ouzounian: I absolutely do not tweet. I don't want to enter into the trivial, mindless discussions that I see happening with it. I see what it does to J. Kelly Nestruck at the *Globe and Mail*. I see him being tempted to run off at the mouth at 140 characters about everything from the karaoke bar he's at to what he thought about the show he just saw at intermission. That's not what I do.

Maybe I'm an old-fashioned old fart, but I do not think theater criticism, at my level, is about dialogue. As someone who's trained and has worked as long as I have, I have an opinion. You can disagree with that opinion. You can write letters to the editor. If you write me an email using your real name, I will answer you intelligently and respectfully every time. But I think the comments section under all the online reviews is one of the worst things that has ever happened to theater criticism. It lets trolls hide, and it's usually the same trolls time and time again.

Most of social media is not liberating anybody. It's not doing anything for those of us who are in the positions of authority. It's letting other people have a free shot at us. They think, I'm going to post 140 words on Richard Ouzounian's *Twitter* feed that will be so brilliant that the world will stop and realize I should be the next critic. That's not how it goes, and you just wind up wasting your time. I did *Facebook* for a little, but I found it was more of a social exercise than anything else.

I recently had a huge argument about this with J. Kelly Nestruck. It was the time of year when we get leaks about what'll happen next season at the Shaw Festival and Stratford Festival, and we both happened to get the same leaks on the same night. Kelly tweeted the names of three shows that he heard were being done next season at Stratford. I went out, did a little more homework, and found out who was directing them, how they were fitting in the season, and who would probably be in them, and I wrote a piece online later that evening. That's journalism. Just tweeting the titles of the plays is gossipy pissing in a barrel.

Twitter is great for revolutionary movements, to get people stirring in the street. But when was the last time something artistically important happened on *Twitter*? It makes you realize that Ira Glass (from the radio show *This American Life*) randomly said "Shakespeare sucks." It becomes the scandal of the day, and then it's forgotten. It doesn't do anything for real dialogue, and that's why I don't waste my time on it.

Robert Faires: I'm trying to get better at it, but I haven't used it an awful lot. I've tried to up my game in the last year or so, but I'm an old dog for whom that particular new trick is proving harder to learn than I expected. Over the years, I've gotten slower, while the pace at which the world is moving has picked up, so I'm at a disadvantage. There are a lot of things I just don't think of doing because I'm still in the mode I learned way back. It doesn't always occur to me to get on *Twitter* and throw 140 characters out about something, like letting people know I just saw a show or that a review is coming. I'm hardwired to write in what's probably the most old-fashioned way possible. I have been trying to break myself of that habit, but what little success I've had has been modest.

Don Aucoin: You go where the readers are, and social media is where the readers are. The *Globe* sends out my stuff on *Twitter*. I also post my reviews on *Facebook*. I've got 530 *Facebook* friends, and I try to engage them in a dialogue about theater. I'm not boosterish, but if something's worth seeing, I will say so.

Eric Grode: I think people should use as many platforms as they can— as long as they have legitimate things to say on those platforms. I can instantly tell which critics are tweeting only because someone at their office ordered them to do a certain number of tweets per week. They don't get tons of followers because their heart isn't really in it.

The best thing about social media is that we no longer have a situation where the artists create a piece, the critics come in and pass judgment, and that's the end of the discussion. I am in favor of the artists having a chance to respond. I am in favor of audience members having a chance to respond. And if the critic decides to respond back, I don't see any harm in that either. You can easily go down the rabbit hole and spend too much time in that realm, but I think it's healthy for everyone to be held accountable for their opinions. Social media can be a great outlet to engage with your readers.

Roma Torre: I've been advised (or I should say encouraged?) to tweet a lot. And I do somewhat. But to be honest, I don't have the time to share any more than what I write in my reviews. I spend a lot of time crafting each review. There's really no point in saying much more on *Twitter* or *Facebook*. It would almost be like stealing my own thunder. There's obviously a way to share my thoughts on social media, but I hate to be redundant, and I'm just not into writing anything else unless I have a good reason.

Elisabeth Vincentelli: I'm not on *Facebook* at all. The whole idea of friending someone on *Facebook* is really hard. It can be such a can of worms when you're *Facebook* friends with publicists and actors, and it's just really complicated for me to navigate that. But I am on *Twitter*, and I enjoy it. Somehow it feels different. *Twitter* is more of an open field. Following someone has less baggage than friending. I've also gotten embroiled in some *Twitter* wars, which are very fun.

Thom Geier: I tweet my reviews and theater news as well. It's part of the job now. For many people, *Entertainment Weekly* is more than just the print edition that's stapled together and mailed to them, or that appears at the newsstand. People experience *Entertainment Weekly* on their tablets, on our website, on their phones, on *Twitter*. There are many different ways they can access it now, and social media is one of them. It's a way to draw people who might not otherwise be aware that we cover theater, except for it popping up on their *Twitter* feed.

Steven Suskin: I feel like I'm always fighting deadlines, so why do more writing on social media?

Frank Rizzo: I hear from readers through social media. They have wonderful things to say and share, and sometimes it results in other stories. The idea of the critic in the ivory tower is offensive to me. There's nothing more fun than a good old-fashioned argument about something that we all feel passionate about. What you don't want to do is become irrelevant. You don't want to not be a part of that culture.

Jesse Green: I don't know about you, but I get instructed by my publication on using *Twitter* and *Facebook*. Jerry Saltz, our art critic, is one of the biggest *Facebook* destinations of any critic in the world. The rest of us are in awe and mystified because we don't know how to do that. Theater critics are going to have to learn how to leverage their voices electronically, but I'm hopeful that we can figure out a way to do it without cheapening the brand. I'm not there yet. I tweet and post when I have a review. I basically just say, "Here's my review." Apparently, that's not sufficient, but I haven't figured out what else to do—or perhaps I have and I am just unwilling.

Howard Shapiro: I was a really early tweeter. I started five years ago, not long after tweeting had started. The *Inquirer* made a decision that we were going to tweet our reviews. I find that *Twitter* is a really good way to tell people about something out there and to lead them to it. It's helpful for critics to say, "My review is ready." What you're really saying is, "You might be interested in reading this."

11. Online 203

Michael Riedel: I'm not a *Facebook* person. I don't use *Instagram*. I don't tweet. I'm old-fashioned. I rely on my sources. I still believe in calling people, talking to people, chatting with people, going over to see people at their offices, hanging out with them at lunch. I don't think there's any substitute for that kind of old-fashioned "lay work," as we used to call it. People are much more forthcoming when you meet them face-to-face.

The big change for me is that I now can only have exclusives for stuff that is deeply under wraps. You can't really have exclusivity over something that's very dramatic, that happened in front of a lot of people, because all the people that are there can tweet about it. I'm not breaking those kinds of stories anymore. Back in the day, when I had a really good scoop about something that happened in the theater the night before, I would put it in the paper the next day. I would own that story for the rest of the day, and people had to follow me. But now someone can tweet something that happened at the theater, and then everyone else is following the tweet. There's nothing I can do about it. It's the way of the world.

Peter Marks: I went on *Twitter* three or four years ago. My feed is made up of people in the theater world. It's made me more human to them. As a result, I'm more relaxed about talking with them. I've learned how my reviews land, what about my reviews is useful to other people, and which ones have the most impact. I've learned a lot about what's going on in the theater, and the issues that are most important to the people out there, like how there are so few female directors. You get to hear voices from the groups you're not a part of.

Today at a newspaper, you have to be your own delivery system. You can't hope that your review is going to get read just by posting it on a website. I post almost every review on *Twitter,* hoping it will get some readers that way. It's a clicks thing. I tweet back at people who make a statement about the theater that I don't agree with, or that I do agree with. I tweet observations about the state of the theater. I tend to limit my tweets to theater. I don't tweet about politics.

Robert Feldberg: For a while, we were being encouraged to write blogs, so I did, but I didn't find it useful professionally. If a sports writer is constantly updating what's going on with a game, there's an audience of sports fans for that. With the theater, I'm already expressing my opinion in my review. Other than that, I'm not quite sure what a blog would be like. If there's some breaking news, I could send something out, but there isn't much of that in the theater.

Michael Musto: I resisted it for years, but later found it's a good way to drum up traffic and increase my audience. I resent when you only seem to be valued by the amount of people that click on your article, but you have to be realistic and realize that if your piece isn't read by lots of people, then you're pretty much irrelevant and obsolete. A lot of critics have now found that they also have to peddle their work. They have to hawk it to the masses. It's demeaning, but that's the way it is now in the journalistic marketplace. You're a writer and a self-promoter, and sometimes you're a bill collector, too.

Jason Zinoman: As print institutions decline, it becomes more important to have your own personal brand. I just sold a new book. When you talk to publishers, they look at how many *Twitter* followers you have. That's also true in Hollywood for actors. It's the world we live in now. I was asked to go on *Twitter* by my editor. I started begrudgingly, and now I'm addicted to it. You need to learn how to use the form. You can reach a huge number of people and have a really interesting dialogue. There are also some downsides. You have to be careful what you say. Things can be taken wildly out of context. You can't make certain arguments in short form.

12

Spider-Man

MATT WINDMAN: *Was it appropriate for so many theater critics to review* Spider-Man: Turn Off the Dark *before it officially opened on Broadway?*

Eric Grode: I was in the New York Drama Critics' Circle when there was a debate about reviewing *Spider-Man* while it was still technically in previews. It seemed to me like a tempest in a teapot. If I remember correctly, the producers asked for a not-unreasonable grace period, which the critics granted, and then they asked for a massive one, like another couple of months, and that's when critics started bum-rushing the theater. It's not unusual for producers to say, "We need another 10 days or two weeks because this show is really complicated." A lot of organizations will honor that. For the most part, critics will be reasonable when they're given reasonable requests, and they'll be less reasonable when they're given unreasonable requests.

Jesse Oxfeld: If I remember correctly, Jeremy Gerard and Linda Winer were the first to write about the show. I wrote about it soon after that, and then everybody starting writing about it a couple of weeks later. The point when everybody wrote about it was on a date that had been scheduled as opening night before the producers delayed it yet again.

There was a New York Drama Critics' Circle meeting where the matter was discussed. There was a letter from the show's press agent, Rick Miramontez (or maybe it was from the producers via Rick Miramontez), asking the Drama Critics' Circle to agree to abide by their new designated opening date. There was some discussion, and the official answer was that we would make our own decisions with our individual editors. The big question was when the *Times* was going to review it. The *Times* does not allow its critics to be members of the Drama Critics' Circle. There was a fear that the *Times* was going to go ahead and jump the embargo, and everyone else didn't want to have to review it after the *Times*. The general reaction was, "My editor is going to be really pissed off at me if we are scooped by the *Times*."

Michael Dale: When it became known that the *Times* was going to review *Spider-Man* before it opened, I discussed it with my editor and wrote a column about why I was not going to review the show before I was invited to do so. As a reviewer, I believe I am an invited guest. And frankly, I don't want to review anyone who doesn't want to be reviewed. I believe in letting the artists do what they need to do at their own pace and offering my opinion when it's requested.

David Cote: With *Spider-Man*, there were discussions among the critics about what to do. Some of my colleagues were zealous and outraged about the embargo situation. They wanted to break in and file a review. I understand that. But at the same time, I believe in the sanctity of the right of artists to develop their work in peace. Of course, the whole thing was decided when certain reviewers went in and tipped everyone's hand. Then no one wanted to be left out in the cold. I wasn't so happy about it. Still, it was kind of fun and naughty to buy your ticket and sneak in.

Jeremy Gerard: I was the first critic to review *Spider-Man*. I think I went back four times in total. All my reviews pretty much said the same thing because it was a piece of shit from beginning to end. But if the review was written before opening night, I made that clear in the review. I've always gone my own way, and many of my colleagues have vehemently disagreed with me. When I wrote my first review of *Spider-Man*, the *New York Times* attacked me by name, even though they eventually also broke the embargo.

David Sheward: The critics had a right to go in and see the show before it officially opened because it had been in previews for such a long time. The producers delayed the opening night two or three times. Enough was enough, and we deserved to be able to write a review. The show still was a mess at that point, and the public deserved to know that the show was a mess.

Howard Shapiro: When we bought our own tickets, it showed a kind of individualism. It showed that were willing to abide by social conventions with producers for only so long. At some point, we felt we were being toyed with and abused. So we said, "You've broken social convention, so now we have no social convention." Previews don't last 100-plus days. The social convention is that there's an opening night. We get invited on opening night or right before it, we sit where you tell us to sit, and then we write our reviews. We give you a review, and you give us a seat. But that convention didn't cover endless previews where so many people had already seen the show and were telling each other about it. I thought that showed individualism on the part of the critics. I was really proud of the critical community.

Adam Feldman: I did not feel that the critics should have reviewed the Julie Taymor version before it was officially open. I wrote an appeal at the time suggesting that we give them more time to continue developing it before we stepped in with our opinions, but I completely understand why my colleagues felt differently. By that point, it had reached an absurd point in the preview period. They were charging a lot of money for people to see it, and it was very problematic creatively and functionally.

Marilyn Stasio: Do I think the critics overstepped by writing about *Spider-Man* while it was still in previews? I don't know. It was important for the trade press to write about it. I hope *Variety* covered it well. It was something for people in the business to know about—to see what could go wrong, and to realize how important it is to finance your show and set down limits. I don't know why it was covered in the *Times* or the press in general in that way. I don't know why people were so taken with it. There have been all kinds of abominable productions that should never have opened. There's something people want to know about Marie Antoinette going to the guillotine. They like to watch that kind of thing.

David Finkle: *Spider-Man* is a part of the story of contemporary criticism. It was a very big show. Money seemed to be no object to the director, so we kept hearing about how much was being spent. If Julie Taymor had her way, if the producers had said, "Okay, put on the show you want, and we'll only open it when you're finished with it," she'd probably still be working on it today. It challenged critics in a way that was kind of silly. It put us in a position of saying, "How long will you keep throwing good money at something that sounds so bad? We're going to come. You've fiddled enough with this thing." Jeremy Gerard went first. Then Linda Winer went. And then Julie Taymor was fired. At that point, I felt I should see her version because I would have to write about the show when it finally did open, and the reader would want to know how the final version compared to her version. I paid for a ticket, but the real hardship was sitting through it twice.

Michael Schulman: The preview period serves a purpose. It takes a couple weeks for a live performance to get its sea legs. I know some TV critics who refuse to review the pilot episode of a new television show. At the same time, it's like a deal that critics have with the producers to wait until the preview period has passed, and in exchange, they'll get free tickets for the dates that the producers preordain, when the show has reached some kind of finishing point. The whole thing with *Spider-Man* was how it was in previews for months and people were paying full price for tickets. It was a very unique circumstance where the deal was betrayed or abused. The critics felt they had an ethical obligation to go and review what people were paying to see.

Jesse Oxfeld: The producers of *Spider-Man* were asking people to spend a lot of money on tickets for months and months. If you're a reviewer, you owe an obligation to your readers to tell them whether this is something they should or should not be spending money on and why. The whole existence of *Spider-Man* was built around a series of incredibly marketable names, from Spider-Man to Bono. It was specifically designed so that people would want to see it regardless of what Ben Brantley or Robert Feldberg or Jesse Oxfeld might say about it. We live in a market-driven society. Everything that happens around us is based on carefully-calculated marketing campaigns. What color shirts they have at the Gap this week, or what they're putting on the menu at the Olive Garden, has all been focus-grouped and tested in terms of how to get people to spend their money.

Peter Marks: The theater critics were symbolically saying, "There are only so many times you can manipulate the system before we have to take things into our own hands." *Spider-Man* was extreme in every way: the length of the preview process, the problems with the show, the amount of money spent, the degree of publicity. They were all outsized. Was it the right decision to go in and review it when we did? In retrospect, I don't know. At the time, it felt right. It went to the question of who really determines when a show is ready. There are people paying $150 dollars to see the show, so why shouldn't we be there?

Jason Zinoman: To me, the biggest thing *Spider-Man* revealed was that we have this system where there are press performances for critics. There's this sense that a long preview period is set in stone, but I don't think that's true. There's no reason why shows couldn't rehearse before they start charging a hundred dollars for tickets. I thought the press did a really good thing. It was an instance where the producers were abusing the preview period. We needed to react by breaking the embargo and doing what journalists need to do. People were talking about the show. It was important, and it needed to be covered.

Jeremy Gerard: Going back to my days at *Variety*, I have always felt that theater critics allow themselves to be too manipulated by producers. Tryout periods go on too long. It's ridiculous for shows that have already been done at other places to have extended preview periods. I've had a longstanding feud with the way the Public Theater is run because they pick and choose what shows critics can be invited to, especially with their Under the Radar Festival. They bring in shows that have been reviewed all over the place, and then they say that the New York critics can't review some of them. Last summer, I reviewed the musical *The Bridges of Madison County* at the Williamstown Theatre Festival—much to the horror of the Williamstown people, who had made agreements with the creative staff that no New York reviewers would be allowed to see it. I think that's preposterous, particularly at a time when the notion of national critics and local critics has become completely blurred by the Internet. There's no other area of journalism where we let the subjects of our pieces tell us what we can or cannot write about.

12. Spider-Man

MATT WINDMAN: *Did the* Spider-Man *ordeal demonstrate the power or powerlessness of theater critics today?*

Michael Schulman: I think it showed the power of the theater critics. The show survived longer than people thought it would, but the reaction of the critics was very negative, and that undeniably had an impact.

Adam Feldman: *Spider-Man* is a hard case to extrapolate any general conclusions from. It was vastly more expensive than anything that came before it. It had an unusual combination of very high-powered creative forces and an inexperienced producer. The scale of everything made it all wilder than it might have been otherwise.

David Cote: It got some of the worst reviews in history. But if you were to go to the Foxwoods Theatre and ask anybody in the theater about the reviews, they would have looked at you blankly. They don't read reviews. They see a brand—Spider-Man—and they go, like sheep. So the complete impotence of the critics to have an effect on the show was kind of depressing.

Marilyn Stasio: I don't think the theater critics killed *Spider-Man*. It was the press in general. You're confusing theater reviewing with backstage gossip. A lot of what passes for theater criticism these days is really gossip.

Eric Grode: With *Spider-Man*, it's important to separate the critical response from the media response. That all gets lumped together in a lot of people's minds. There was a *New Yorker* cover on *Spider-Man*. David Letterman dealt with *Spider-Man*. Those things weren't reviews. That was just the media having its 15 minutes.

Gordon Cox: It showed the threat of the increasing irrelevance of theater critics, which is why so many critics went to review the show early—to take a stand against a production that had been perceived as pushing them around. I'm not entirely certain they were proved to be irrelevant because the show eventually did close. There was a match-up between the reviews and word-of-mouth that eventually led the production to peter out. It didn't turn into the next *Wicked*.

Alexis Soloski: Criticism isn't helpful for some events. You can write a review of a Barnum and Bailey circus, but people aren't going to decide whether or not to see it because you said it's good or bad. They're going to see it because there are lions and tigers and a motorcycle in a flaming wheel, and that's fine.

Peter Marks: What did it mean when tourists kept seeing it, even after the critics said it was terrible? Spider-Man is a superhero. You can't beat him, you know? A high-flying superhero trumps reviews. In any event, critics shouldn't decide when shows open and close. Why should that be our responsibility? Classical music critics don't close orchestras. Why is there a business component to a theater critic's job? Why is it left to theater critics to have a commercial responsibility? No one expects movie critics to sell tickets. Nobody expects a dance critic to keep a ballet company going. People talk about the power of this or that theater critic to sell a show or close a show, but no one talks about a music critic being able to cancel a concert.

Helen Shaw: *Spider-Man* pointed to a cultural shift on Broadway that has long since happened. In the 1950s, 1960s, and somewhat in the 1970s, Broadway had that beautiful appeal to post–G.I. Bill Middle America, which wanted something highbrow-to-middlebrow to make them feel like they were a part of the national culture. That culture is now gone—and it's gone forever. What's on Broadway now isn't a national conversation. *Spider-Man* did become part of that pop culture conversation. It wasn't about the powerlessness of theater critics. It was about the fact that there is still something marvelous and exciting about a flop, about Broadway, and about backstage chaos.

Ben Brantley: If you look back, *Abie's Irish Rose* was despised by every critic who reviewed it. It was the laughing stock of the critics, but it went on to become one of the longest-running plays in Broadway history. A lot of the musicals that have endured forever like *Cats* were not much loved by the critics. There are always things that slide under the radar. *Spider-Man* was big. It was something unto itself. It just kept running. And at the same time, we were writing so many stories publicizing the show. It became news. Going to see it was like going to a news event.

Steven Suskin: Family musicals and extravaganza musicals are pitched to a different, broader audience that doesn't usually go to the theater. With those shows, it doesn't matter what the critics say. Those people don't read the critics to decide what to see. If you look back at the reviews for *Les Miz* and *Phantom*, you'll see that the reviews were not good. Is it a bad thing that a show with bad reviews is such a hit? As for *Spider-Man*, most of us simply said that it wasn't any good, and the ultimate audience response was not favorable enough to prevent it from failing.

Peter Filichia: In 1966, there was a musical about Superman: *It's a Bird ... It's a Plane ... It's Superman*. Stanley Kauffmann, the *Times* theater critic at the time, called it the best musical of the season. One of the best things about the musical was its lyrics. There's a lyric where Lois Lane wonders if she should forget about Superman because he's never going to marry her. She says she should look for "a homey type who'll stay around/a guy with both feet on the ground." Needless to say, that's funny because Superman flies. There's no lyric in *Spider-Man* that can touch that. Its lyrics are generic. *Spider-Man* was not called the best musical of the season by the *Times*. In fact, I think it was called one of the worst musicals of all time, and yet it ran for three years, while *Superman*, with the blessing of the *Times*, ran only 129 performances. The power of the theater critic is not what it once was.

Elisabeth Vincentelli: *Spider-Man* wasn't about the critics at all. The critics were completely irrelevant. I recently read the book by Glen Berger (the show's book-writer) about what happened behind the scenes at *Spider-Man*, and the critics play very little part in the book. There's a mention of when the critics went in to review it, but it's kind of irrelevant. The reviews were largely irrelevant. *Spider-Man* was its own thing. It was such an oddity in so many ways that it can't be used as a lesson for anything.

Rob Weinert-Kendt: Ultimately, *Spider-Man* couldn't save itself from itself. It was a doomed project from the start. The production, to its benefit and ultimate detriment, ran away from anyone being able to control it. It had rock stars and Julie Taymor. The critics were just a small part of that story. There was no way critics could control that narrative—not least because *Spider-Man* had press agent Rick Miramontez being the referee, making the story happen, even when it was not flattering to the production. Critics weren't going to be the referees. But like in sports, they're the commentators. They're going to have a take on it. And fans at home might throw their beers at the TV, to use that analogy, and say, "You're full of it."

Terry Teachout: Even with a big-budget commodity musical, critics can have an influence. It's almost possible to bulletproof a show if the commodity is popular enough, and if you spend enough money on it, but that is not normal. I think the critics made a difference with *Spider-Man*, but I don't care if people want to see it. I care to the extent that the commodity musical is increasingly crowding out better kinds of musicals on Broadway. But then again, I don't spend most of my time on Broadway. If I did, I'd kill myself. Broadway is just a small part of American theater, and it is not the most important part. I'm perfectly fine with people spending lots of money on shows that I don't like. It's their money. That's their business.

Elysa Gardner: I don't really think the reviews affected it much at all. At the end of the day, I don't think critics can kill a show. Frank Rich was called "the butcher of Broadway" in the 1980s, but Andrew Lloyd Webber still had his hits.

Charles Isherwood: *Spider-Man* was indicative of the current state of Broadway in the sense that there are more and more shows that are impervious to criticism. They are brand-tested before they even get to Broadway. They're adaptations of popular movies or collections of songs from popular artists. What the critics think of these kinds of shows is immaterial. If they strike a chord with an audience, they're going to run whether critics like them or not. If they're second-rate and word of mouth is not particularly good, then eventually they're going to close at a loss, like *Spider-Man* did. It played for a considerable amount of time, but it came nowhere near to making back its investment.

Leonard Jacobs: When I was in high school, there was a show called *Merlin*, which was one of the last shows to play the Mark Hellinger Theatre.

The magician Doug Henning and Chita Rivera were in it, and Nathan Lane had a small role. The preview period went on and on. If my memory serves, the critics started going to review it before the opening, and there was a lot of outrage over it. It didn't make a bit of difference one way or the other. The show was terrible.

Matthew Murray: I do think that *Spider-Man* showed that the critics still do have power. The odds are excellent that the show wouldn't have received an overhaul had the critics not publicly weighed in on what was going on. It seems as though everyone involved thought they could get away with it, and the critics didn't let them, and they deserve credit for that. But—and I realize I'm in the minority with this opinion—I think the critics lighting the fuse on the eventual overhaul really hurt the show in the long run because the changes that were later made were almost universally for the worse. To my reading, a lot of other critics didn't get what the show was trying to do, and therefore weren't assessing it and nudging it along fairly. And so the creative team, which clearly needed help, ended up doing things that weakened the show in every imaginable way. The critics may have been responsible for a different *Spider-Man*, but they were also responsible for a worse *Spider-Man*.

13

Regrets and Advice

MATT WINDMAN: *Considering the current challenges for theater critics, do you wish you had done something else with your life?*

Jason Zinoman: Almost certainly.

Michael Dale: I have a lot to regret about my life. Getting free tickets to every show on Broadway isn't one of them.

John Lahr: I did do something else with my life. I didn't make my living writing drama criticism. I wrote books and movies and the occasional play. If I was only tossing out opinions, I'd be in bad shape. I didn't start out being a theater critic. I didn't even think you could make a living writing criticism until I went to Oxford.

Gordon Cox: Do I think I'll be doing this for the rest of my life? Who knows? Where this industry is going is totally unpredictable, but I've gotten quite a bit out of it.

Jeremy Gerard: I've been very lucky because since 1975, I have always found a way to earn a pretty good living as a journalist. I'm basically doing what I've always done, but I've been able to accommodate myself to changes in technology. Of course, I would be giving a very different answer if I was still looking for work after losing my job at *Bloomberg*. I have seen great pain inflicted on a lot of my colleagues. I'm no better than they are, and a lot of them are seriously struggling and facing challenges that we shouldn't have to at our age. Unfortunately, it's not limited to critics or even to journalists. We live in dire times for a lot of people.

Ronni Reich: It's hard to say because my original goal was to pursue a career as an opera singer. Compared to that, I think I made the more appropriate personal choice, even in this economy. But knowing what I know now, it might have given me some pause. I am at an age where, if I wanted to, I could theoretically go back to school and start over, but this just feels like such a perfect thing that I wouldn't change it.

Alexis Soloski: I would have made different choices if I knew it would be this difficult.

Ben Brantley: No. This is what I really enjoy doing. If it stopped tomorrow, I'd feel very grateful to have done it for as long as I have.

Charles Isherwood: Oh lord, yes. I came to journalism through a series of circumstances. It wasn't really a career path I specifically pursued. I ended up working at a magazine straight out of college. Once on that path, one job led to another, and this is where I ended up. That being said, if I had seen that the rise of the Internet was going to undermine the economic model of journalism, I certainly would have done my very best to switch tracks 20 years ago. But unfortunately, that's not the way life works.

David Cote: No. I wouldn't change a thing. I have been doing this for 14 years, and I'm sort of amazed that I'm still doing it. It's a career. I tell people, "I'm paid to sit on my ass and look at theater," and that's kind of wonderful. Although it hasn't made me rich, it has made me very happy, and it's helped me immensely over the years.

As far as what might be next if the gravy train stops—and by gravy, I mean a tiny, dried-up piece of gravy in the corner—I don't know what I would do next. Do I think I should have gotten my PhD years ago? Yes, I do. The thing about theater critics is they live for the moment and in the moment, and for the eight o'clock curtain and the deadline the next day. It's a drug. Then you wake up and realize that 20 years have passed, and you didn't have a Plan B. That's scary, but a hell of a lot of fun.

Elisabeth Vincentelli: I don't know how to do anything other than writing, though I may have used my writing skills in another way. But what's done is done. I'm past my midcareer point. I think it's more of a problem for the younger generation, which doesn't have many options.

Peter Marks: I regret what's happening to other theater critics, but I don't regret doing it. Being on the aisle seat at the theater is fascinating. I don't regret a moment I spend in almost any theater. It's a great job. There are hassles, downsides, pitfalls, nervous-making moments, and things that are on the line and at stake, but it's been an amazing experience.

David Rooney: I think I would have thought more seriously about a job offer I got while I was still at *Variety*. Not long after I moved to New York from Rome at the end of 2002, I was offered a really interesting job in film development. It probably would have doubled my salary. I said no at the time because it involved a move to L.A., and I have no interest in living there. It also felt slightly disloyal. *Variety* had moved me to New York. They were putting me through the green card process, and I had loyalty back then to a company that had provided me with opportunities. Knowing what I know now, I probably would have thought more seriously about the proposal. Whether or not I had stuck with that career path, it would have opened up more opportunities for me and provided a little more security. Theater writing is a very narrow niche.

I'm now in my early fifties. It's scary to look down the pipeline and think, I have 20 more years of work left in me. Am I going to be able to scratch out a living doing this for that amount of time? I also own property in New York. I have financial responsibilities. I'm not getting any younger, which means healthcare becomes more of a concern.

Michael Musto: Nobody knew in advance that journalism would become the equivalent of selling typewriters and pencils, but it's still there. It's still vital. You can still make a living at it. I can't imagine doing anything else. So no, I would not have chosen any other path.

Peter Filichia: As Charles Kringas says in *Merrily We Roll Along*, "I like money a lot.... I mean, it's better than not...." However, money has never been the motivating factor for me. When I was in high school, everyone was being told to go into engineering, but that's of no interest to me. There's a part of me that feels like I'm not working at all when I'm writing.

Richard Ouzounian: Becoming a critic was a late-in-life turn for me. I got into it at age 50. I didn't know how long it was going to last. The fact that I'm still doing it 15 years later is a compliment to me, the paper, the business, and the city I live in. If someone is 25 years old now and thinking of being a theater critic, I'd ask them to think long and hard and to realistically look around. When I hear all about these universities offering degrees in theater criticism and dramaturgy, I wonder where their students are going to work.

Adam Feldman: I could've gone in different directions with my life in a gazillion different ways. I don't think that's a productive way of thinking. I've very much enjoyed being a theater critic, and I hope to continue being a theater critic for many years to come. That's really all there is to it. If, for some reason, it becomes impossible for me to continue doing that, then I will do something else. There are lots of things I would like to write about. But no, if I could go back in time and change one thing I've done in my life, it would certainly not be the choice of writing about theater.

Terry Teachout: I never planned to be a theater critic. When the *Wall Street Journal* approached me, I had never done it before. If you're asking me the question more generally, then no, I would not have gone into journalism. No one in his right mind, had he been able to look forward to the situation as it is now 25 or 30 years ago, would have assumed there would be a job for him. I'm terribly lucky. There's only one *Wall Street Journal*, and I'm its only drama critic. Those are not good odds.

Roma Torre: The state of theater criticism has nothing to do with whether I want to continue being a theater critic. I do it because I love the theater.

Matthew Murray: As far as theater criticism itself is concerned, I consider it only one part of my life, and not even necessarily the biggest part. It's something I do, but it's not everything that I am. Even after it became clear

I'd never make a ton of money at it or work for the *Times*, I didn't think it was a bad choice. I wouldn't be half the person I am today without it.

Zachary Stewart: Every profession has challenges in this ultra-disruptive economy. At least we get to sit comfortably in a darkened theater and be entertained (sometimes). It's not shoveling coal.

MATT WINDMAN: *What advice do you have for aspiring theater critics?*

Michael Musto: See as many shows as you can see. Write down your thoughts about the shows, even if it's just for yourself or your *Facebook* friends. That's how you become a critic. You learn by doing. The cream rises in this society, and your work will get noticed if you're a little aggressive in promoting yourself. And if that's what you were meant to do, you will find a job, even in this diminished landscape.

If you are not passionate about the theater, don't do it. If you just think it might be cute, or if you liked *Mamma Mia!*, that's not going to be good enough. You have to like the whole breadth of what the theater provides: from musicals to Shakespeare to original dramas. You have to really love it because you are going to be spending a lot of time sitting there in the dark, and it can become torture if you're not into it.

David Sheward: Have another job that pays you, like maybe a job writing in some other capacity that is in demand and that you'll get a salary for.

Michael Dale: Try acting instead. You'll be more likely to get work.

Elisabeth Vincentelli: Find a backup plan to make money because the chances of you making a living and supporting yourself from it are so slim. It's not economically viable at all. There was a moment of glory from the 1990s up to the mid–2000s when you could support yourself writing, but that moment is gone. We're back to the Dark Ages of having three jobs at once. It's very depressing. You might be able to write a few theater reviews here and there, but you have to be ready and willing to write articles about a whole bunch of other things that are not necessarily of interest to you.

Alexis Soloski: I tell students it's a marvelous hobby, but I do not encourage them to pursue it as a career.

Leonard Jacobs: Diversify your talent and skills. You're ultimately a better writer if you know something about the world above and beyond the latest revival of *The King and I*. When I was unemployed, I made a conscious decision to broaden my palette of writing. I wrote about business, music, art, architecture, and dance. I'm not necessarily trained in any of those things, but I'd go to a museum, see an exhibit, do some research, and try to write intelligently about it.

Young theater critics need to think broadly. Can they write a news article? Can they do a Q&A? Can they write an op-ed? Can they write about sports? Can they write about the law or politics? Do they have any interests

13. Regrets and Advice 217

or areas of expertise other than theater? What else can they do to become a more sellable commodity in the world of journalism? If all they want to do is write reviews, that's a niche within a niche—the larger niche being arts journalism, the smaller niche being theater journalism.

As for established theater critics who have worked at a newspaper for 10, 20, or 30 years and suddenly find themselves without a job, I don't know what they're going to do. I don't know how you turn around when you're 50 or 55 years old and you've been a working theater critic for 25 years. What do you do? I really have no idea. I know many of them. If that's you, and if you're not of retirement age, I think you're fucked.

Charles Isherwood: The chances of forging a full-time career as a critic are dwindling by the minute, but I would certainly encourage young people to study criticism because it's a way of developing writing skills and analytical skills, which are important in many realms of culture and business. I would just caution them that no matter how passionate you are, there's no guarantee that you will be able to have a career in writing about theater.

Ben Brantley: I don't want to be downright discouraging. I find it heartening that there are still people who want to be theater critics. There's still a romance about it, at least for a few kids out there. You should see all you can, read all you can, and get your words out there however you can. Today, someone can start posting on their own online in way that I couldn't. But in terms of practical career advice, I don't really know. What can I tell them? Where do you go?

David Rooney: I'd say, "Back off, Eve Harrington!" But seriously, I would advise them to think very carefully about how much they want to do this because it's really a tough field. It would be very hard to make a living out of it. There is a lot of bravado in young people who sign up for journalism courses and think, I'm going to be a critic. But it's becoming harder and harder. I don't know whether there will eventually be a turnaround. I don't have that kind of foresight.

I would tell them to think about having other skills to supplement criticism. You can be lucky and land a great gig as a chief film or theater critic at the *New York Times*, the *Washington Post*, the *Wall Street Journal*, or the *New Yorker* and you can make that pay, but that handful of dream jobs is tiny. More and more, newspaper owners are looking at those jobs and thinking, Do we really need this as a salaried position? A lot of the second-tier newspapers have already made those cuts.

I think the people who are going to make a go of it are the ones who are able to do other things. Don't just be a purist and say, "I want to be a critic specializing in only this discipline." You have to be able to write features, profiles, and non-review think pieces. I suspect both the successful upstarts and the survivors are going to be the ones who are savvy about using social media to enhance their personal brand as writers, which I have to confess I'm not very enterprising about.

Howard Shapiro: I don't think criticism is dying. It's changing. The whole nature of it is changing. It will survive in some form because people want it. I teach an arts criticism course once a year in the journalism department at Temple University. Out of the 20 students in each class, at least five are already getting paid for writing criticism. They're not making a lot, but they're getting some money.

David Cote: Read, read, read. See, see, see. Write, write, write. Consume as much theater criticism as you can. See as much as you can. Start a blog. Get free theater tickets. But don't expect anyone to pay you for it. I would say it's next to impossible to find a good paying job as a theater critic, so you might want to think more broadly about journalism. Maybe you want to be an arts journalist who has the opportunity to write theater criticism as well. To be a specialist is not necessarily a desirable thing anymore. You want to be a generalist. Maybe you want to do arts journalism and build a career that way. But again, getting a staff position on a paper or magazine is extremely hard, so prepare for many years of freelance work, not making money, and hoping a job will open up.

John Simon: I would say to forget about it because in most cases, there are no jobs available. Of course, it's already a bad sign if you're asking whether to do it or not. The only people who have a chance are the ones who don't ask. They go ahead and do it. There has to be a very strong propulsion to do it.

Helen Shaw: I tell students to start writing. I give them a list of places to try submitting their stuff to. I think writing is very useful. And if a student spends five years writing theater criticism, there will be zero downside. There are actual physiological benefits to writing and engaging and thinking in that way. But I'm very upfront about how I have to work several jobs to support my theater criticism habit.

Michael Schulman: I don't know if I could wholeheartedly recommend to a young person today to pursue theater criticism unless the model is changed to give people more opportunities. That's not to say I don't encourage people to follow their interests and passions. But if a college student came up to me, I would say to beware that theater criticism is a dwindling natural resource. I would say that it's very unlikely that you're going to be able to do it as a full-time job. There are places to do it, but not a lot. I would tell them to diversify. Don't put all your eggs into the basket of being a theater critic because your survival depends on being able to write about other things and adapting to what there is a market for. I know so few people who are able to support themselves as just theater critics or theater journalists. I've never even tried to do that.

Frank Rizzo: Just do it. When I started out, I had to crawl my way to the middle, but you could have an impact pretty quickly now if you're clever and if you can build an audience. There are more possibilities now. What I'd like to think is that younger critics will have even more ideas on how they can connect to a larger audience out there. The potential for a new era of theater criticism is there. That's the good news in all of this terrible news.

Steven Suskin: I would dissuade them. It's great if you love it, but train yourself to do something that will pay a living wage. If you can supplement that with theater criticism, that's fine.

Richard Zoglin: Just start writing, even if it's for nothing, and try to establish your name and reputation. If you're good, somehow or other, you will be rewarded for it. I have to believe that. You have to get your stuff published somewhere and hope that somehow a way will materialize where you can make money at it.

Rob Weinert-Kendt: Write as much criticism as you can, in whatever venue you can, even if it's on your own blog. There's no barrier to just starting to do it. I would caution them from getting ahead of themselves and thinking that they're professionals and sending articles to editors. They shouldn't expect to make a living at it. If you really are passionate about making a living at it, you might have to think about covering something more diverse than just theater, or doing more than just criticism, like becoming a theater academic. For example, Tom Sellar is now the new *Village Voice* critic, and he teaches at Yale. If you look at many playwrights, the way they make a living is having an academic gig, and then they write their plays. We're in a similar boat.

Robert Faires: I got so much encouragement from people who had been professionals before me, and I got such a leg-up on what being a professional theater critic meant from them. I would love to think that people are going to be following in my footsteps. I would love to help them in the same way. I just don't know what the profession will look like in the next 15 or 20 years. I don't think I could send a young person over to a daily newspaper in this or any other city and say, "This is where you get your start." There will always be freelancers writing about theater for my paper for as long as it exists, but I don't know if that's a stepping stone into the profession or simply one more aspect of a freelancer's life.

Adam Feldman: I would warn them about the economic challenges and the rapidity with which the landscape is shifting. The professional model of journalism changes all the time as the methods of media distribution change, and we have no way of anticipating how that will continue to change in the future. It does seem less stable than it used to be. On the other hand, we don't know how many hidden possibilities will open up in ways that could be very productive, very satisfying, and maybe even financially advantageous.

Jesse Green: I'd try to discourage them, as I try to discourage anyone who expresses a desire to go into the arts, but I don't really mean it. I say it as a kind of test. You should become a writer only if you must because it won't be easy. Beyond that, you're really asking what kind of skills someone should have or acquire and how to acquire them. You have to learn to write well. And you have to develop an interest in the world that is larger than your interest in the theater. If you do not have an interest that is larger than the theater, you cannot be interesting in the theater. Therefore, don't major only in theater or theater criticism. Have a profound and deep understanding of literature, or another field, or several other fields. Read great criticism of the past. Pursue a valuable life. And, back to the beginning, learn to write. That's the most important thing—and the hardest.

John Lahr: It's like when people come up to you and say, "I want to be a writer." What do you say to that? You say good luck. If you're lucky enough to ride those rapids and go down the stream without tipping over, it's a fabulous ride, but the marketplace is going to test you very quickly. If you can't make a life or a career doing it, you should stop. The battle won't be worth the prize. There's no sin in stopping. You can move on to something else. Having drama criticism is necessary, but it's such a small field. I could never in good faith say to someone who wants to be a theater critic, "Keep at it and you'll make it someday." I don't think anybody can really make it now. I just don't think the opportunity is there, and I don't think it's going to get any better.

Maybe the way to do it is to do something else. Write a biography. Follow a theme through someone's plays. If that gets noticed, you've got a calling card. I don't think that just submitting a series of short opinions to a publication will get you anywhere. I was incredibly lucky because I wrote a biography of my father when I was 27 years old, and it was on front page of the Sunday *Times*. I had a calling card. If I didn't have that, this whole thing wouldn't have happened.

Marilyn Stasio: Why would I dissuade them? If it didn't work out, they would still know a hell of a lot about theater. Maybe they could do something else in the theater. There's nothing wasted when you throw yourself with a passion into something that you love. If that's what you love, if that's what you want to pour your life savings, work, heart, and soul into, then do it. Don't censor yourself from something you love because you think you'll never get hired. That's sad. Do it anyway. Something will come out of it.

Terry Teachout: I never recommend to anyone who's interested in working in journalism to shoot for a job like the one I have. My experience, which dates all the way back to the 1970s, is not relevant to a millennial who is trying to figure out how to make a living in the arts. I tell them that if this is something they want to pursue, they should make sure they know more than one discipline, more than one branch of the arts, so that their potential value will be greater than if all they know about is theater. That's already a good thing for theater critics because theater encompasses all of the arts.

Beyond that, I give them the usual professional advice. Seek every opportunity to publish, whether paid or not. Practice your instrument. Make art. Get involved. Get your hands dirty in the making of art. Find out what it takes to put a performance on. Find out what it feels like to go onstage. It doesn't have to be theater, but it needs to be something. You really have to put yourself on the line. Otherwise, you're not going to have the standing that you need in order to sit in judgment, insofar as that's what we do. That's more important than anything else. It's even more important than the large body of knowledge that's central to being a critic. You can fuse that experiential knowledge with your knowledge of whatever art form you're writing about. You ought to get yourself in the position where somebody's reviewing you. Then you'll know what it feels like when you're on the other side of the typewriter.

Zachary Stewart: Be as honest and insightful as you can without alienating your editors and the people signing your paycheck. You need to make rent, but you also don't want to trade away your credibility because once you do, you can never have it back.

David Finkle: I would tell them to see as much theater as they can and write about it. Send it to newspapers they'd like to write for. You never know when an opening will pop up. Look at the Roger Ebert story. He was working as a sports writer at the *Chicago Sun-Times*. They lost their movie critic and said, "How would you like to review movies?" You never know.

Matthew Murray: Theater does not exist on the page. It exists on the stage, and that's where you have to experience it. See professional (Broadway, Off-Broadway, regional) plays. See college and high school plays. See community theater. See everything you can, even if it's not your favorite genre: plays, musicals, operas, dance shows, mime, circuses, performance art. See old plays: the Greeks, the Romans, Shakespeare. See new plays. If you are a serious theater critic, you won't be able to pick and choose what you see, so you need to know as much as you can about everything that's out there. And you can augment this by having at least a passing familiarity with other related disciplines: art, architecture, music, fashion, choreography. Eventually, they'll all play a role in some theater you see.

Then, once you've done that, figure out what you think about what you've seen and how you can communicate that to others. Tell them who you are and why that's important. Make them see the play through your eyes. Whatever you think about a play, you'll bring to it something that no one else in the world possibly can. It's scary at first, but don't shy away from it. Embrace it. Embrace who you are and what you have to say, and don't let anyone tell you that you shouldn't be saying it. If you know your stuff and you've done your homework, your perspective is just as valuable as theirs, and maybe even more so.

Jason Zinoman: In a way, it's a better time than ever for people getting started. If you work hard, you can make a name for yourself pretty quickly. Don't necessarily wait for institutions to give you a platform. Get out there. Write and get better. Freelance as much as possible. Doing some reporting is useful, too. To get really good, you need to do it a lot. And fail. And mess up. Just like an actor or a playwright, you have to focus on your craft. The fun thing about this job is that if you're a curious person, there's an endless amount of interesting things. You can never stop learning.

When you're starting out and young, you have to balance the things that you want to do with the things that you have to do for money. You need to settle on a ratio for that in your mind and stick to it. That ratio can change as you develop in your career. For a long time, I thought, 50 percent of what I'm doing is what I want to do, and 50 percent of what I'm doing is what I need to do.

Hilton Als: Please keep writing. Do it out of your love for the theater.

Epilogue

It is now February of 2016. Since I completed work on this book a few months ago, the *New York Daily News* and *New York Post* have severely reduced their theater coverage. Frank Rizzo (*Harford Courant*) and Christine Dolen (*Miami Herald*) have retired, and Richard Ouzounian (*Toronto Star*) is on the verge of retiring, which brings into question the future of theater criticism at all of those publications.

In the coming years, we will see more of the same. Mainstream publications will continue to cut back on theater criticism. Except for just a few writers at the *New York Times* and other major regional papers, theater criticism will die out as a full-time profession or even a part-time paying gig. But thanks to countless reviews on the Internet (of varying quality and credibility) theatergoers may not care or even notice.

The straw that would break the camel's back would be if the *New York Times* scaled back its theater coverage. But barring any unforeseen circumstances, this seems unlikely to occur. As much as people may bemoan the overwhelming power of the *Times*, no other outlet publishes as many reviews of consistent quality. And if the *Times* did scale back, what other outlet would be capable of filling the void?

I am slowly becoming more optimistic about the role that non-paid reviewers on the Internet can have. If they regularly write about theater, and if they do it with knowledge, passion, and wit, they can conceivably establish themselves as legitimate critics. There are plenty of people out there who love theater and are willing to write reviews in exchange for press tickets, or for nothing whatsoever. By just posting a link to their reviews via *Facebook* or *Twitter,* they can peddle their reviews to their social media followers, who may be potential theatergoers. And if their writing is good enough, maybe they can find a way to get paid for their writing (via sponsors or advertising or getting hired by another party).

In a way, this makes theater criticism into more of a meritocracy. In the past, a critic got access to readers only by being published in a newspaper.

The paper brought readers to the critic. Going forward, the critic will need to attract readers on his or her own. The critics who manage to stand out may be the best writers, if not those that skilled at self-publicity.

A fine example is the user Jesse21 on the discussion board *All That Chat*. Since 2008, Jesse21 has written a review of about 600 to 800 words for every new Broadway show, posting each review right before the show officially opens. Since he apparently does not receive complimentary press tickets, he is under no obligation to wait until the press embargo is lifted, and he can beat other critics to the punch. I, along with many others who check out *All That Chat* on a daily basis, look forward to his straightforward, well-developed reviews.

My own reviews are also part of the trend of non-professional theater criticism to a certain extent. I have never been a full-time theater critic, and at this point, I never expect to be one. I balance writing theater reviews with the demands of a full-time legal career. I go to a show virtually every night of my life and churn out countless reviews out of my love of seeing theater, just like many others out there.

Bottom line: the theater will change. Theater criticism will change. But regardless of the changes, we need to hold on to our journalistic standards and ethics. We need to turn out reviews that will earn the respect and attention of different kinds of readers. If we can manage that, there could be a meaningful future for theater criticism.

Index

Abie's Irish Rose 210
Act One 149
Actors' Equity Association 45, 69, 196
After Dark 41
Agee, James 17
Al Hirschfeld Theatre 151
Albee, Edward 92
All About Eve 52, 162
All That Chat 46, 126, 133, 163, 180, 195–198, 224
Als, Hilton 7, 25, 56, 58, 62, 73, 84, 94, 105, 109, 115, 120, 125, 127, 135, 145, 180, 198, 222
America (magazine) 42
American Idol 13, 28
American Place Theatre 64
American Theater Web 10, 180, 193
American Theatre (magazine) 2, 10–11, 42, 65, 126
American Theatre Critics Association 3, 185, 19
American Theatre Wing 88, 176
amNewYork 3, 11, 144, 187
Angels in America 27, 33, 42
Anna in the Tropics 118
Annie 142
The Apple Family Plays 148
A.R.T. Institute 20, 40
Associated Press 171
Atkinson, Brooks 18, 98–99, 107
Atkinson, Jayne 127
Aucoin, Don 7, 23, 26, 38, 55, 57, 59, 66, 77, 110, 121, 126, 136, 141, 148, 158, 182, 189, 201
August: Osage County 117–118
Austin Chronicle 9, 46, 113
Ayckbourn, Alan 119–120

Bacalzo, Dan 7, 62, 95, 119
Backstage 9–10, 36, 38, 42, 45, 163, 167, 175
Baldwin, Alec 182
Barnard Bulletin 41
Barnes, Clive 39, 116
Bart, Peter 37, 108
Benanti, Laura 150
Bennett, Michael 67
Bentley, Eric 20, 25, 79
Bergen County Record 8, 129
Berger, Glen 211
Bergman, Ingmar 154
Bernard, Jami 41
Betrayal 178
Bezos, Jeff 164
Billy Rose Theatre Division 175
Bishop, Andre 172
Bishop, Kelly 41
Blanchett, Cate 145
The Blonde in the Thunderbird 118
Bloomberg 8, 10, 109, 165, 166, 173–174, 213
Bock, Jerry 152
Bono 208
The Book of Mormon 11, 16, 123, 127
Boston After Dark 30
Boston Globe 7, 39, 55, 89, 110, 126, 201
Boublil, Alain 124
Bradshaw, Thomas 52
Brantley, Ben 7, 15, 17–18, 23, 27, 35, 48, 55, 57, 62, 67, 70–71, 76, 85, 90, 98, 107, 110, 113, 117, 121, 126, 131, 136, 140, 144, 147, 151–152, 162, 177, 186, 193, 196–199, 208, 210, 214, 217
Brecht, Bertolt 74, 95, 149

225

226 INDEX

The Bridges of Madison County 86, 122, 208
The Broadway Association 186
Broadway.com 8–9, 42, 45, 164
Broadway League 88
Broadway World 8, 38, 190
Broadway Yearbook 44
Brook, Peter 72
Brooklyn Academy of Music 2, 126
Brown, Jason Robert 94
Brown, Scott 7, 21, 24, 27, 43–44, 54, 56, 72, 78, 85
Brown, Tina 33, 181
Brustein, Robert 19–20, 32, 39, 43, 79
Bucks County Playhouse 71
Burton, Richard 118
Buscemi, Steve 74

Cabaret 136
Camino Real 117
Canby, Vincent 165
Caroline, or Change 120
Cassidy, Claudia 18–19, 85, 97
Cats 210
CBC 31
Chapman, John 23
Chenoweth, Kristin 120
Chicago Sun-Times 90
Chicago Theater Movement 16, 34
Chicago Tribune 9, 11, 16, 18, 33–34, 37
A Chorus Line 41, 122
Christian Science Monitor 10, 40, 108
Christiansen, Richard 16, 37
City Center 100
Clurman, Harold 25, 32, 71, 79
Clyde Fitch Report 8–9, 175
CNN 181
Coleman, Cy 10
Colin Quinn: Unconstitutional 92
Collins, Gail 55
Columbia Daily Spectator 40–41
Columbia University 10, 35, 40–41, 49
Cote, David 7, 14, 19, 22, 38, 51–52, 54, 56, 60, 66, 74, 76, 84, 91, 94, 106, 111, 113, 118, 130, 132, 135, 140, 144, 147, 151, 153, 159, 168, 181, 190, 200, 206, 209, 214, 218
Coward, Noel 36
Cox, Gordon 8, 51, 84–85, 132, 137, 178, 182, 185, 209, 213
Craig, Daniel 178

Crain's New York 176
Croce, Arlene 17
Cromer, David 118, 120, 138, 157
Cruz, Nilo 118
Cunningham, Dennis 168
The Curious Incident of the Dog in the Night-Time 155
Curtain Up 187, 193

Daisey, Mike 198
Dale, Michael 8, 14, 22, 38, 49, 52, 55, 57–58, 65, 66, 70, 75, 82, 88, 100, 107, 110, 113, 118, 121, 130–131, 145, 157, 160, 206, 213, 216
Dallas Morning News 174
The Dance of Death 86
Davidson, Gordon 42
Deadline 8, 130, 173, 174
Death of a Salesman 136
deBessonet, Lear 74
Denby, David 51
Denby, Edwin 17
Disney 66, 120
Dogeaters 119
Dolen, Christine 4, 8, 76, 90, 95, 101, 114, 118, 131, 139, 147, 153, 170, 181, 190, 199, 223
Dorfman, Ariel 181
Doubt 5
Downtown News 42
Doyle, John 156
Drabinsky, Garth 31
Drama Desk 88, 193
The Drowsy Chaperone 31
The Duck Variations 34
Dziemianowicz, Joe 8, 27

Ebert, Roger 221
Edelstein, Gordon 116
Elle 7, 35
The Empty Space 72
Encores! 100, 120
Eno, Will 90, 144
Entertainment Weekly 7–8, 43, 112, 129, 202
Eugene O'Neill Theater Center 9, 76, 193
Eustis, Oskar 172

Facebook 79, 163, 165, 194, 199–203, 216, 233

Feiffer, Jules 33
Feingold, Michael 25, 171
Feldberg, Robert 8, 26–27, 51, 53, 63, 69, 83, 96, 104, 129, 185, 187, 197, 203, 208
Feldman, Adam 8, 18, 24, 44, 48, 61, 68, 78, 88, 91, 106, 111, 116, 119, 123, 127, 130, 140, 145, 155, 160, 184, 192, 195, 206, 209, 215, 219
Felker, Clay 32
Fiddler on the Roof 36
Fifth Row Center 22
Filichia, Peter 2, 4, 8, 15, 23, 30, 56, 61, 67, 71, 74, 80, 93, 97, 109, 116, 145, 152, 171, 183, 199, 210, 215
Finkle, David 8, 25, 120–121, 169, 184, 207, 221
Fleming, Mike 173
Follies 80, 122
Footloose 86
Foreman, Richard 144
Foster, Sutton 149
Foxwoods Theatre 209
Foy, Eddie, Jr. 138
Franco, James 26, 131
Fun Home 5
A Funny Thing Happened on the Way to the Forum 137

Gardner, Elysa 8, 26, 53, 57, 61, 69, 78, 87, 91, 106, 108–109, 122, 127, 136, 141, 157, 159, 211
Geier, Thom 8, 69–70, 81, 112, 129, 138, 157–158, 191, 198, 202
Genet, Jean 145
George Washington University 83
Gerard, Jeremy 4, 8, 14, 19, 22, 48, 52–53, 61, 64, 67, 101, 130, 169, 173–174, 183, 187, 197, 205–208, 213
Gerroll, Daniel 120
Ghosts 120
Giamatti, Paul 74
Gigot, Paul 36
Gilbert, Matthew 55
Gingold Theatrical Group 74
Girls in Trouble 60
Glass, Ira 201
The Glass Menagerie 19, 37, 80, 116
Globe and Mail 170, 194, 200
Globe Theatre 136, 184
Glory Days 123

Good People 59
Good Person of Szechwan 148
Goodman, John 74
Goodman Theatre 117
Grantland 188
Green, Jesse 8, 13, 21, 24, 26, 43, 57, 59, 63, 74, 80, 84, 97, 102, 111, 116, 125, 132, 137, 149, 169, 190, 196, 202, 220
Greenberg, Clement 17
Grode, Eric 8, 29, 48, 128, 191, 194, 196, 201, 205, 209
Guardian 8, 10, 109, 187
Guettel, Adam 94
Guider, Elizabeth 172
Gypsy 20, 39, 98, 135, 159

Haimes, Todd 172
Hair 8, 30, 62
Hamilton 4, 5
Hamlet 97, 112, 136, 160
Harrington, Eve 217
Harris, Leonard 31
Hart, Moss 143
Hartford Courant 10, 40, 99, 127, 223
Hartford Stage 38
Harvard Crimson 80
Harvard Gay & Lesbian Review 44
Hays, Charlotte 35
Hazlitt, William 19
Hedda Gabler 139
Heilpern, John 41
Henning, Doug 212
Henry, William A., III 42
Henry V 61
Herman, Jerry 11
Hicklin, Aaron 176
Hilton, Perez 4, 9, 56, 65, 86, 115, 142, 147, 199
The History Boys 123
Hitchcock, Alfred 155
Hitchens, Heather 176
Hoelterhoff, Manuela 173–174
Holler If Ya Hear Me 86
Hollywood Reporter 10, 40, 108, 130, 171–172, 181
Hot Seat 21
Hudson Review 32
Huffington, Arianna 181, 183
Huffington Post 11, 130, 182–184
Huneker, James Gibbons 18

Hurwitt, Robert 4, 9, 46, 50, 80, 96, 104, 113, 167, 188

Ibsen, Henrik 127
If/Then 119
Imus in the Morning 71
Inge, William 71
Instagram 165, 199, 203
Into the Woods 74
Irina's Vow 110
Irving, Amy 120
Isherwood, Charles 9, 21, 26, 35, 57, 60, 62, 65, 71, 89, 94, 97, 99, 107–108, 117, 132, 139, 140, 143–144, 151, 153, 157, 164, 180, 189, 194, 196, 199, 211, 214, 217
It's a Bird...It's a Plane...It's Superman 210

Jackman, Hugh 83, 150, 169
Jacobs, Leonard 9, 16, 59, 64, 66, 72, 87, 95, 98, 108, 121, 145, 160, 175, 183, 187, 197, 211, 216
Jefferson, Margo 59
Jenkins, Jeffrey Eric 3
Jesse21 196, 224
John, Elton 57
Johnson, Samuel 183
Jones, Chris 4, 9, 14, 19, 23, 27, 37, 52, 54, 58, 69, 71, 76, 85, 90, 97, 100, 105, 110, 114, 118, 121, 126, 132, 139, 147, 153, 157–158, 164, 167
Joseph and the Amazing Technicolor Dreamcoat 31

Kael, Pauline 17–18, 35, 165, 178
Kane, Sarah 140
Kansas City Star 36
Kauffmann, Stanley 115, 210
Kaufman, George S. 70–71
Kelly, Kevin 39, 76, 89
Kennedy, Louise 39
The Kentucky Cycle 42
Kerr, Walter 19–20, 23, 71, 98, 151, 190
Kilgallen, Dorothy 70
The King and I 216
King Lear 136, 146, 154
Kinky Boots 122
Kipness, Joseph 67
Kissel, Howard 18
Klein, Stewart 168

Krugman, Paul 56
Kushner, Jared 41
Kushner, Tony 33, 95

La MaMa 38
LaBute, Neil 133
Labyrinth Theater Company 145
Lady Day at Emerson's Bar & Grill 149
Lahr, Bert 9, 152
Lahr, John 9, 18, 20, 24–25, 32, 51, 57–58, 69, 71, 73, 79–80, 91, 96, 103, 106, 108–109, 116, 119, 123, 127, 130, 133, 138, 140, 150, 156, 159, 178, 184, 195, 198, 213, 220
Lane, Anthony 58, 127
Lane, Nathan 137, 150, 152, 212
Lansbury, Angela 39
La Rocco, Claudia 64
Laurents, Arthur 44, 159
Law, Jude 160
Leight, Warren 150
Lessing, Gotthold Ephraim 36
Lestat 57
Letterman, David 209
The Light in the Piazza 94
Lincoln Center 95–96
Lincoln Center Festival 145
Lindsay, Robert 152
Lindsay-Abaire, David 59
The Lion King 120
Lipton, Brian 9, 90, 137, 193
"Little Man" 104, 113
A Little Night Music 39
Long Day's Journey Into Night 57
Long Wharf Theatre 36, 38
Los Angeles Times 8, 11, 33, 35, 42, 96, 133
Lucas, Craig 123
Luker, Rebecca 150
LuPone, Patti 135
Lyons, Jeffrey 168

Ma Rainey's Black Bottom 39
Mac, Taylor 148
Macbeth 95, 155
The Maids 145
Mamet, David 5, 16, 34, 133
Mamma Mia! 216
The Man Who Came to Dinner 36, 70
Manhattan East 32
Mantle, Burns 23

Marat/Sade 32
Mark Hellinger Theatre 211
Marks, Peter 4, 9, 14, 45, 49, 58, 63–64, 69, 75, 79, 82–83, 90, 93, 98, 103, 107, 112, 116, 119, 123, 128, 131, 133, 138, 143, 150, 156, 159, 164, 167, 177, 190, 195, 198, 203, 208, 209, 214
Martin, Bob 31
Marx, Jeff 44
Massey, Kyle Dean 131
Mayer, Michael 156
McCarter, Jeremy 40
McCarthy, Mary 18
McCarthy, Todd 172
McDonagh, Martin 87
McDonald, Audra 122, 131, 149
McKellen, Ian 86, 146
McNally, Terrence 61
McNulty, Charles 167
Me and My Girl 152
Mencken, H.L. 63
Merlin 211
Merrily We Roll Along 80, 215
Metropolitan Opera 100
Miller, Arthur 18, 92, 133
Miramontez, Rick 205, 211
Mirren, Helen 86
Les Misérables 43, 124, 210
Miss Saigon 124
Mr. Burns, a Post-Electric Play 177
Moliere 50
A Moon for the Misbegotten 69
Moss, Adam 174
Mostel, Zero 137
Mother Courage and Her Children 95
Mothers and Sons 61
Murphy, Donna 133
Murray, Matthew 9, 21, 46, 55, 58, 71, 75, 91, 97, 104–105, 112, 117, 124, 126, 133, 135, 156, 192, 212, 215, 221
The Muscles in Our Toes 145
The Music Man 98
Music Theatre International 8, 171
Musto, Michael 9, 41, 49, 52, 56, 59, 64, 68, 77, 85–86, 96–97, 118, 122, 126, 131, 148, 155, 162, 176, 183, 190, 195, 203, 215–216
My Name Is Rachel Corrie 128, 131

Nathan, George Jean 7, 9–10, 18–19, 80, 196

Nation 25, 189
National Critics Institute 9, 76
National Institute of Dramatic Art 37
National New Play Network 13
National Observer 79
National Playwrights Conference 76
Neighborhood Playhouse 45
Nelson, Richard 148
Neuwirth, Bebe 93
New Criterion 125, 175
New Group 52
New Haven Journal-Courier 39
New Jersey Newsroom 10, 176
New Republic 20, 25, 32, 47, 189
New Society 33
New York (magazine) 7–10, 10, 21, 26, 32, 41, 43–44, 56, 125, 168–169, 174, 187
New York City Department of Cultural Affairs 176
New York Daily News 8, 10–11, 22–23, 34, 35, 41, 65, 160, 168, 223
New York Drama Critics' Circle 8, 10, 62, 87–88, 165, 205
New York Herald Tribune 19, 32, 65
New York International Fringe Festival 40
New York Journal-American 165
New York Observer 9, 23, 41, 96, 127, 169, 170–171
New York Native 45, 63
New York Philharmonic 161
New York Post 4, 8, 10–11, 35, 39–40, 62, 65, 68, 99, 101, 106, 108, 130, 168, 193, 223
New York Press 9, 175
New York Sun 8, 40–41, 128
New York Times 2, 7–11, 19–21, 25, 30, 38, 41, 43, 46–47, 59, 65, 70, 83, 88–90, 107, 112, 125, 127, 129, 159, 163–164, 169, 172–176, 187, 190, 199, 206, 217, 223
New York Times Book Review 11, 70, 175
New York University 10, 46, 65
New Yorker 7–10, 18, 25, 27, 33, 35, 45, 51, 57, 62, 101, 103, 106, 108, 119, 125–128, 168, 184, 187, 190, 209, 217
Newman, Paul 168
News 12 Long Island 43
Newsday 8, 11, 34–35, 65, 187
Nicholas, Mike 156

INDEX

Nieman Reports 25
Nightingale, Benedict 22
The Normal Heart 45
Norton, Elliot 76, 89
NPR 31, 173
NY1 7, 11, 43, 114, 128, 168
NYTheatre.com 193

Obie Awards 76, 83
The Odd Couple 48, 53
Off Broadway 5, 16, 49, 52, 65, 76, 88, 145, 176, 221
Off Off Broadway 16, 38, 49, 66, 76, 88, 140
O'Hara, Kelli 149
Oklahoma! 17
Oliver! 36
Once 95, 142, 155
110 in the Shade 122
O'Neill, Eugene 20, 69
Ontological-Hysteric Theater 38, 144
Open House 90
Orton, Joe 9, 33
Osmond, Donny 31
Our Town 118, 138, 168
Out 9, 42, 176
Ouzounian, Richard 4, 9, 19-20, 31, 59, 65, 98, 115, 127, 133, 137, 142, 170, 183, 191, 194, 200, 215, 223
Oxfeld, Jesse 9, 21, 23, 41, 67, 80, 96, 127, 170, 183, 187, 197-198, 205, 207-208
Oxford University 32, 213

Pacific Overtures 39
Pacino, Al 74
The Pajama Game 138
Paris Opera House 83
Parker, Dorothy 18, 57
Parks, Suzan-Lori 139
Paulus, Steve 43
PBS 10
The People in the Picture 133
Peter and the Starcatcher 155
Peters, Bernadette 135
The Phantom of the Opera 87, 122, 210
Philadelphia Inquirer 10, 40, 79, 131, 173, 202
The Pillowman 87
Pinter, Harold 25, 33, 178
Pippin 131

The Pirate Queen 124
Playbill 11, 44
PM 65
Politico 188
Portantiere, Michael 9, 58, 73, 119, 122, 142, 147, 159, 186
Porter, Fairfield 17
Prick Up Your Ears 33
Project Shaw 72
Propst, Andy 10, 16, 21, 23, 27, 50, 54, 72, 94, 101, 105, 107, 180, 189, 193
P.S. 122 38
Public Theater 74, 95, 119, 126, 148, 208

Queen 86, 141

Rabbit Hole 118
Radcliffe, Daniel 131
Raidy, William A. 45
A Raisin in the Sun 138-139
Reader's Digest 32
Record-Journal 38
Reich, Ronni 10, 63, 96, 121, 129, 143, 150, 156, 169, 178, 185, 213
Remnick, David 198
Repertory Theatre of Lincoln Center 33
The Resistible Rise of Arturo Ui 74
Reuters 173
Reynolds, Jonathan 60
Rich, Frank 21, 35, 54, 80, 83, 107, 152, 211
Richard III 136, 148
Richards, David 89
Ricks, Christopher 32
Ridley, Clifford A. 79
Riedel, Michael 4, 10, 13, 21, 27, 31, 35, 50, 54-55, 60, 65, 68, 70, 80, 83, 86, 89, 105, 107, 116, 120, 126, 143, 150, 164, 184, 198, 203
Rivera, Chita 41, 212
Rizzo, Frank 10, 14, 39, 60, 76, 92, 94, 99, 119, 127, 139, 141, 144, 190, 202, 219, 223
Roberts, Julia 150
Robinson, Marc 36
Rocky 109, 127, 142
The Rocky Horror Show 118
Rodgers & Hammerstein 68
Rooney, David 4, 10, 37, 50, 108, 129, 165, 171-172, 181, 186, 214, 217

Rorem, Ned 28
Roundabout Theatre Company 133
Rudin, Scott 123, 142, 172
Ruhl, Sarah 121–122, 133
Rush, George 35
Rylance, Mark 148–149

St. Ann's Warehouse 126
Saltz, Jerry 202
San Francisco Chronicle 9, 46, 113
San Francisco Examiner 9, 46
Sarris, Andrew 178
Scheck, Frank 10, 21, 26, 28, 40, 68, 86, 93, 101, 106, 108, 111, 114, 130, 132, 145, 151, 158, 172
Schonberg, Claude-Michel 124
Schulman, Michael 10, 16, 25–26, 43, 51, 53, 57, 62, 67, 83, 85, 91, 101, 111, 122, 126, 137, 142, 152, 155, 186, 198, 207, 209, 218
Seasons of Discontent 20
Second City 97
Seesaw 67
Sellar, Tom 219
Shakespeare, William 5, 37, 50–51, 94–95, 137, 146, 148, 150, 201, 216, 221
Shakur, Tupac 86
Shalhoub, Tony 149
Shapiro, Howard 4, 10, 14, 23, 40, 49, 53, 55, 57, 69, 72, 79, 83, 85, 92, 95, 109, 117, 122, 131, 136, 142, 152, 154, 160, 173, 178, 186, 191, 202, 206, 218
Shaw, George Bernard 13, 71, 79, 178
Shaw, Helen 10, 13, 20–21, 23, 29, 40, 50, 54, 61, 64, 74, 76, 83, 87, 100, 110, 141, 144, 147, 152, 158, 168, 183, 191, 199, 210, 218
Shaw Festival 84, 200
Sheed, Wilfrid 64
Shelley, Carole 41
Sheward, David 10, 38, 61, 92, 120, 140, 148, 153, 178, 197, 206, 216
Show Business 44
Side Man 150
Siegel, Joel 168
Signature Theatre 123
Simon, John 5, 10, 15, 18, 20–22, 28, 32, 48, 50–51, 54, 56, 64–66, 70, 75, 84, 95, 100, 109, 114–115, 118, 121, 125, 131, 140, 146, 154, 166, 174, 177, 196, 218
Simon, Neil 53, 69

Simonson, Robert 1–2
Sixteen Wounded 60
Slate 188
Sleep No More 119
Small Tragedy 123
Smash 71
Smile, Smile, Smile 116
SoHo Weekly News 41
Soloski, Alexis 10, 18, 36, 49, 52, 56, 61–62, 66, 72, 76, 86, 90, 95–96, 105, 109, 113, 126, 131, 140, 144, 147, 151, 157, 166, 171, 186, 197, 209, 213, 216
Sommer, Elyse 187, 193
Sommers, Michael 4, 10, 13, 18, 21, 25–26, 31, 45, 52, 62, 71, 83, 84, 92, 98, 103, 138, 147, 163, 171, 176, 186, 187
Sondheim, Stephen 80, 94
The Sopranos 55
The Sound of Broadway Music 152
The Sound of Music 150
Sourd, Jacques le 18
Spamalot 52
Specter, Michael 126
Spider-Man: Turn Off the Dark 120, 181, 205–212
Spring Awakening 5, 117, 124
STAGES 40
Star-Ledger 8, 10, 31, 45, 92–93, 129, 171, 176
Stasio, Marilyn 11, 64, 73, 82, 89, 97, 99, 130, 136, 142, 146, 156, 169, 171, 184, 207, 209, 220
Stone, David 187
Stefanova-Peteva, Kalina 3
Stewart, Patrick 146
Stewart, Zachary 11, 13, 22, 26, 38, 48, 52, 55, 65, 70, 77, 83, 87, 90, 100, 105, 107, 109, 113, 120, 122, 130–131, 135, 141, 144–145, 147, 151–152, 157, 159, 170, 177, 182, 216, 221
Stoppard, Tom 49, 71, 122, 133
Stratford Festival 4, 84, 200–201
Streep, Meryl 39, 95
A Streetcar Named Desire 94
Stritch, Elaine 9, 150
Studio Theatre 46
Suskin, Steven 11, 16, 18, 20, 22, 44, 51, 56, 85, 102, 110, 115, 121, 125, 130, 136, 141, 149, 152, 155, 162, 184, 193, 202, 210, 219
Syracuse University 9, 48

TalkinBroadway.com 9, 46, 126
Taylor, Elizabeth 118
Taymor, Julie 181, 206–207, 211
Teachout, Terry 11, 17, 21, 28, 36, 51–52, 63–64, 67, 71, 75, 82, 86, 91, 95, 104, 107, 109, 115, 120, 123, 129, 133, 143, 145, 150, 152, 157–158, 161, 163, 177, 185, 188, 194–195, 197–198, 211, 215, 220
The Tempest 74
Temple University 10, 218
Theater Talk 10, 44, 71
TheaterMania 7–10, 38, 187
TheaterWeek 2, 30, 35
Theatre Journal 119
This American Life 201
Thomson, Virgil 17, 33
Three Days of Rain 150
Thrill Me 122
Timbers, Alex 83
Time (magazine) 11, 28, 42, 128, 200
Time Out 2, 7–8, 10–11, 37–40, 42, 45, 47, 91, 106, 110–111, 127, 129, 133, 162, 168, 187, 200
TimeLine Theatre Company 123
Titus Andronicus 169
Tony Awards 9, 25, 53, 77, 85, 87–89, 122, 148
Toronto Star 9, 31–32, 127, 223
Torre, Roma 11, 15, 19, 24, 43, 56, 63, 68, 71, 77, 87, 102, 105, 111, 114, 123, 128, 142, 149, 155, 160, 168, 183, 201, 215
Total TV 43
Truffaut, François 71
Twelfth Night 136, 148–149
The 25th Annual Putnam County Spelling Bee 124, 139
Twitter 49, 129, 165, 168, 194, 197–204, 233
Tynan, Kenneth 9, 19, 58, 79, 178

Ulysses 138
Uncensored John Simon 174
Uncle Vanya 136
Under the Cooper Beech 3
Under the Radar Festival 208
University of Arizona 39
USA Today 8, 11, 34, 127

Vanity Fair 7, 35
Variety 2, 8–11, 14, 36–38, 40, 44, 49, 62, 99, 101, 108, 119, 129–130, 139, 166, 171–173, 187, 196, 207–208, 214
Viertel, Jack 120
Village Voice 2, 7–10, 30, 33, 35–36, 41, 76, 125–126, 131, 171, 176, 219
Vincentelli, Elisabeth 11, 14, 18, 21–22, 39, 60, 62, 64, 96, 101, 106, 111, 114, 117, 122, 131, 133, 136, 141, 145, 148, 153, 166, 182, 191, 193, 197, 202, 210, 214, 216
Violet 156
Vox 188
Vulture 26, 125

WABC 71
Waiting for Godot 123, 146
Wall Street Journal 11, 36, 91, 120, 129, 168, 173, 197, 199, 215, 217
Wallach, Allan 34
Warp! 34
Washington, Denzel 131, 138–139, 181
Washington Post 9–10, 36, 46, 89–90, 128–129, 164, 188, 217
Wasserstein, Bruce 174
Wasserstein, Wendy 83, 174
We Will Rock You 86, 141
Webber, Andrew Lloyd 211
Weber, Bruce 46
Weekly Standard 125, 175
Weinert-Kendt, Rob 11, 17, 20, 42, 48, 55–56, 65, 70, 77, 92, 96, 102, 106, 113, 115, 133, 137, 148, 155, 167, 178, 191, 198, 211, 219
Weiss, Hedy 90
West Side Story 98
Westchester Guardian 10, 174
What's My Line? 70
Whitehead, Sam 47
Who Calls the Shots on the New York Stages? 3
Who's Afraid of Virginia Woolf? 158
WHYY 173
Wicked 187, 209
Wilde, Oscar 82
Williams, Tennessee 9, 18–19, 25, 37, 80, 117
Williamstown Theatre Festival 208
Wilson, August 39, 47, 91
Wilson, Robert 148
Windman, Matt 1–2, 6, 11, 13, 17, 22, 26, 30, 48, 51, 55, 58, 64, 66, 70, 75, 82, 87, 89, 94, 96, 98, 105, 107, 109, 113,

117, 120, 125, 130–131, 135, 140, 143–145, 151–152, 157–158, 162, 170, 177, 180, 185, 193, 195, 198, 205, 209, 213, 216
Winer, Linda 11, 15, 17–18, 20, 28–29, 33, 49, 62, 66, 73, 82, 97, 103, 107, 112, 128, 187, 205, 207
Witchel, Alex 35
Wolfe, George C. 156
Women's Wear Daily 7, 35
Wonderland 119, 122
Wontorek, Paul 45
Wood, Frank 150
Woollcott, Alexander 70

Yale Repertory Theatre 36, 38–39, 43
Yale School of Drama 7, 36, 43
Yale University 36, 43, 45, 83, 219
Yonkers Tribune 10
York Theatre Company 122
Young, Stark 79
Young Frankenstein 144
You're a Good Man, Charlie Brown 120
YouTube 96

Zinoman, Jason 11, 17, 38, 46, 63, 73, 78, 91, 116, 129, 162, 185, 188, 198, 204, 208, 213, 222
Zoglin, Richard 11, 28, 42, 66, 68, 87, 91, 119, 122, 128, 148, 169, 183, 195, 200, 219
Zorba! 120

www.ingramcontent.com/pod-product-compliance
Ingram Content Group UK Ltd.
Pitfield, Milton Keynes, MK11 3LW, UK
UKHW041943140426
5217IPUK00014B/632